THE JEWS OF ISLAM

The Jews of Islam

BERNARD LEWIS

PRINCETON UNIVERSITY PRESS

PRINCETON, NEW JERSEY

FOR Y, WHO WILL UNDERSTAND

¿No ha de haber un espíritu valiente?
¿Siempre se ha de sentir lo que se dice?
¿Nunca se ha de decir lo que se siente?

—*Francisco de Quevedo*

Contents

Note on Illustrations

ILLUSTRATIONS FOLLOW PAGE 66

My thanks are due to the following institutions and individuals for permission to reproduce pictures of items in their possession.

Israel Museum, Jerusalem: Nos. 1, 6, 7, 8, 9, 10, and 21

Hebrew Union College, Skirball Museum, Los Angeles: Nos. 2, 4, and 5.

Jewish Museum, London: No. 3

British Library, London: No. 11.

Professor Myriam Ayalon, Jerusalem: Nos. 12 and 13.

Jewish Museum of Greece, Athens: Nos. 16 and 17.

Gennadius Library, Athens: Nos. 14, 15, 18, 19, and 20.

No. 16 is taken from *Recueil de cent estampes représentant differentes Nations du Levant* ... (text by) M. De Ferriol, Ambassadeur du Roi à La Porte (Paris, 1714).

No. 20 is taken from Georges de La Chappelle, *Recueil de divers portraits des principales dames de la Porte du Grand Turc* (Paris, 1648).

Foreword

A READING of medieval and modern Jewish history would seem to suggest that Jews in the Diaspora can only flourish, perhaps even only survive in any meaningful sense, under the aegis of one or the other of the two successor religions of Judaism—Christianity and Islam. Virtually the whole panorama of Jewish history, or rather that part of it which is of any significance between the destruction of the ancient Jewish centers and the creation of the new Jewish state, is enacted either in the lands of Islam or in the lands of Christendom. There were occasional Jewish settlements in areas dominated by other civilizations and religions, such as India and China, but—despite the very large measure of tolerance they enjoyed—they did not flourish. They had no great share in the life and culture either of those countries or of the Jewish people, and appear to have produced nothing of any real importance for the one or the other. In India it was only with the advent of Islam that the small Jewish communities of that country received a modicum of attention and played a small part. In the realms of Hinduism, Buddhism, and the religions of the Far East, the Jews remained few and inactive, attracting neither persecution nor favor nor even attention. In Hindu India and in China, Judaism atrophied. When Arnold Toynbee used the term "fossil" to describe the Jews and some other minority groups that survived from the ancient world, he was vehemently criticized. Indeed the term "fossil," applied to something as vibrant as Jewish life in the Middle East, in Europe, and in the Americas, seems an absurdity. It is less absurd when applied to the isolated and immobilized Jewish communities of southern and eastern Asia.

The main centers of Jewish life and activity since the early Middle Ages have always been in the lands of Islam and Christendom. It seems that these two religions share some quality that is conducive to active Jewish life and that is lacking in societies dominated by Hinduism, Buddhism, and other faiths, to which perhaps in our own day we should add communism. Under Christian or Muslim rule, Jewish life has not always been comfortable. Jews may be slighted or hated; they may be despised or oppressed or slaughtered, but they are never ignored. For both Christianity and Islam, and therefore for both Christians and Muslims, the Jews and Judaism have a certain cosmic stature. They are known; they have a place, and indeed an important place, in both the theological and historical scheme of things. For good or for evil, they are seen as significant. The Christians even adopted the Jewish scriptures. The Muslims, though they did not go that far, were prepared to recognize the Jewish scriptures as a corrupt relic of an authentic revelation. For the Christian and the Muslim alike, the Jewish religion was neither alien nor absurd. It was a faith of the same kind as his own, but in an earlier and outdated version. He might punish the Jew for not catching up with his own, final version of God's message; he would not brush him aside as a votary of one minor sect or cult among a multiplicity of others. For the believer, persecution is easier to endure than disregard.

There are, it would seem, certain preconditions required to make possible the kind of cultural symbiosis—and still more the mutual and interacting cultural influences—that gave rise to what is now commonly called the Judaeo-Christian tradition in the Western world, and its equivalent in Islam. Until the twentieth century, when the positions of both Jews and Muslims underwent radical change, the term "Judaeo-Islamic" is at least as meaningful and as valid as "Judaeo-Christian" to connote a parallel and in many ways comparable cultural tradition.

As far as I am aware, the term "Judaeo-Islamic" has been used only by Western scholars and was never adopted either by Jews or by Muslims in the Islamic lands, since neither side saw their relationship in this light. At the present time it is a term of purely historical relevance, since the Judaeo-Islamic tradition no longer exists as a living force. The tradition has been destroyed, and its bearers have gone into exile or to Israel, where the two great branches of the Jewish people, the Jews of Islam and the Jews of Christendom, are meeting again for the first time in centuries and are struggling to create a new synthesis based on their common Jewishness. Their encounter repeats in miniature the clash of the two civilizations from which they come, and the aim of unity will not easily be achieved. The attempt will in part determine, in part be determined by, the parallel effort—so far of little avail—to create a new and different symbiotic relationship between Israel and the Islamic world by which it is surrounded.

In the following pages I have tried to examine the origins, the flowering, and the ending of the Judaeo-Islamic tradition, and to set these processes against the background of both Jewish and Islamic history. At most times and in most places, the Jews of Christendom were the only non-Christian minority in an otherwise wholly Christian land. Under the rule of Islam, in contrast, the Jews were normally one of several religious minorities, usually not the most important. The attitude of Islam to Judaism, of Muslims to Jews, is thus one aspect of a larger and more complex issue. The first chapter is therefore devoted to a general consideration of the relations between Islam and other religions—in theology and in law, in theory and in practice. The second chapter deals with the beginning and formation of the Judaeo-Islamic tradition, and is mainly concerned with the formative and classical periods of medieval Islam. The third chapter concentrates on the Ottoman Empire, the last of the great Islamic world states and the home of large and important Jewish communities; it also touches more briefly on other Muslim states in North Africa and in Asia. The fourth and last chapter, covering the nineteenth and twentieth centuries, takes as its theme the era of Western impact on the world of Islam, and the final phase of the Judaeo-Islamic tradition.

THIS book is based on the Gustave A. and Mamie W. Efroymson Memorial Lectures delivered at Hebrew Union College in Cincinnati, Ohio, in November 1981. I have considerably expanded the material presented in those lectures and added annotations. I should like to express my appreciation to my hosts and to my attentive and well-informed audiences, from whose questions and comments I derived much benefit. My thanks are also due to the *Alliance Israélite Universelle* for permission to use its archives, and to the archives' staff for their patience and courtesy. I am greatly indebted to several friends and colleagues for reading and commenting on earlier versions of this book; to Professors S. D. Goitein, Halil Inalcik, and Itamar Rabinovitch; and to Professors Judith Goldstein and Amnon Cohen, both members of the Institute for Advanced Study in the academic year 1982-83, who generously sacrificed some of their carefully hoarded time to read my drafts. I responded gratefully to some of their suggestions, and apologize to them for resisting others. I would like to thank Mr. Nikola Stavroulakis of Athens for his generous and invaluable advice and help in selecting and procuring illustrations. Finally, a special word of thanks to David Eisenberg, a graduate student in Near Eastern Studies at Princeton University, for his invaluable efforts as a research assistant, and to Ms. Dorothy Rothbard for her uncomplaining typing of innumerable revisions and changes in the long journey from the first draft of the lectures to the final text of the book.

A French version of parts of chapter 1 was published in *Annales* (1980). I would like to offer my thanks to the editors of that journal.

B. L.

September 1983

THE JEWS OF ISLAM

ONE

Islam and Other Religions

Two stereotypes dominate most of what has been written on tolerance and intolerance in the Islamic world.[1] The first depicts a fanatical warrior, an Arab horseman riding out of the desert with a sword in one hand and the Qur'ān in the other, offering his victims the choice between the two. This picture, made famous by Edward Gibbon[2] in his *Decline and Fall of the Roman Empire*, is not only false but impossible—unless we are to assume a race of left-handed swordsmen. In Muslim practice, the left hand is reserved for unclean purposes, and no self-respecting Muslim, then or now, would use it to raise the Qur'ān. The other image, almost equally preposterous, is that of an interfaith, interracial utopia, in which men and women belonging to different races, professing different creeds, lived side by side in a golden age of unbroken harmony, enjoying equality of rights and of opportunities, and toiling together for the advancement of civilization. To put the two stereotypes in Jewish terms, in one version classical Islam was like modern America, only better; in the other it was like Hitler's Germany, only worse, if such can be imagined.

Both images are of course wildly distorted; yet both contain, as stereotypes often do, some elements of truth. Two features they have in common are that they are relatively recent, and that they are of Western and not Islamic origin. For Christians and Muslims alike, tolerance is a new virtue, intolerance a new crime. For the greater part of the history of both communities, tolerance was not valued nor was intolerance condemned. Until comparatively modern times, Christian Europe neither prized nor practiced tolerance itself, and was not greatly offended by its absence in others. The charge that was always brought against Islam was not that its doctrines were imposed by force—something seen as normal and natural—but that its doctrines were false. Similarly on the Muslim side, the claim to tolerance, now much heard from Muslim apologists and more especially from apologists for Islam, is also new and of alien origin. It is only very recently that some defenders of Islam have begun to assert that their society in the past accorded equal status to non-Muslims. No such claim is made by spokesmen for resurgent Islam,[3] and historically there is no doubt that they are right. Traditional Islamic societies neither accorded such equality nor pretended that they were so doing. Indeed, in the old order, this would have been regarded not as a merit but as a dereliction of duty. How could one accord the same treatment to those who follow the true faith and those who willfully reject it? This would be a theological as well as a logical absurdity.

The truth, as usual, is somewhere between the opposing and contrasting stereotypes, and is more complex, more varied, more shaded than either of them.

How tolerant has Islam been in the past? The answers we may give to this question depend very much on the definitions we assign to its terms. What do we mean by Islam? This is neither as easy nor as obvious as might at first sight appear. What do we mean by tolerance? This again has many different definitions and raises many questions, not least of which is our standard of comparison.

The definition of Islam raises problems that are by now familiar. As has often been pointed out, the word "Islam" is commonly used in several different senses. In the first instance it denotes what Muslims conceive as the definitive revelation vouchsafed by God to the Prophet Muḥammad and contained in the holy book called the Qur'ān. This is what might be called the original Islam, a set of doctrines and commandments that is the basis and also the starting point of the religion known by that name.

But the word "Islam," like the word "Christianity," is also used in a second and broader sense to indicate the historical development of that religion after the death of its founder. In this sense the term "Islam" embraces theology and mysticism, worship and ritual, law and statecraft, and the whole complex of what countless Muslims thought, said, and did in the name of their faith. Islam in this sense may be as different from the Islam of the Prophet as, shall we say, the Christianity of the Emperor Constantine and the bishops from the Christianity of Christ—or, we might add, as different as the Judaism of the Talmud from that of the Torah, or the Judaism of today from that of the Talmud.

On the whole, however, the difference was probably less radical in Islam than in either Judaism or Christianity, because of the very different experiences of the founders of the three religions. Moses died before he entered the promised land; Christ died on the cross. Muḥammad attained not martyrdom but power. During his lifetime he became a head of state, commanding armies, collecting taxes, administering justice, and promulgating laws. The resulting interpenetration of faith and power, of religion and authority, has remained characteristic of Islam throughout most of its history. Even so, a great deal happened after the death of the Prophet, and Islam in the empire of the caliphs, like Christianity in the empires of Rome and its successors, evolved into something vastly more complex and more extensive than the original dispensation.

Finally, there is a third meaning in which the term "Islam" is the counterpart not of Christianity but of Christendom. In this sense it denotes not just a religion but a whole civilization, including many things that, as we in the Western world classify them, would not be regarded as religious in any sense. The term "Islamic art," for example, denotes virtually any kind of art produced within the Islamic world and marked by certain cultural and not merely religious characteristics. The term "Christian art" is limited to devotional and ecclesiastical art and would certainly not be extended to include art produced by Christians, still less by non-Christians living within the world of Christendom. Similarly, "Islamic science" means mathematics, physics, chemistry, and the rest, produced within this Islamic civilization and expressed normally in Arabic, occasionally in one of the other languages of Islam. Much of this science, as of this art, is the work not of Muslims but of Christians and Jews living in Islamic lands and constituting a part of the Islamic civilization in which they were formed. In contrast, the term "Christian science" is not used to designate the scientific achievements of Christians and others in Christendom. Indeed, until comparatively recently the term was not used at all, and when it first made its appearance, it was with an entirely different meaning.

Given the centrality and pervasiveness of religion in Islamic life and culture, even in this third sense of the word, the religious element in Islam is greater and more significant than in Christendom. But in this sense the term "Islam" denotes not precept but practice, not the doctrines and commandments of Islam, but the record of Muslim history—a record, that is, of the activities of human beings, their successes and failures, their weaknesses and achievements. And Muslims, like the rest of mankind, sometimes fall short of their own ideals, and sometimes relax their own strict rules. If we look for tolerance or intolerance in both the theory and practice of Islam, the answers may differ according to the definition of Islam that we adopt. They may also differ according to our standard and measure of tolerance.

What indeed do we mean by tolerance? In dealing with such subjects there is an inevitable tendency to assess and evaluate by comparison. If we speak of tolerance in Islam, we shall soon find ourselves measuring tolerance in Islam against tolerance in other societies—in Christendom, in India, in the Far East, or perhaps in the modern West. This is a form of comparison much cultivated by polemicists of various factions. The polemicist can of course make his task much easier by choosing the terms of comparison that suit him best. It is, for example, always easy to demonstrate the superiority of one religion to another by contrasting the precept of the one with the practice of the other. I recall reading a delightful little pamphlet proving that the Islamic caliphate was superior to the American presidency. This was done by the simple device of defining the caliphate in terms of theological and juridical treatises and the presidency in terms of the latest scandals from Washington. It would of course be equally easy, if any-one thought it worth the trouble, to demonstrate the reverse by the same method—by defining the presidency in terms of the constitution, and the caliphate in terms of gossip from medieval Baghdad, which is not lacking in the sources at our disposal.

This kind of comparison, however common, is not very helpful. It may be emotionally satisfying, but it is intellectually dishonest to compare one's theory with the other's practice. It is equally misleading to compare one's best with the other's worst. If, as the term of comparison for Christendom, we take the Spanish Inquisition or the German death camps, then it is easy to prove almost any society tolerant. There is nothing like Auschwitz in Islamic history, but it would not be difficult to name Muslim rulers or leaders worthy to rank with Cotton Mather or Torquemada and thus demonstrate Christian tolerance.

Other, more subtle, forms of loaded comparisons can be achieved by comparing discrepant times, places, and situations. For example, we can compare a medieval society with a modern one, or a believing society in which religion is profoundly important and religious tolerance is a searching test with a secular society in which religion is of minor interest. Tolerance is easy in matters of indifference; it is much more difficult in those that deeply concern us. A glance at the effective limits on freedom of expression in academic life even in the most advanced present-day democracies will illustrate this point.

Though other disparities have displaced religion as the main source of conflict and therefore of repression in our modern society, the term "tolerance" is still most commonly used to indicate acceptance by a dominant religion of the presence of others. Our present inquiry is limited to one question: How did Islam in power treat other religions? Or, to put it more precisely, how did those who, in different times and places, saw themselves as the upholders of Muslim authority and law, treat their non-Muslim subjects?

Whether this treatment deserves the name of tolerance depends, as already noted, on the definition of terms. If by tolerance we mean the absence of discrimination, there is one answer; if the absence of persecution, quite another. Discrimination was always there, permanent and indeed necessary, inherent in the system and institutionalized in law and practice. Persecution, that is to say, violent and active repression, was rare and atypical. Jews and Christians under Muslim rule were not normally called upon to suffer martyrdom for their faith. They were not often obliged to make the choice, which confronted Muslims and Jews in reconquered Spain, between exile, apostasy, and death. They were not subject to any major territorial or occupational restrictions, such as were the common lot of Jews in premodern Europe. There are some exceptions to these statements, but they do not affect the broad pattern until comparatively modern times and even then only in special areas, periods, and cases.

Islam has often been described as an egalitarian religion, and in many senses it is indeed such. If we look at the changes made by Islam at the time of its advent in seventh century Arabia; still more, if we compare the Muslim world in medieval times with caste in India to the east or with the entrenched aristocratic privilege of Christian Europe to the west, then Islam does indeed appear as an egalitarian religion in an egalitarian society. In principal and in law, it recognizes neither caste nor aristocracy. Human nature being what it is, both tend to obtrude themselves on occasion; but when this happens, it is in spite of Islam and not as part of it, and such departures from equality have repeatedly been condemned by both traditionalists and radicals as non-Islamic or anti-Islamic innovations.

All in all there was far greater social mobility in Islam than was permitted either in Christian Europe or Hindu India. But this equality of status and opportunity was limited in certain important respects. The rank of a full member of society was restricted to free male Muslims. Those who lacked any of these three essential qualifications—that is, the slave, the woman, or the unbeliever—were not equal. The three basic inequalities of master and slave, man and woman, believer and unbeliever, were not merely admitted; they were established and regulated by holy law. All three groups of inferiors were seen as necessary, or at least as useful, and all had their places and functions, even if occasional doubts were expressed about the third. Though there was general agreement on the need for slaves and women, there was at times some question about the need for unbelievers. The common view, however, was that they served a variety of useful purposes, mostly economic.

A major difference between the three is the element of choice. A woman cannot choose to become a man. A slave can be freed, but by the choice of his master, not his own. Both the woman and the slave are thus in a position of involuntary—for the woman also immutable—inferiority. The inferiority of the unbeliever, however, is entirely optional, and he can end it at any time by a simple act of will. By adopting Islam he becomes a member of the dominant community, and his status of legal inferiority is at an end. True, in the earliest Islamic period there was some social differentiation between the Arab Muslims who founded the Empire and the non-Arab converts who appeared among their subjects, and traces of these differences remained in the formulations of the law.[4] But in general, these early distinctions were forgotten, and in most times and places the perceived differences between old Muslims and new converts did not go beyond the bounds of familiar social snobbery. The status of inferiority to which the unbeliever was subject was thus entirely voluntary; from a Muslim point of view it might indeed be described as willful. For the Muslim, Jews and Christians were people who had been offered God's truth in its final and perfect form, of which their own religions were earlier, imperfect, and abrogated forms, and yet had willfully and foolishly rejected it.

Of the three victims of social inferiority, therefore, the unbeliever was the only one who remained inferior by his own choice. He was also the one whose disabilities were on the whole the least onerous of the three. Other things being equal, it was more comfortable to be a free male unbeliever than a woman or a slave in Muslim society. Perhaps for this very reason it was felt to be more necessary with an unbeliever than with a woman or a slave to enforce or at least visibly to symbolize the status of inferiority. Of this more in a moment.

The history of the relations between the Muslim state on the one hand and its non-Muslim subjects and, later, neighbors on the other begins with the career of the Prophet. The Qur'ān and the Muslim tradition tell us about Muḥammad's dealings with the Jews of Medina and of the northern Hijaz, with the Christians of Najrān in the south and some other Christians in the north, and with the pagans who constituted the majority of the Arabian population. For pagans the choice was clear: Islam or death. For Jews and Christians, possessors of what were recognized as revealed religions, based on authentic though superseded revelations, the choice included a third term: Islam, death, or submission. Submission involved the payment of tribute and the acceptance of Muslim supremacy. Death might be commuted to slavery.

At an early stage in his career as ruler of Medina, the Prophet came into conflict with the three resident Jewish tribes. All three were overcome and, according to the Muslim tradition, two were given the choice between conversion and exile, and the third, the Banū Qurayẓa, between conversion and death. The bitterness generated by the opposition of the Jewish tribes to Muḥammad is reflected in the mostly negative references to Jews in the Qur'ān and in the biography and traditions of the Prophet.[5]

A different situation arose with the capture in the year 7 of the Hijra (corresponding to A.D. 629) of the oasis of Khaybar, about ninety-five miles from Medina. This oasis, inhabited by Jews, including some who had settled there after being driven out of Medina, was the first territory conquered by the Muslim state and brought under its rule. The Jews of Khaybar capitulated to the Prophet after about a month and a half of hostilities, and were granted terms by which they were allowed to remain in the oasis and to cultivate their lands; but they were to hand over one-half of the produce to the Muslims. This agreement became a *locus classicus* for later legal discussions of the status of conquered non-Muslim subjects of the Muslim state. Its force as a leading case was not affected by the subsequent expulsion of the Jews of Khaybar in the time of the caliph 'Umar I (634-644).[6]

Contacts with Christians during the lifetime of the Prophet were rather less important and very much less contentious than with Jews. The Prophet's relations with Christian tribes and settlements in the northern Hijaz, and later in southern Arabia, were in general regulated by agreements, the most famous of which was that concluded with the Christians of Najrān. By its terms the Christians were permitted to practice their religion and run their own affairs, on condition that they paid a fixed tribute, gave hospitality to the Prophet's representatives, provided supplies to the Muslims in time of war, and refrained from usury. No doubt because of the rather more peaceful relations between the Prophet and the Christians, references to them in the Qur'ān are more favorable than to Jews. A much-quoted passage reflects the Prophet's differing experiences with the followers of the two earlier religions: "You will surely find that the most hostile to the Believers are the Jews and the idolators, while those who have the greatest affection to them are the ones who say: 'We are Christians' " (V,86). Other passages in the Qur'ān and elsewhere dealing with Jesus, while not accepting Christian doctrines on Christ's nature and mission, nevertheless share the Christian view of the Jewish rejection. Toward the end of the Prophet's life, the expansion of the Muslim state brought it into contact and sometimes into conflict with Christian tribes, and a somewhat less benign attitude toward Christians is reflected in Muslim scripture and tradition. But in general, while these on the whole express a far more sympathetic attitude toward Christians than toward Jews, the subsequent development of Islamic law makes no such distinction between the two.

The political problem posed by the relations between Muslim and non-Muslim was already clear in the lifetime of the Prophet, and the principles for its solution are contained in the Qur'ān. As chief magistrate and later ruler of the community of Medina, the Prophet had Jewish subjects; as sovereign of the Islamic state he had relations with both Christian and Jewish neighbors in other parts of Arabia. Already at the beginning, the question was seen as one of power—the rules to be followed by the Muslim state in its dealings with non-Muslim subjects, neighbors, and ultimately conquests, and the larger principles from which these rules derive. The Qur'ān speaks clearly and unequivocally on these issues and contains the nucleus of what later became an elaborate system of legal regulations.

But Muḥammad became a statesman in order to accomplish his mission as a prophet, not vice versa, and it is clear that the more strictly religious aspect of these relationships was also a prime concern. Here too the Qur'ān is very instructive. Unlike most earlier religious documents, it shows awareness of religion as a category of phenomena, and not merely as a single phenomenon.[7] There is not just one religion; there are religions. The word used in Arabic is *dīn*, obviously related to the Hebrew and Aramaic word meaning law. In both Judaism and Islam, religion and law, though not identical, largely overlap. Our modern word "religion" comes from the Latin, but the Latin *religio* and the Greek *threskeia* mean rather different things. The notion of religion as a class or category, in which Islam is one and in which besides Islam there are others, seems to have been present from the advent of the Islamic dispensation. The Qur'ān contains a number of passages in which the new religion defines itself against others— a normal way of self-definition, for communities as well as individuals. A much-cited phrase describes the Muslims as a *umma dūn al-nās*, a people or a community distinct from the rest of mankind. Islam is defined against Christianity by verses rejecting the incarnation and the trinity, against Judaism by passages abandoning some of the Jewish dietary laws. Far more important than the rejection of Christianity or Judaism, however, was the rejection of paganism—the main enemy against which the Prophet fought and from which he won the main body of his converts. Inevitably, the struggle against paganism brought Islam closer to Judaism and Christianity, seen, if not as allies, then as kindred faiths opposed to a common adversary.

Something of this sense of kinship can be discerned, at least in later times, in the consciousness of all three communities. There are passages in the Qur'ān that have been interpreted by later commentators and exegetes as an acceptance of religious pluralism, even of coexistence. Though the precise meaning of some of these passages in the original text has recently been challenged, there can be no doubt about the consensus of Muslim opinion. Thus, for example, the verse *la ikrāha fi'l-dīn* (II,256), "there is no compulsion in religion," has usually been taken to mean that other religions should be tolerated, and that their followers should not be forced to adopt Islam. Recently a European scholar has argued that this phrase is not a commendation of tolerance but rather an expression of resignation—an almost reluctant acceptance of the obduracy of others.[8] One may argue for or against this interpretation of the original meaning of the Qur'anic words, but even if we accept this version, it does not affect the way in which the verse was normally and regularly interpreted in the Islamic legal and theological tradition. The same may be said of the well known verse *lakum dīnakum walī dīnī* (CIX,6), "To you your religion, to me my religion." Here again there may be some uncertainty as to what precisely these words conveyed in their original context, but a common subsequent interpretation was to use this as proof-text for pluralism and coexistence. Another Qur'anic verse (II,62) appears to offer even more striking support: "Those who believe [i.e., the Muslims], and those who profess Judaism, and the Christians and the Sabians, those who believe in God and the Last Day and act righteously, shall have their reward with their Lord; there shall be no fear in them, neither shall they grieve." At first sight, this verse might seem to treat the four monotheistic and scriptural religions as equal. While such an interpretation is excluded by other passages in the Qur'ān, this verse nevertheless served to justify the tolerated position accorded to the followers of these religions under Muslim rule.

A much-cited example of other, more negative, passages occurs in V,51: "O you who believe, do not take the Jews and Christians as friends [or perhaps allies—the word is *aw-*

liyā']; they are friends of one another, and whoever among you takes them as friends will become one of them." This and other similar verses reflect the periods when the Prophet was in conflict with both religions. A well-known verse of the late period deals with the need for the holy war against the unbelievers and the imposition on them of a poll tax (Qur'ān, IX,29): "Fight against those who do not believe in God or in the Last Day, who do not forbid what God and his Prophet have forbidden or practice the true religion, among those who have been given the Book, until they pay the *jizya* [poll-tax] from their hand, they being humbled ('*an yadin wahum ṣāghirūn*)." These four words have recently been the subject of several studies, curiously enough written almost entirely by Jewish, mostly Israeli scholars, offering new interpretations of what these Arabic words really mean or could originally have meant.[9] But here again what concerns us is not the original meaning of the verse but the way in which it was interpreted in historic Islam. On this there is little doubt. The normal interpretation was that the *jizya* was not only a tax but also a symbolic expression of subordination. The Qur'ān and tradition often use the word *dhull* or *dhilla* (humiliation or abasement) to indicate the status God has assigned to those who reject Muḥammad, and in which they should be kept so long as they persist in that rejection. Thus, in a passage on the Children of Israel, we read: "They were consigned to humiliation and wretchedness; they brought the wrath of God upon themselves, and this because they used to deny God's signs and kill His Prophets unjustly and because they disobeyed and were transgressors" (II,61).

The imposition of the *jizya*, and more especially the manner of its payment, are usually interpreted in this light. The words '*an yadin wahum ṣāghirūn* are explained symbolically. Thus, for Maḥmūd ibn 'Umar al-Zamakhsharī (1075-1144), author of a standard commentary on the Qur'ān, the meaning of these words is that "the *jizya* shall be taken from them with belittlement and humiliation. He [the *dhimmī*, i.e., the non-Muslim subject of the Muslim state] shall come in person, walking not riding. When he pays, he shall stand, while the tax collector sits. The collector shall seize him by the scruff of the neck, shake him, and say: 'Pay the *jizya!*', and when he pays it he shall be slapped on the nape of his neck."[10] Other authorities add similar details—such as, for example, that the *dhimmī* must appear with bent back and bowed head, that the tax collector must treat him with disdain and even with violence, seizing his beard and slapping his cheeks, and the like. A piece of symbolism prescribed in many law books is that the *dhimmī*'s hand must be below, the tax collector's hand above, when the money changes hands. The purpose of all this is made clear by a fifteenth-century jurist of the rigorous Ḥanbalī school who, after prescribing these and similar acts of ritual humiliation to be performed in public "so that all may enjoy the spectacle," concludes: "Perhaps in the end they will come to believe in God and His Prophet, and thus be delivered from this shameful yoke."[11]

In contrast to the commentators and other theologians, the jurists are less ferocious and more concerned with the fiscal than the symbolic aspect of the *jizya*. Abū 'Ubayd (770-838), author of a classical treatise on taxation, insists that the *dhimmīs* must not be burdened beyond their capacity, nor must they be caused to suffer.[12] The great jurist Abū Yūsuf (731?-808), the chief qāḍī of the caliph Hārūn al-Rashīd, rules explicitly against such treatment: "No one of the people of the *dhimma* should be beaten in order to exact payment of the *jizya*, nor made to stand in the hot sun, nor should hateful things be inflicted upon their bodies, or anything of that sort. Rather, they should be treated with leniency."

Abū Yūsuf was not, however, in favor of coddling the taxpayers: "They should be imprisoned until they pay what they owe. They are not to be let out of custody until the *jizya* has been exacted from them in full. No governor may release any Christian, Jew, Zoroastrian, Sabian, or Samaritan unless the *jizya* is collected from him. He may not reduce anyone's payment by allowing a portion to be left unpaid. It is not permissible for one person to be exempted and for another to have to pay. That cannot be done, because their lives and possessions are guaranteed safety only upon payment of the *jizya*, which is comparable to tribute money."[13]

Several points must be noted in considering these and other similar passages. First, the jurists, with their more humane and also more practical attitude, belong to the early period of Islam, when it was confident and expanding; the commentators cited were writing in a period of contraction and constraint, when Islam was under threat both at home and abroad. Second, there can be no doubt that it is the attitudes of the jurists, rather than of the commentators and other theologians, that more accurately reflect the practice of Muslim rulers and administrators. Most of these, in the treatment of *dhimmīs* as in many other matters, failed to meet the exacting demand of their religious advisers and critics. The rules that some of the ulema laid down on the collection of the *jizya* and related matters belong more to the history of mentalities than of institutions. They have their own kind of importance, which becomes greater in times of crisis or defeat.

In general, these prescriptions again illustrate the need that was felt to remind the unbeliever of an inferiority that he might otherwise be tempted—and even permitted—to forget. No such reminder was needed for the woman or the slave.

After the death of the Prophet, the sway of Islam was extended across a vast territory reaching from the Atlantic in the west to the borders of India and China, and at times even beyond these borders, in the east. In these newly acquired territories there were large, important, and established religious communities; there were also old established legal and administrative systems regulating how these communities were treated. The most important of these systems—indeed the only ones encountered during the early formative centuries of the Islamic state—were those inherited from the ancient empires of Persia and of Rome.[14] The overwhelming majority of the new subjects of the Islamic state were Christians of various churches. Iraq, though part of the Persian Empire, was predominantly Nestorian Christian. Syria, Palestine, the whole of North Africa, and the Muslim acquisitions in Europe had all formed part of the Christian Roman Empire. In all these countries there were Jewish minorities, sometimes of considerable size. In Iran, too, there were Christian as well as Jewish populations, but the majority of the Iranians professed the religion of Zoroaster or one of its variants.

In the early centuries of Islamic rule, there was little or no attempt at forcible conversion, the spread of the faith being effected rather by persuasion and inducement. The rate and scale of conversion are difficult to assess from the available evidence, and some scholars have argued that as late as the Crusades, non-Muslims still constituted a majority of the population. It is clear, however, that large numbers of Christians, Jews, and Zoroastrians adopted the Muslim religion and became part of Islamic society.[15]

There are significant differences in the fates of the three religions after the Muslim conquest. Zoroastrianism fared worst. The pre-Islamic Persian state, unlike the Christian state, was completely overcome and destroyed, and all its territories and peoples were brought within the embrace of the Islamic caliphate. The Zoroastrian priesthood had been closely associated with the structure of power in ancient Iran. Deprived of this association, and possessing neither the stimulation of powerful friends abroad enjoyed by the Christians nor the bitter skill in survival possessed by the Jews, the Zoroastrians fell into discouragement and decline. Their numbers dwindled rapidly, and it is striking that they took little or no part in the Iranian cultural and political revival that occurred under the aegis of Islam in the tenth century and thereafter.

Christianity was defeated, not destroyed by the rise of Islam and the establishment of the Islamic state. But the processes of Arab settlement, of conversion to Islam and assimilation to the dominant culture, gradually reduced the Christians—when and at what stage is impossible to say—from a majority to a minority of the population. In some places, notably in Central Asia, southern Arabia, and North Africa, where Christianity before the advent of Islam had occupied a significant or even, in the last-named, a dominant position, it died out completely. For many Christians, the transition from a dominant to a subject status, with all the disadvantages involved, was too much to endure, and large numbers of them sought refuge from subjection by adopting Islam and joining the dominant faith and community. Judaism in contrast survived. Jews were more accustomed to adversity. For them, the Islamic conquest merely meant a change of masters, in most places indeed for the better, and they had already learned to adapt and endure under conditions of political, social, and economic disability. In the core countries of the Middle East, in Egypt, Syria, Lebanon, Palestine, and to a lesser extent Iraq, Christianity showed greater endurance than in North Africa, and Christian minorities survived in significant numbers. The reason may be that in these countries the Christians enjoyed the same advantage, if we may call it that, as the Jews: experience in survival. In Iraq they had been subordinate to the dominant Zoroastrian faith; in Egypt and the Syrian lands, though sharing the Christian religion with the rulers of the Byzantine Empire, they were of different sects and subject to discrimination and even at times to persecution. For many of the adherents of the Eastern churches, the advent of Islam and the transfer of their countries from Christian to Muslim rule brought a marked improvement in their circumstances, and a greater degree of religious freedom than they had previously enjoyed.

The further expansion of Islam brought the authority of the Muslim state beyond the heartlands of the Middle East and North Africa, which were also the homelands of Christianity and Judaism, into new areas where these religions had little or no impact. Buddhists and Hindus in Asia, animists in Africa south of the Sahara and of Ethiopia, now came within range of Muslim power. For the Muslim, these were polytheists and idolators, and were therefore not entitled to tolerance. For them the choice was between Islam and death, which later might be commuted to enslavement at the discretion of their captors.

In the vast empire which they created by conquest, the Muslims at first found themselves as a dominant but small minority. Their religion provided them with certain basic religious principles by which to rule their subject populations;

the older regimes which they had replaced bequeathed them traditions, procedures, and even personnel with which to put these principles in practice, or to modify them. Certain features of the situation in the former Persian and Byzantine lands that constituted the new Islamic caliphate are very relevant to the understanding of Muslim policies toward other religions.

Perhaps most important, the Middle Eastern region was and had for long been one of ethnic and religious pluralism. True, the Greek orthodox Christian masters of the Byzantine Empire and the Persian orthodox Zoroastrian masters of the empire of Iran had been trying, in the not-so-distant past, to impose their faith and identity on other religious and ethnic groups. But these efforts had failed, and the resulting tensions and resentments made the Muslim conquerors more welcome, and their presence, after the conquest, more acceptable. Apart from one episode, of brief duration and minor significance, the Arab Muslim rulers of the new empire did not repeat the errors of their predecessors but instead respected the pattern of pluralism that had existed since antiquity. This pattern was not one of equality, but rather of dominance by one group and, usually, a hierarchic sequence of the others. Though this order did not concede equality, it permitted peaceful coexistence. While one group might dominate, it did not as a rule insist on suppressing or absorbing the others. The new dominant group was variously defined—at first as Arab Muslims, then simply as Muslims. And with the replacement of an ethno-religious by a purely religious definition, access to the dominant group was open to all, thus making it possible, in the course of the centuries, for a dominant minority to become an overwhelming majority.

This change, too, was facilitated by a feature observable in the Middle East through most of its recorded history—a pattern of fluctuation, of change, even of fusion between the different communal, national, territorial, cultural, and legal identities. It is an essential part of human behavior to divide the world into ourselves and the rest. The ancient Middle East had known many such divisions—kinsmen and strangers, Jews and gentiles, Greeks and barbarians, citizens, metics, and aliens, as well as others. A classification already familiar to Jews and Christians was between believers and unbelievers. In Islamic times this came to be by far the most important line of division, overshadowing all others.

Both these groups were of course subdivided in various ways. The subdivisions of the believers do not concern us here. The unbelievers are subdivided, in most Muslim theoretical discussions of the subject, by two broad classifications, one theological, the other political. The theological classification is between those who follow a monotheistic religion based on revelation, and those who do not. The possessors of such a revelation are known as *ahl al-kitāb*, the people of the book, a term commonly used of the Jews, but also applicable to other religious communities possessing recognized scriptures.

The Qur'ān recognizes Judaism, Christianity, and a rather problematic third party, the religion of the Sabians,[16] as earlier, incomplete, and imperfect forms of Islam itself, and therefore as containing a genuine if distorted divine revelation. The inclusion of the not very precisely identified Sabians made it possible, by legal interpretation, to extend the kind of tolerance accorded to Jews and Christians much more widely, first to Zoroastrians in Persia, later to Hindus in India and other groups elsewhere. Communities professing recognized religions were allowed the tolerance of the Islamic state. They were allowed to practice their religions, subject to certain conditions, and to enjoy a measure of communal autonomy. Those who were not so qualified, in other words those classified as polytheists and idolators, were not eligible to receive the toleration of the Islamic state; for them, indeed, according to the law, the choice was the Qur'ān, the sword, or slavery.

A difficult problem is presented by monotheistic religions that arose after the advent of Islam, especially those that emerged from within the Muslim community, such as the Bahā'īs in Iran and the Aḥmadiyya in India. The followers of such religions cannot be dismissed either as benighted heathens, like the polytheists of Asia and the animists of Africa, nor as outdated precursors, like the Jews and Christians, and their very existence presents a challenge to the Islamic doctrine of the perfection and finality of Muḥammad's revelation. Muslim piety and Islamic authority have always had great difficulty in accommodating such post-Islamic monotheistic religions.

The political classification was between those who had been conquered or who had submitted themselves to the power of Islam and those who had not. In Muslim law and practice, the relationship between the Muslim state and the subject non-Muslim communities to which it extended its tolerance and protection was regulated by a pact called *dhimma*, and those benefiting from this pact were known as *ahl al-dhimma* (people of the pact) or more briefly, *dhimmīs*.[17] By the terms of the *dhimma*, these communities were accorded a certain status, provided that they unequivocally recognized the primacy of Islam and the supremacy of the Muslims. This recognition was expressed in the payment of the poll tax and obedience to a series of restrictions defined in detail by the holy law.[18]

The second category of unbelievers in this political classification consists of those who have not yet been conquered and are not subject to Muslim power. Lands where Muslims rule and the Islamic law prevails are known collectively as the *Dār al-Islām*, the House of Islam; the outside world, inhabited and also governed by infidels, constitutes the *Dār al-Ḥarb*, the House of War. It has this name because between the realm of Islam and the realms of unbelief there is a canonically obligatory perpetual state of war, which will continue until the whole world either accepts the message of Islam or submits to the rule of those who bring it. The name of this war is *jihād*, usually translated as "holy war," though the primary meaning of the word is striving or struggle, hence struggle in the cause of God. There are some parallels between the Muslim doctrine of *jihād* and the rabbinical Jewish doctrine of *milḥemet mitsva* or *milḥemet ḥova*, with the important difference that the Jewish notion is limited to one country whereas the Islamic *jihād* is worldwide.[19]

A non-Muslim from the *Dār al-Ḥarb* may be permitted to visit the Muslim lands and even to reside there for a specified period of time, for which he receives what is known in Muslim

law as an *amān*, a kind of grant of safe conduct. The holder
of an *amān* is called *musta'min*. This denotes the legal status
of the non-Muslim from outside who comes as a merchant or
envoy and stays for a while under Muslim rule. He is not a
dhimmī and is not subject to the poll tax and other disabilities.

The Muslim law books discuss in some detail the granting
of *amān*—when, by whom, to whom, and on what conditions
it may be granted. The *amān* was in principle given for a
limited period, and the visitor from outside who became a
permanent resident changed his status from *musta'min* to
dhimmī. In fact, however, the *amān* was normally renewed
on a yearly basis and resident communities of foreign merchants were allowed to retain that status. Citizens of a foreign
state could benefit from a collective *amān* accorded to their
government. Interestingly, the status of *musta'min* was on
some interpretations limited to Christian citizens of Christian
states. European Jews traveling in the Ottoman Empire were
sometimes, especially later, treated as citizens or subjects of
their countries, benefiting from the collective *amān* accorded
to them at other times as Jews, on the same footing as Ottoman
Jews, with both the advantages and disadvantages of this different status. In some Ottoman documents the phrase *kâfir
yahudisi* (the infidel's Jew) is used to designate Jews who are
subjects of Christian states. Similarly, in Persia, Sunni Muslim
subjects of the Russian czars were not allowed to benefit from
the extraterritorial privileges accorded to Russian subjects but
were treated as Sunni Muslims—not always an improvement
in a Shīʿī Muslim state.[20]

The discussions both of *dhimma* and *amān* relate to the
position of the non-Muslim resident or visitor in Muslim territories. The position of the Muslim, whether as resident or
as visitor, in non-Muslim territory is another matter. It is
discussed very little in the classical Islamic sources for the
good reason that the question rarely arose. In the early centuries of Islam, when the basic principles of Muslim law and
theology were formulated, Islam was advancing steadily all
the time. Territory might be briefly lost in the course of military operations, but it was always swiftly recovered. There

seemed no good reason to doubt that the advance of Islam would continue until, in the not too distant future, the holy war achieved its ultimate goal and all the world was incorporated into the House of Islam. The possibility of retreat, of the loss of territory and populations to infidel rule, simply did not occur to the men of the heroic age.

By the mid-eighth century it was becoming clear that the advance of Islam had come to a stop, and the notion of a frontier, and of dealings with more or less permanent authorities on the other side of it, came to be accepted. Though from time to time there was a resurgence of the *jihād* and a new wave of conquest, the final victory in the *jihād* was postponed from historical to eschatological time.

But worse was to come. What began as a pause became a halt and in time the halt gave way to a retreat. With the Christian recovery in Portugal, Spain, and Sicily and the arrival of the Crusaders in Syria and Palestine, Muslim territories were conquered by Christian armies and Muslim populations fell subject to Christian sovereigns. The resulting problem was much discussed by Muslim jurists, particularly of the Mālikī school, predominant in North Africa and among the Muslims of Sicily and the Iberian peninsula. There were different opinions on the obligations of Muslims who found themselves under non-Muslim rule. Some authorities took a lenient view. If a non-Muslim government was tolerant, that is, if it allowed Muslims to practice their religion and obey their laws and thus live a good Muslim life, then they might stay where they were and be law-abiding subjects of such a ruler. Some opinions go further and permit Muslims to remain even under an intolerant ruler, if necessary pretending to adopt Christianity but preserving their Islam in secrecy.

The opposing, more severe, view is formulated in a classical text, a *fatwā* or responsum written by a Moroccan jurist named Aḥmad al-Wansharīsī and issued shortly after the final conquest of Spain by the Christians. The *fatwā* addresses the question: May Muslims remain under Christian rule or must they leave? His answer is unequivocally that they must leave— men, women, and children alike. If the Christian government from which they are departing is tolerant, that makes it all the more urgent that they should leave, since under a tolerant Christian government the danger of apostasy is greater. Al-Wansharīsī dramatizes his ruling in the phrase: "Rather Muslim tyranny than Christian justice."[21]

This formulation was more rhetorical than real, since for the most part Christian justice was not on offer. There was no *dhimma* for Muslim residents in Europe, no *amān* for Muslim visitors. For a while Christian rulers in Spain and Italy, inspired by the example or perhaps fearing the reprisals of the surviving Muslim states with Christian subjects on European soil, treated their Muslim (and also Jewish) subjects with a measure of tolerance. But the final expulsion of the Moors removed both the example and the incentive, and Muslims, like Jews, were given the choice, if they wished to live, of exile or apostasy.

Inevitably, the great struggles between Christendom and Islam in the Reconquista and the Crusades brought a sharpening of religious loyalties and antagonisms, and a worsening of the position of minorities—Jewish as well as Christian—under Muslim rule. Even so, in this as in many other things, Islamic practice on the whole turned out to be gentler than Islamic precept—the reverse of the situation in Christendom.

The early history of the *dhimma*, or more broadly of the restrictions imposed on the tolerated non-Muslim subjects of the Muslim state, is full of uncertainties. The Muslim historiographic tradition ascribes the first formulation of these regulations to the caliph ʿUmar I (634-644) and preserves what purports to be the text of a letter addressed to him by Christians in Syria indicating the terms on which they are willing to submit—the disabilities they are prepared to accept and the penalties to which they make themselves liable if they violate these undertakings. According to this account, when the caliph was shown this letter he agreed to the terms with two additional clauses.

Though the so-called "pact of ʿUmar" was frequently cited both by Muslim and *dhimmī* writers as the legal basis of the relationship between the two sides, the document can hardly be authentic. As A. S. Tritton pointed out, it is not normal for the vanquished to propose the terms of surrender to the victors, nor is it likely that Syrian Christians in the seventh century, who knew no Arabic and undertook not to study the Qur'ān, would echo its language and provisions so faithfully. Some of the clauses clearly reflect developments of a somewhat later period, and it is not unlikely that in this as in many other aspects of early Muslim administrative history, some measures that were really introduced or enforced by the Umayyad caliph ʿUmar II (717-720) are ascribed by pious tradition to the less controversial and more venerable ʿUmar I.[22]

However, while this and other similar documents may in themselves be partly or wholly fabricated, they nevertheless reflect the development, in the course of the early centuries, of the policy of maintaining a certain differentiation between the dominant group and the various subordinate groups. The origins of many of these restrictions seem to go back to the very first period of the Arab conquests, and to be military in nature. When the Muslims first conquered immense territories and were a tiny minority of conquerors amid a vast majority of the conquered, they needed security precautions for the protection of the occupying and governing elements. As with so many of the practices of the early period, their actions, even though determined by immediate considerations of expediency, were sanctified and incorporated in the holy law, so that what began as security restrictions became social and legal disabilities. These restrictions involved some limitation on the clothes that *dhimmīs* might wear and the beasts they might ride, and forbade them to bear arms. There were limits on the building and use of places of worship. They were not to be higher than mosques; no new ones were to be built but only old ones restored. Christians and Jews were to wear special emblems on their clothes. This, incidentally, is the origin of the yellow badge, which was first introduced by a caliph in Baghdad in the ninth century and spread into Western lands in later medieval times.[23] Even when attending the public baths, non-Muslims were supposed to wear distinguishing signs suspended from cords around their necks, so that they might not be mistaken for Muslims when disrobed in the bathhouse. (Under Shīʿa rules, they were not allowed to use the same bathhouses.) The need to distinguish arose especially in the case of Jews, who shared with Muslims the rite of circumcision. The non-Muslims were required to avoid noise and display in their ceremonies, and at all times to show respect for Islam and deference to Muslims.

Most of these disabilities had a social and symbolic rather than a tangible and practical character. The only real economic penalty imposed on the *dhimmīs* was fiscal. They had to pay higher taxes, a system of discrimination inherited from the previous empires of Iran and Byzantium. There are varying opinions among scholars as to how hard the payment of these extra taxes bore on them. Where we have documentary evidence, as in the eleventh-century Geniza documents from Cairo, it would seem that for the poorer classes at least the burden was heavy.[24] However, since the rate of the *jizya* was fixed in gold by Holy Law, it became progressively less of a burden with the steady rise of prices and incomes through the centuries. In addition to the poll tax, *dhimmīs* were in principle, though not always in practice, called upon to pay a higher rate than Muslims in other taxes—in certain periods including even tolls and customs duties.

Apart from taxation, there was one other economic disability that often weighed very heavily on the non-Muslim subjects. This arose from the laws of inheritance. The general rule of Muslim law was that difference of religion was a bar to inheritance. Musims could not inherit from *dhimmīs*, nor could *dhimmīs* inherit from Muslims. A convert to Islam could therefore not inherit from his unconverted kinsmen, and on his own death only his Muslim heirs could inherit from him. If he reverted to his previous religion before his death, he ranked as an apostate, and his estate was forfeit. The rule that a Muslim cannot inherit from a *dhimmī*, while accepted by the four canonical schools of Muslim jurisprudence, was not admitted by all the doctors of Holy Law. Some of them held that in inheritance as in marriage, there is a necessary inequality, and that while a *dhimmī* may not inherit from a Muslim, a Muslim may inherit from a *dhimmī*. Some Shīʿa jurists went so far as to maintain that a Muslim heir will always preempt *dhimmī* heirs, and thus if a *dhimmī* died leaving a number of *dhimmī* heirs and a single Muslim heir, the latter alone could inherit to the exclusion of all others. The application of this rule, particularly in periods of forced conversion, could cause considerable hardship. It was the subject of frequent complaint among the Jews of Iran.[25]

In their own internal affairs, the *dhimmīs* normally enjoyed some autonomy, being subject to their own chiefs and judges, and living, at least in family, personal, and religious matters, according to their own laws. In relations between *dhimmīs* and Muslims, they were treated unequally. A Muslim could marry a free *dhimmī* woman, but a *dhimmī* man could not marry a Muslim woman. A Muslim could own a *dhimmī* slave, but a *dhimmī* could not own a Muslim slave. While the second of these limitations was often disregarded, the first, touching a far more sensitive point, was enforced with the utmost rigor, and any violation of it was severely punished and by some authorities treated as a capital offense. A similar position existed under the laws of the Byzantine Empire, according to which a Christian could marry a Jewish woman, but a Jew could not marry a Christian woman under pain of death. Likewise, Jews in Byzantium were forbidden to own Christian slaves on whatever grounds. The laws of the Muslim state assimilated the position of its Christian and Jewish subjects to that previously held by the Jewish subjects of Byzantium, but with some alleviation for both. The evidence of a *dhimmī* was not admissible before a Muslim court, and most schools— but not the Ḥanafīs—put a lower value on *dhimmīs* than on Muslims in the compensation or bloodwit to be paid for an injury.[26]

On the other hand, apart from the fiscal and occasionally the testamentary burden, *dhimmīs* were not subject to any economic disabilities. They were not barred from any occupations, nor were they forced into any others. There were no restricted professions and, besides the Hijaz, the Muslim holy land, and a few sanctuaries elsewhere, there were no restricted places. Except in Morocco and sometimes in Iran, *dhimmīs* were not confined to ghettos either in the geographical or in the occupational sense. Though Christians and Jews tended on the whole to form their own quarters in Muslim cities, this was a natural social development and not, like the ghettos of Christian Europe, a legally enforced restriction. The only significant exception in early times was the decision of the caliph ʿUmar I to expel the Jews and Christians from Arabia, so that only Islam would be professed in the holy land of its birth.[27] This decision seems to have applied only to the Hijaz, since Jewish and for a while Christian communities remained in southern and eastern Arabia.

However, just as the minorities tended to congregate in certain places, so too we find them concentrating in certain professions, more particularly in those requiring skills that the Muslims needed and either did not possess themselves or did not care to acquire. In certain periods the *dhimmīs* were heavily engaged in trade and finance, vocations scorned by hero military societies; in some periods, particularly in the later centuries, they were well represented in what one might call the dirty trades. These included such tasks as cleaning cesspools and drying the contents for use as fuel—a common Jewish occupation in Morocco, Yemen, Iraq, Iran and Central Asia. Jews were also found as tanners, butchers, hangmen, and other similar disagreeable or despised occupations. As well as the more obvious dirty jobs, these *dhimmī* professions included what was also, for a strict Muslim, something to be avoided—namely, dealing with unbelievers. This led at times to a rather high proportion of non-Muslims in such occupations as diplomacy, commerce, banking, brokerage, and espionage. Even the professions of worker and dealer in gold and silver, esteemed in many parts of the world, were regarded by strict Muslims as tainted and endangering the immortal souls of those engaged in them.

The question of the employment of non-Muslims in high government positions was a sensitive one, and is probably the commonest single form of complaint. A few *dhimmīs*, in both earlier and later times, managed to reach positions of great power and influence under Muslim sovereigns. Much greater numbers served in the middle and lower ranks of the state bureaucracy. This was of special importance in a society where access to the economic activities of the state was the surest— at times the only—road to riches. A saying attributed to the caliph 'Umar I is relevant: "Do not appoint Jews and Christians to public office because in their religion they are people of bribes. But [in Islam] bribes are not lawful."[28] The attitude of the doctors of the law to the employment of *dhimmīs* is unequivocal, as for example in this responsum from a thirteenth-century jurist:

QUESTION: A Jew has been appointed inspector of coins in the treasury of the Muslims, to weigh the dirhams that come and go and to test them, and his word is relied upon in this. Is his appointment permissible under the Holy Law or not? Will God reward the ruler if he dismisses him and replaces him with a competent Muslim? Will anyone who helps to procure his dismissal also be rewarded by God?

ANSWER: It is not permissible to appoint the Jew to such a post, it is not permitted to leave him in it, and it is not permissible to rely on his word in any matter relating to this. The ruler, may God grant him success, will be rewarded for dismissing him and replacing him with a competent Muslim, and anyone who helps to procure his dismissal will also be rewarded. God said, "O you who believe, do not take intimates from among those who are not of your own people, for they will spare no pains to corrupt you; what they desire is what makes you suffer; their hatred appears in their mouths, but that which is hidden in their breasts is greater. We have made the signs clear to you, if you can understand" (Qur'ān, III,114). The meaning of this is that you should not adopt outsiders, that is, unbelievers, and allow them to penetrate to your innermost affairs. "They will spare no pains to corrupt you." This means that they will not refrain from anything which is in their power to cause you harm, damage, or injury. "Their hatred appears in their mouths," for they say, "We are your enemies."[29]

Despite such rulings and polemics, however, the practice of employing non-Muslims was and remained almost universal—for pragmatic rather than theoretical reasons. They were useful, and that was enough; Muslim rulers and their spokesmen did not normally find it necessary or expedient to justify the practice. There is, however, an interesting story preserved in the scribal tradition and attributed to the time of the caliph ʿUmar I. The caliph, who was in the mosque, asked Abū Mūsā, the governor of Kūfa, to send his secretary to the mosque to read him some letters that had arrived from Syria. Abū Mūsā replied that the secretary could not enter the mosque. ʿUmar asked: "Why, is he in a state of ritual impurity?" "No," replied Abū Mūsā, "but he is a Christian." The caliph was shocked, slapped his thigh in indignation and said to Abū Mūsā: "What is the matter with you? May God strike you! Don't you know the words of Almighty God: ʿO you who believe, do not take the Jews and the Christians as friends' (V,51). Why couldn't you take a genuine Muslim?" To which Abū Mūsā replied: "His religion is his, his secretaryship is mine." Abū Mūsā's meaning is clear—a man's religion is his own affair; his employer's concern is only with his professional skill. The narrator of this story, however, gives the caliph the last word: "I will not honor them when God has degraded them; I will not glorify them when God has humiliated them; I will not bring them near when God has set them far away."[30] This distinction between a man's religious affiliation, which might be disapproved, and his professional competence, which might be useful, was rarely expressed but often applied.

The fiscal penalization of the unbeliever is basic to the perceived relationship between the two sides, and is central to the *dhimma* as a whole. Unlike most of the other restrictions of the *dhimma*, it rests on a clear text in the Qurʾān, and is well authenticated and established in the oldest traditions and historical narratives. In the earliest period, when, in accordance with the usage of the time, the Muslims would have been entitled to treat the conquered people as booty and sell them into slavery, the procedure adopted, of imposing a poll tax, was an action at once of prudence and of clemency. The point is clearly made in an early treatise on taxation citing a letter allegedly written by the caliph ʿUmar I to one of his governors:

> Neither you nor the Muslims who are with you should treat the unbelievers as booty and share them out [as slaves] . . . if you take the poll tax from them you have no claim on them or right over them. Have you considered, if we take them and share them out, what will be left for the Muslims who come after us? By God, the Muslims would not find a man to talk to and profit from his labors. The Muslims of our day will eat [from the work of] these people as long as they live, and when we and they die, our sons will eat [from] their sons forever, as long as they remain, for they are slaves to the people of the religion of Islam as long as the religion of Islam shall prevail. Therefore, place a poll tax upon them and do not enslave them and do not let the Muslims oppress them or harm them or consume their property except as permitted, but faithfully observe the conditions which you have accorded to them and all that you have allowed to them.[31]

poll-tax only!

The fiscal differentiation between believer and unbeliever remained in force throughout the Islamic world until the nineteenth century, and was never at any time or place allowed to lapse. The other restrictions, in contrast, seemed to have varied very considerably in their application. On the whole one gets the impression that they were more often disregarded than strictly enforced. Partly, no doubt, such laxness may be attributed to limited powers a medieval state was able to exercise over the mass of its subjects, but partly also to a genuine disinclination on the part of rulers to enforce the more irksome and humiliating restrictions.

All in all, though sometimes alleviated, this pattern of restriction became part of the Islamic way of life. As in many other societies and situations, its symbolic purpose was to demonstrate who belonged, however remotely, to the dominant group and who did not, and to maintain the distinction between the two.

The extent to which these restrictions were relaxed or enforced was determined by many factors, one of the most important being the strength or weakness of the Muslim state. It is easier to be tolerant when one feels strong than when one feels weak and endangered. The relationship between Muslims and *dhimmīs* was affected by the state of relations between Islam and the outside world. We shall hardly be surprised to find that from the time of the Crusades onward, as the Muslim world, compared with the Christian world, became weaker and poorer, the position of the non-Muslim subjects of the Muslim states deteriorated. They suffered from a more rigorous enforcement of the restrictions and even from a degree of social segregation—something that had not often happened previously.[32]

Their position was in general tolerable but insecure. Humiliation was part of the pattern. The Qur'ānic words *dhull* and *dhilla*, meaning lowliness, abasement, abjectness, are often used by Muslim writers to denote the humility that was felt to be appropriate for the non-Muslim and more especially the Jewish subjects of the state. This is amply attested both in medieval sources and by a succession of Western travelers to the Islamic lands.[33]

In considering the long record of Muslim rule over non-Muslims, a key question is that of perception and attitudes. How did Muslims view their *dhimmī* subjects? What did they see as the normal relationship between themselves and those subjects? What departures from these norms did they see as calling for action—and what action?

One important point should be made right away. There is little sign of any deep-rooted emotional hostility directed against Jews—or for that matter any other group—such as the anti-Semitism of the Christian world. There were, however, unambiguously negative attitudes. These were in part the "normal" feelings of a dominant group toward subject groups, with parallels in virtually any society one cares to examine;

in part, more specifically, the contempt of the Muslim for those who had been given the opportunity to accept the truth and who willfully chose to persist in their disbelief; in part, certain specific prejudices directed against one or other group and not against the rest.

On the whole, in contrast to Christian anti-Semitism, the Muslim attitude toward non-Muslims is one not of hate or fear or envy but simply of contempt. This is expressed in various ways. There is no lack of polemic literature attacking the Christians and occasionally also the Jews.[34] The negative attributes ascribed to the subject religions and their followers are usually expressed in religious and social terms, very rarely in ethnic or racial terms, though this does sometimes occur. The language of abuse is often quite strong. The conventional epithets are apes for Jews and pigs for Christians.[35] Different formulae of greeting are used when addressing Jews and Christians than when addressing Muslims, whether in conversation or in correspondence. Christians and Jews were forbidden to give their children distinctively Muslim names and, by Ottoman times, even those names that were shared by the three religions, such as Joseph or David, were differently spelled for the three.[36] Non-Muslims learned to live with a number of differences of this sort; like the sartorial laws, they were part of the symbolism of inferiority.

Shi'ite Muslims are further concerned with the question of ritual purity. Purity (*tahāra*) and impurity (*najāsa*) are matters of great importance for practicing Muslims. Defilement, according to Muslim jurists, produces a state of ritual impurity and may result from sexual intercourse, menstruation, and childbirth; from micturition and defecation; or from contact with unclean things or creatures such as wine, pigs, carrion, and certain discharges from the body. Among the strict Shī'a, non-Muslims also fall into this category, and contact with them, or with clothes, food, or utensils handled by them, causes ritual impurity requiring purification before undertaking religious or ritual duties.[37] Some authorities in Iran were even stricter on the question of ritual purity. Thus the first of a set of rules dating from late nineteenth-century Iran forbids

Jews to go out of doors when it rains or snows, presumably for fear lest the rain or snow carry the impurity of the Jews to the Muslims.[38] Such obsessive concern with the dangers of pollution by unclean persons of another group is virtually limited to Iranian Shiʿism and may be influenced by Zoroastrian practices. It is unknown to mainstream Sunni Islam.

By the early years of the twentieth century such beliefs and the resulting practices were gradually being forgotten. More recently, however, they have again been remembered. The Āyatollāh Khomeinī, in a widely circulated book written for the guidance of Muslims in ritual and related matters, observes: "There are eleven things which make unclean: 1. urine; 2. faeces; 3. sperm; 4. carrion; 5. blood; 6. dog; 7. pig; 8. unbeliever; 9. wine; 10. beer; 11. the sweat of a camel which eats unclean things." In a gloss on number 8 he adds: "The entire body of the unbeliever is unclean; even his hair and nails and body moistures are unclean." There is, however, some relief: "When a non-Muslim man or woman is converted to Islam, their body, saliva, nasal secretions, and sweat are ritually clean. If, however, their clothes were in contact with their sweaty bodies before their conversion, these remain unclean."[39]

To some extent the distinctive clothing or headgear worn by various subgroups within Islamic society served for internal at least as much as for external recognition, and in many situations might have conveyed no hostile intention. From very ancient times until, in some regions, the present day, various sectarian, regional, ethnic, tribal, and other groups have retained and even prized the cut or color or style of their clothing and headgear, which marked them off as different from other people and therefore, presumably in their own estimation, as superior. Pride in identity is normal among human social groups, even among those subject to discrimination or persecution. Distinctive clothing also serves a useful purpose by facilitating mutual recognition and claims to solidarity or support. Already in the seventh century B.C., the Prophet Zephaniah (I,8) records that "in the day of the Lord's sacrifice," God will punish "all such as are clothed with strange

apparel." Similarly, the Talmud urges Jews not to dress like
Persians, that is, like the masters of the empire in which they
lived.[40]

NB:
Abu ʿIsa

From the beginnings of Islam, the Muslim authorities are
virtually unanimous in their instruction to the believers:
"*Khālifūhum*"—differentiate yourselves from them—that is,
the unbelievers—in dress as in manners and customs.[41] And
since Muslims might not dress like unbelievers, it follows that
unbelievers should not adopt or imitate the attire of Muslims.
This principle was by no means always strictly enforced, but
its disregard was a common grievance of the ulema. Even the
usually calm and tolerant Ebussuud Efendi, chief mufti of the
Ottoman Empire in the time of Sultan Süleyman the Magnificent, was provoked to a rare display of anger by the violation
of this rule in his day, as is shown in a responsum, quoting
standard authorities:

> QUESTION: If a ruler prevents the *dhimmīs* who live among
> the Muslims from building high and ornamented houses,
> riding horses inside the city, dressing themselves in sump-
> tuous and costly garments, wearing kaftans with collars and
> fine muslin and furs and turbans, in sum from deliberate
> actions to belittle the Muslims and exalt themselves, will
> that ruler be rewarded and recompensed by God?
>
> ANSWER: Yes. The *dhimmīs* must be distinguished from
> the Muslims by their dress, their mounts, their saddles, and
> their headgear.[42]

The restrictions on clothing imposed on the *dhimmīs* were
drawn from several different sources and inspired by more
than one motive. In one sense, they no doubt retained and
confirmed certain styles of dress that had previously been—
or subsequently become—the accepted form of vestimentary
self-expression of the groups themselves. In early Islamic times,
there was, from the Muslim side, a necessary security consideration—that of mutual recognition and protection among
the Muslims themselves, when these were still a tiny ruling
minority. By medieval times, this need had disappeared, but

the Ottoman advance into Christian Asia Minor and then into Christian southeastern Europe brought it back again.

Finally, there was a third consideration, which became more important and perhaps dominant in the later centuries: the desire to humiliate, to remind the *dhimmī* of his inferiority, and to punish him if he ever tried to forget his quality and his place.

The stigma of inferiority is expressed in a number of ways. The requirement that Jews and Christians, their families, and their slaves wear cloaks and headgear of distinctive colors is not in itself necessarily hostile. However, the requirement that they wear a patch of a different color on their outer garments is clearly intended to degrade as well as to differentiate. The same is true of Moroccan regulations requiring Jews to go either barefoot or to wear straw slippers when they wandered outside the ghetto.

Of rather more significance are the regulations designed to show, and indeed to stress, that the *dhimmīs* do not belong to the arms-bearing classes.[43] The *dhimmī* must ride an ass, not a horse; he must not sit his beast astride but sidesaddle, like a woman. Most serious of all, he must carry no weapons, and is therefore always at the mercy of any who choose to attack him. While armed assault on *dhimmīs* is comparatively rare, there is always a sense of danger, as well as of inferiority, for those who may not bear arms in a society where it is normal to do so. The *dhimmī* was not alone in this disability, which also affected some other social groups, notably in the Arabian peninsula. He was, however, the most vulnerable. The *dhimmī* cannot and indeed may not defend himself even against such petty but painful attacks as stone throwing, done mainly by children—a form of amusement recorded in many places from early until modern times. The *dhimmī* had to rely on the public authorities to protect him from attack or other harm, and while this protection was often, indeed usually, given, it inevitably faltered in times of trouble or disorder. The resulting feeling of endangerment, of precariousness, is frequently expressed in *dhimmī* writings.

A similar expression of inferiority, this time more symbolic than substantial, is in the regulations regarding the attire of *dhimmī* women. The regulations forbidding them to wear luxurious garments or costly jewels were only sporadically enforced, and in any case were paralleled by restrictions imposed on Muslim women. But one difference is clearly a mark of inferiority. Free Muslim women going out of doors were required to keep their faces covered by some sort of veil. *Dhimmī* and slave women were permitted to go barefaced, and sometimes even required to do so. There are some sets of regulations that actually forbid the women of the *dhimmīs* to wear veils.[44] The association of the uncovered face with slave women and of the veiled face with virtue and propriety is clear. The sentiment expressed in these rules is clearly the same as that which inspired Western conventions, in the recent past, concerning the exposure of the female bosom. At a time when standards in the cinema and television were stricter than they are now, it was acceptable to display bare-breasted women if they were regarded as primitive natives of some remote place. It was forbidden to display them if they were white and, so to speak, civilized.

A common feature of all these regulations, Sunni and Shī'a alike, is the concern to maintain and more especially to symbolize the social inferiority of the *dhimmīs*, and the corresponding superiority of the Muslims. The symbols of inferiority were sometimes of greater importance than the reality, and surely—at least for the wealthy—more irksome. While in general the purpose of the clothing restrictions imposed on the *dhimmīs* was social and, in a sense, political, some other considerations may occasionally have intruded. An Ottoman *fermān* of 1568, responding to a wish expressed by the qāḍī of Istanbul for a stricter enforcement of the rules, notes as a reason given by the qāḍī that the extensive purchase by *dhimmīs* of the kind of headgear, footwear, and clothing worn by Muslims had led to a sharp increase in the prices of these commodities, thus causing injury to the Muslim population:

Order to the Qāḍī of Istanbul:

Whereas you sent a letter to my Threshold of Felicity, in which you informed me that Jewish and Christian men and women, among the infidels residing[45] in the God-guarded city of Istanbul, are wearing garments of fine, fringed cloth, buying fine turbans and binding them in the style of cavalry officers (*sipāhī*) and the like, wearing kaftans of atlas and cotton and other fine cloths and adopting the same kind of shoes and slippers as Muslims, with the result that the prices of turbans, cloths, and footwear has risen beyond reach, and in which you requested that infidels be prevented from dressing like Muslims—

And whereas, in reply to this, my imperial decree had already previously been written and sent, concerning the dress of the infidels—

Therefore I now command that when this present arrives, you proceed in accordance with my previously sent imperial decree, and ensure that henceforth neither Jew nor Christian nor any other infidel be allowed to wear fine clothes, as set forth above, and in contravention of my previously issued noble command.

(Given to the Inspector of Markets)
                    21 Safar 976/15 August 1568.[46]

A consideration of the highest importance was that the *dhimmīs* should show respect not only for Islam but also for each and every individual Muslim. Provisions to this effect were usually incorporated into the sets of regulations that from time to time were drawn up by religious authorities or promulgated by Muslim rulers to specify and itemize the restrictions arising from the *dhimma*. Sometimes the provisions were set forth in surprising detail. Thus in a twelfth-century work from Seville in Spain, dealing with the regulation of markets, we read:

A Muslim must not massage a Jew or a Christian nor throw away his refuse nor clean his latrines. The Jew and the Christian are better fitted for such trades, since they are the trades of those who are vile. A Muslim should not attend to the animal of a Jew or of a Christian, nor serve him as a muleteer, nor hold his stirrup. If any Muslim is known to do this, he should be denounced.[47]

A set of conditions the mullahs wished to impose on the Jews of Hamadān in Iran, in about 1892, are even more specific:

A Jew must never overtake a Muslim on a public street. He is forbidden to talk loudly to a Muslim. A Jewish creditor of a Muslim must claim his debt in a quavering and respectful manner. If a Muslim insults a Jew, the latter must drop his head and remain silent."[48]

If respect for the persons of Muslims was a social obligation, failure in which would lead to unpleasantnesss and possibly to severe reprisals, lack of respect for the Islamic faith itself, its book, or its founder could be a capital offense. Muslim books of jurisprudence devote considerable attention to the question of "the *dhimmī* who insults Islam"—to the definition of the offense, known technically as *sabb*, the proofs required to sustain a charge, and the punishment imposed.[49] In general, the Shiʿites and, among the Sunnis, the Ḥanbalī and Mālikī schools, are more severe, prescribing the death penalty; the Ḥanafīs and to some extent the Shāfiʿīs are more lenient, being content in some cases with flogging and imprisonment. The Turkish jurist Ebussuud Efendi prescribes the death penalty only for habitual and public offenders, and is at some pains to insist that it should not be given lightly. Clearly concerned to avoid frivolous and malicious prosecutions, he lays down that an offender cannot be treated as habitual "merely on the word of one or two persons." The habitual character of the offense must be made known to the authorities by "disinterested Muslims"; the word he uses is *bīgaraz*—literally, without grudge or malice. "When it becomes manifest that it is habitual, the offender may be put to death." Otherwise, "severe flogging and long imprisonment are enough." Similarly, while Ebussuud prescribes death for the offender who defames or belittles the Prophet, he notes that this applies where the offense is public and broadcast, and that the unbeliever is not held guilty under this head merely for stating "that which constitutes his unbelief," that is, for rejecting Muḥammad's prophetic mission. With these reservations, the *dhimmī* who publicly insults the Prophet must be put to death, since "it is not for this that we granted him the *dhimma*."[50]

There were indeed some seekers for martyrdom who attained their wishes in this way. Often, the offenders were demented or drunk; sometimes the accusation and punishment might be due to political needs, popular pressures, or even private vengeance. In general, prosecutions and condemnations for this offense were not common, but they occurred, from time to time, until well into the nineteenth century, and the fear of denunciation must have been a big factor in keeping the *dhimmīs* in their place. Edward Lane, who was in Egypt from 1833 to 1835, after noting the improvement in the position of Egyptian Jews under the rule of Muḥammad ʿAlī Pasha, remarked: "At present, they are less oppressed; but still they scarcely ever dare to utter a word of abuse when reviled or beaten unjustly by the meanest Arab or Turk; for many a Jew has been put to death upon a false and malicious accusation of uttering disrespectful words against the Kuran or the Prophet."[51]

A famous case occurred in 1857 in Tunisia. A Jew of very humble status, by the name of Batu Sfez, was charged with insulting Islam while in a state of intoxication. If tried by Ḥanafī law, then the state school in Tunisia, he would have been let off with a lesser penalty. Instead, the ruler took the exceptional measure of referring the case to the far more rigorous Mālikī court, thus ensuring a death sentence. According to contemporary observers, the reason was that the ruler had recently ordered the execution of a Muslim soldier for robbing and murdering a Jew. The execution of the Jewish offender was thus seen as a necessary demonstration of evenhandedness.[52] Though the criminal prosecution of this offense has in most places ceased, criticism, or even discussion, of Islam by a non-Muslim is still a very sensitive subject.

Shiʿites in Iran were far less tolerant than their Sunni contemporaries in the Ottoman Empire. Expulsion, forced conversion, and massacre—all three of rare occurrence in the Sunni lands—were features of life in Iran up to the nineteenth century. Western travelers comment frequently on the abject and miserable status of the non-Muslim subjects of the shāhs. In general, it is significant that, with the striking exception of Spain and Arabia, Islamic regimes were more tolerant at the center than at the periphery, indeed becoming more repressive the further they were from the heartlands of Islamic civilization. Life for non-Muslims was usually better in Egypt or Turkey, Syria or Iraq than in North Africa and Central Asia.

Perhaps the clearest indication of the perception of the *dhimmīs* as of lower and humbler status is their use as a paradigm of discrimination and inferiority. A Shiʿite author accused the Caliph ʿUmar of introducing racial discrimination between Arab and non-Arab Muslims in marriage; by restricting the rights of the latter, he was treating them "like Jews or Christians."[53] A Syrian historian, noting that the North Africans who conquered Egypt in the tenth century were discriminating against soldiers of Eastern (not North African) origin, observed that "our brethren the easterners among them have become like the *dhimmīs* among the Muslims."[54] An eighteenth-century Damascene diarist, recording the arrest and rough handling by janissaries of a Muslim Sharīf, a descendant of the Prophet, commented that he was treated "as though he were one of the Jews. . . ."[55] The same perception is reflected in a common oath formula: "[If what I say is not true], may I become a Jew. . . ."

As well as the negative side, there is also a positive side. Relations between these communities and the Muslim state were regulated by law, by the *dhimma*, and seen as a contractual relationship. Both Qurʾān and *ḥadīth* insist strongly on the sanctity of treaties, and on the need to respect the lives and property of those persons or groups, called *muʿāhad*, with whom a treaty (ʿahd) has been concluded. Some early jurists at least regarded the *dhimma* as a form of treaty, covered by these prescriptions. A letter ascribed to the famous Syrian Arab jurist al-Awzāʿī (d. 774) is instructive. The Arab governor of Lebanon had crushed a rebellion among the Christians, and al-Awzāʿī accused him of acting with indiscriminate harshness. The governor, he said, had expelled *dhimmīs* from Mount Lebanon who had had no part in the rebellion:

"You killed some, and sent others back to their villages. How can you punish the many for the sins of the few and deprive them of their homes and property, when God has decreed that 'none shall bear another's burden' (Qur'ān, VI,164). The best counsel to observe and follow is that of the Prophet ... who said: 'If anyone oppresses a *mu'āhad* and burdens him beyond his capacity, then I myself will be his accuser [on the Day of Judgment].' "[56]

In this context the term *mu'āhad* clearly includes the *dhimmī*. In later writings, less importance is given to the contractual and bilateral character of the *dhimma*, which is seen rather as a concession granted by the Muslim state to a group of those over whom it rules. As such, however, it is still part of the Holy Law of Islam and must be respected and defended by any good Muslim. The Holy Law conferred a certain status on the followers of these religions. They were, therefore, entitled to that status in accordance with God's law.

If the law forbade them to rise above it, it also forbade Muslims to drag them down below it, and from time to time this principle was explicitly reaffirmed. In the early eleventh century, we are told, the Fatimid caliph al-Ẓāhir

> issued a rescript ... which was read before the people, expressing his good intentions toward all and reaffirming that all persons entrusted with authority in the service of the state and in the administration of justice must base themselves on what is right, pursue justice in all that comes before them and concerns them, defend the peaceful and upright, and pursue wrong-doers and troublemakers. He also said that he had heard of a fear among the people of the protected religions, the Christians and Jews, that they would be compelled to pass to the religion of Islam and of their resentment at this, since there should be no constraint in religion (Qur'ān, II,256). He said that they should remove these imaginary fears from their hearts and be assured that they would enjoy protection and care and retain their position as protected communities. Whoever among them wishes to enter the religion of Islam by the choice of his own heart

and by the grace of God, and not for the purpose of self-advancement and aggrandizement, may do so and be both welcome and blessed; whoever prefers to remain in his religion, but not the backslider, has protection and safeguard, and it is the duty of all members of the [Muslim] community to guard and protect him.[57]

In the following century, that is, in the period of the Crusades, a jurist ruled on the question of whether a Muslim ruler may deport his *dhimmī* subjects. The answer was that he may, but only if there is good reason, whether for their own protection or in the interests of Muslim security:

If the Imam wishes to move the people of the protected religions [*ahl al-dhimma*] from their land, it is not lawful for him to do so without justification, but it is lawful if there is justification. The justification in our time is that the Imam may fear for the safety of the people of the protected religions at the hands of the infidel enemy [*ahl al-ḥarb*], since they are helpless and have little strength, or he may fear for the safety of the Muslims at their hands, lest they inform the enemy of the points of weakness of the Muslims.[58]

An Ottoman *fermān* issued by Sultan Mehmed III, dated March 1602, very clearly states the obligations of the Muslim state toward the *dhimmīs*. It begins:

Since, in accordance with what Almighty God the Lord of the Universe commanded in His Manifest Book concerning the communities of Jews and Christians who are people of the *dhimma*, their protection and preservation and the safeguarding of their lives and possessions are a perpetual and collective duty of the generality of Muslims and a necessary obligation incumbent on all the sovereigns of Islam and honorable rulers,

Therefore it is necessary and important that my exalted and religiously inspired concern be directed to ensure that, in accordance with the noble Sharīʿa, every one of these communities that pays tax to me, in the days of my imperial state and the period of my felicity-encompassed Caliphate, should live in tranquillity and peace of mind and go about their business, that no one should prevent them from this, nor anyone cause injury to their persons or their possessions, in violation of the command of God and in contravention of the Holy Law of the Prophet.[59]

The need to uphold the Holy Law by which the status of the *dhimmī* is established and protected was a common concern of Muslim jurists, and even of rulers. The Ottoman period, about which, thanks to the survival of archives, we are much better informed, gives numerous examples of successful appeals by members of the minorities to the forces of law and order, to protect them against mob violence. Sometimes the forces of law and the forces of order may not be in complete accord, and there are occasions when the minorities take refuge with one from the other. In an Ottoman provincial center, law and order were represented, respectively, by the qāḍī, the judge, and the *vali*, the governor. The one was buttressed by the ulema, the other by the armed forces. At different times we find members of the minorities seeking the help of a righteous judge against an oppressive ruler, and at other times calling on a fair-minded ruler to save them from the incitements of bigoted ulema. The latter rarely included such government-appointed officers as the qāḍī however, and more often than not the *dhimmīs* were able to count on the support of both the administrative and religious authorities. Trouble arose—in later centuries with increasing frequency—when these authorities themselves lacked power and were unable to maintain order or enforce the law.

Sometimes, when a persecution occurred, we find that the instigators were concerned to justify it in terms of the Holy Law. The usual argument was that the Jews or the Christians had violated the pact by overstepping their proper place. They had thus broken the conditions of the contract with Islam, and the Muslim state and people were no longer bound by it.

This concern appears even in violently anti-*dhimmī* literature. Particularly instructive in this respect is that anti-Jewish poem of Abū Isḥāq, written in Granada in 1066. This poem, which is said to have been instrumental in provoking the anti-Jewish outbreak of that year, contains these significant lines:

> Do not consider it a breach of faith to kill them
>   the breach of faith would be to let them carry on.
> They have violated our covenant with them
>   so how can you be held guilty against the violators?
> How can they have any pact
>   when we are obscure and they are prominent?
> Now we are the humble, beside them,
>   as if we were wrong, and they right!
> Do not tolerate their misdeeds against us
>   for you are surety for what they do
> God watches His own people
>   and the people of God will prevail.[60]

Outrage is the dominant theme of the poem. But in striking contrast to the anti-Semitism of Christendom, Abū Isḥāq even in his outrage does not refuse Jews the right to life, livelihood, and the practice of their religion. As a jurist he is aware that these rights are guaranteed by the Holy Law and incorporated in the *dhimma*, which is a binding legal contract. Abū Isḥāq does not seek to deny or even to minimize the contract. On the contrary, he is at some pains to reassure his hearers, and no doubt himself, that in robbing and killing Jews they would not be acting illegally—that is to say, they would not be violating the provisions of a contract established and sanctified by the Holy Law of Islam, and thus imperiling their souls in the hereafter. It is the Jews, he argues, who have violated the contract that has, therefore, ceased to be binding on the Muslims. The Muslims and their rulers are absolved from their obligations under the *dhimma* and are thus free to attack, kill, and expropriate the Jews without illegality, that is, without sin.

Diatribes such as Abū Isḥāq's and massacres such as that in Granada in 1066 are of rare occurrence in Islamic history. In general, the *dhimmīs* were allowed to practice their religions, pursue their avocations, and live their own lives, so long as they were willing to abide by the rules. Significantly, it is during the nineteenth and twentieth centuries, when the *dhimmīs* were no longer prepared to accept or respect the rules, that the most violent and bloody clashes have occurred.

Even in earlier times, however, when the rules were understood and accepted by both sides, there were occasional difficulties. Sometimes these led to violence, to what one side might call persecution and the other chastisement. Such violence was rare. Much more frequent was a tightening of the rules—the stricter enforcement of restrictions that had previously been allowed to lapse, or even the imposition of new restrictions. A classification and possibly a typology of such repressions, or at least of the arguments advanced on the Muslim side to justify or to explain them, may throw some light on the larger problem of how tolerance was understood and practiced.

The commonest case is that of the pious and rigorous ruler who makes good the errors of his impious and lax predecessors, and restores the community to the authentic Islamic way. The paradigm of such a ruler is the Umayyad caliph ʿUmar II whose biography, as told by later historians, contains what became the standard themes of an Islamic restoration. At recurring intervals in Islamic history, movements or individual rulers inaugurate periods of strict and militant orthodoxy. In such times there is an insistence on the purification of Islam, on the need to remove the accretions and innovations that have corrupted and distorted the faith in the course of the centuries, and to return to the true, authentic Islam of the Prophet and his companions. The proper subordination of the unbeliever and the rigorous enforcement of the restrictions imposed on him are an obvious part of any such pious restoration. This does not require the persecution of the unbeliever; on the contrary, biographers and historians of pious rulers usually insist on the fairness and justice with which the *dhimmīs* are treated. But justice requires that they be kept in the place which the law assigns to them, and not be permitted to go beyond it.

ʿUmar II is credited with a stricter enforcement of the fiscal and other restraints on the non-Muslims and with taking steps to exclude them from positions of power and influence they had been permitted to occupy under his predecessors. It is not impossible that ʿUmar II was responsible for introducing some of the restrictions traditionally attributed to ʿUmar I. The restriction of *dhimmī* rights was coupled with the extension of the rights accorded to non-Arab converts to Islam, who were now in large measure accorded the equality they had previously claimed and which the Arab aristocracy had hitherto withheld from them.

The historical circumstances of ʿUmar II's reforms are significant. A vast Arab naval and military expedition sent to capture Constantinople had failed disastrously, and the Umayyad Empire faced a moment of crisis. The war imposed new and heavy economic burdens; the destruction of the Arab army under the walls of Constantinople deprived the government of the means to impose its will by force. Umayyad rule, at all times challenged by pious and other Muslim dissidents, could well have been in danger of overthrow. When the caliph Sulaymān (715-717), who had launched the expedition, died, the Umayyad family, always distinguished by political skill, chose as his successor the one Umayyad prince with a reputation for piety and with the ability to rally Muslim opinion to the support of the dynasty by pursuing policies close to their beliefs.

Similar considerations may have guided the Abbasid caliph al-Mutawakkil (847-861). In Muslim historiography he is credited with putting an end to the domination of the deviant and persecuting Muʿtazila school, favored by the previous caliphs, and returning to authentic Islamic doctrine and practice. These changes may not be unrelated to the need to mobilize popular support against his own pretorian guards, who were threatening his rule and even his person. In a decree issued in 850, we read:

> It has become known to the Commander of the Faithful that men without judgment or discernment are seeking the help of *dhimmīs* in their work, adopting them as confidants

in preference to Muslims, and giving them authority over the subjects. And they oppress them and stretch out their hands against them in tyranny, deceit, and enmity. The Commander of the Faithful, attaching great importance to this, has condemned it and disavowed it. Wishing to find favor with God by preventing and forbidding this, he has decided to write to his officers in the provinces and the cities and to the governors of the frontier towns and districts that they should cease to employ *dhimmīs* in any of their work and affairs or to adopt them as associates in the trust and authority conferred on them by the Commander of the Faithful and committed to their charge. . . .

Do not therefore seek help from any of the polytheists, and reduce the people of the protected religions to the station which God has assigned to them. Cause the letter of the Commander of the Faithful to be read aloud to the inhabitants of your district and proclaim it among them, and let it not become known to the Commander of the Faithful that you or any of our officials or helpers are employing anybody of the protected religions in the business of Islam.[61]

The main purpose of this and other similar measures seems to have been to reduce the encroachment of non-Muslims on the Muslim state and their arrogation to themselves of an authority that would rightfully belong to Muslims alone. At the same time, al-Mutawakkil

gave order that the Christians and the *dhimmīs* in general be required to wear honey-colored hoods and girdles; to ride on saddles with wooden stirrups and two balls attached to the rear; to attach two buttons to the caps of those who wear them and to wear caps of a different color from those worn by the Muslims; to attach two patches to their slaves' clothing, of a different color from that of the garment to which they are attached, one in front on the chest, the other at the back, each patch four fingers in length, and both of them honey-colored. Those of them who wore turbans were to wear honey-colored turbans. If their women went out and appeared in public, they were only to appear with honey-colored head scarfs. He gave orders that their slaves were to wear girdles and he forbade them to wear belts. He gave orders to destroy any churches which were newly built, and to take the tenth part of their houses. If the place was large enough it was to be made into a mosque; if it was not suitable for a mosque it was to be made into an open space. He ordered that wooden images of devils should be nailed to the doors of their houses to distinguish them from the houses of the Muslims. He forbade their employment in government offices and on official business where they would have authority over the Muslims. He forbade their children to attend Muslim schools or that any Muslim should teach them. He forbade the display of crosses on their Palm Sundays and Jewish rites in the streets. He ordered that their graves be made level with the ground so that they should not resemble the graves of the Muslim.[62]

There is no evidence of any violent persecution of non-Muslims under al-Mutawakkil, nor is it clear how far, how wide, and how long those restrictions were enforced. The frequent pious complaints of their disregard and occasional pious attempts to reimpose them both suggest that their application was for the most part lax and intermittent.

There were many later rulers who followed the model of ʿUmar II. One such was the Ottoman sultan Bayezid II (1481-1512), whose reign marked something of a reaction against the policies of his father and predecessor Mehmed the Conqueror. Mehmed had opened, so to speak, a window to the West. He had shown favor to both Greeks and Jews, and had even extended patronage to artists and scholars from Christian Europe.[63] Bayezid, reputed to be a man of great piety and much under the influence of the ulema, changed all that. The paintings his father had accumulated in the palace were removed and sold, while the Christian and Jewish courtiers and functionaries were sent about their business. According to a Jewish source, the sultan gave orders to close synagogues that had been built in Istanbul after its capture by the Turks and were thus in breach of the rules of the Holy Law permitting *dhimmīs* to retain only those places of worship they had possessed before the conquest and forbidding them to build new ones. This may be related to specific measures, reported by Muslim sources, resulting from demographic changes. Certain districts that had been predominantly non-Muslim were intensively settled by Muslims. In some of these areas, churches and synagogues, previously tolerated, were seen as offensive to the new majority, and steps were taken to close them or transfer them elsewhere. In this as in other cases, action to curtail the presumption of the *dhimmīs* earned the approval of pious chroniclers. It is striking, however, that it is this same Sultan Bayezid II who, in 1492 and after, permitted and even encouraged great numbers of Jews from Spain and Portugal to settle in the Ottoman realms and to rebuild their lives after their expulsion from their homelands.[64]

The paradox is apparent, not real. The strict application of the Sharī'a imposed certain restrictions on the non-Muslim communities, and limited or precluded their participation in the processes of government. It did not require—indeed, it did not permit—that they be persecuted, in the sense that they be prevented from practicing their religions, living according to their own customs, or earning their livelihood. It was indeed during the reign of the stern and rigorous but just and pious Bayezid II that the greatest Jewish immigration into the Ottoman lands took place.

Once again it may be noted that the severities of Sultan Bayezid coincided with a period of grave external and internal threats to his throne. His brother Jem, an unsuccessful rival claimant to the throne, had fled to Europe, where the pope and some of the Christian princes were trying to use him in a combined attack on the Ottoman territories and the Ottoman throne. His relations with both his Muslim neighbors were bad. There were disputes with the Mamluk sultans who ruled over Egypt and Syria, while in the east the new militant Shi'ite dynasty in Iran threatened Bayezid not only with warfare on his border but with sedition and upheaval among his own Muslim subjects. Against the double threat of Christian

Crusades from the west and Shiʿite subversion from the east, Bayezid needed the rewards of piety both from above and and from below.

Under the rule of Bayezid's successors the position of the subject communities improved, but a new moment of danger came during the reign of Murad III (1574-1595). Again the pattern is much the same: a predecessor seen as overindulgent to the *dhimmīs*, religious and military problems at home and abroad; measures against some *dhimmīs* seen as unduly rich or powerful; orders to close unauthorized places of worship; and the reintroduction of the old rules concerning clothing and headgear. According to a report by a Venetian cleric, the sultan at one point decided to kill first all the Jews and then all the Christians in his empire, but was dissuaded by his mother and the grand vizier. This story is confirmed neither by Jewish nor by Turkish sources, and seems inherently improbable.[65] What is well attested is the normal pattern of such interludes of religious severity—the restriction on fine clothes, the prescription of a special kind of hat, the closure of new places of worship deemed illegal, and the like.

The *dhimmīs* may also suffer—and rather more seriously—under another kind of religious regime, very different from that of pious and rigorous exponents of a return to the good old ways. From time to time, especially in periods of great upheaval and disorder, Messianic and millenarian movements have appeared in the lands of Islam, which sometimes destroyed old regimes and swept new rulers and even dynasties into power, through revolution often followed by conquest. One of the most successful of these was the movement known as the Almohads, founded by a Berber religious leader called Muḥammad ibn ʿAbdallāh ibn Tumart in the second and third decades of the twelfth century. In 1121 he was recognized by his followers as the Mahdī, the divinely appointed leader who is to restore Islam to the true path and inaugurate the kingdom of heaven on earth. Under the Mahdī's successors the power of the Almohads spread from the valleys of the High Atlas where it had begun, and by the late twelfth century they were masters of most of Muslim North Africa and Spain. The Mes-

sianic fervor of the Almohads could not tolerate any deviation
from their particular version of Islam. Muslims who would
not submit were ruthlessly purged, while Jews and still more
Christians were denied the tolerance prescribed by the Sharī'a.
It was probably at this time that Christianity was finally ex-
tirpated from North Africa. Jews, too, suffered badly in both
North Africa and Spain and—exceptionally in Muslim history
west of Iran—were given the choice between conversion, exile,
and death.[66]

The later Almohads modified their stance and permitted the
dhimmīs to practice their religion in accordance with the law.
Their position was, however, permanently worsened, especially in North Africa, where Christians disappeared and Jews
were subject to the severest and most rigorous interpretation
of the *dhimma*. The enthronement of the Safavids, a militant
Shi'ite dynasty with Messianic claims, in Iran at the beginning
of the sixteenth century also led to a worsening in the position
of the non-Muslims, Jews, Christians, and Zoroastrians. Under the Safavid shāhs they were subject to frequent vexations
and persecutions, and at times to forced conversion.[67]

A parallel to earlier Islamic messianism may be discerned
in some modern movements, expressed in national and social
rather than religious terms, but ascribing an analogous role
to the charismatic leader and to the doctrine that he proclaims.
Like those who reject God's final revelation and its latest
renewal, so too those who cannot rally or will not be identified
with the cause may no longer be accorded tolerance.

To these religiously or ideologically motivated forms of
repression one may add a third, also derived from the sovereign's initiative, but inspired by limited and practical rather
than by large and moral considerations. The usual reason is
shortage of money. When a ruler is in financial straits, a simple
way of raising funds is to enforce some disagreeable and previously forgotten restriction, or to impose a new one on the
non-Muslims, who are then usually willing to persuade the
ruler, by means of a suitable gift, to rescind his decree.

In all these situations the repression is initiated by the ruler,
sometimes to placate popular sentiment, more often in re-

sponse to his own moral or political needs. Sometimes, however, the attack on the *dhimmīs* originated with the populace, and it was mostly on these occasions that it involved physical violence. The commonest reason by far for such outbreaks in premodern times was that the *dhimmīs* were not keeping their place, that they were acting arrogantly, that they were getting above themselves. This brings us to one of the fundamental political ideas of Islam—the idea or ideal of justice. In most Muslim political thought the central duty of government, the main justification of authority and the cardinal virtue of the good ruler, is justice. The definition of justice has varied in Islamic history. In the earlier period, justice usually meant the enforcement of God's law, that is, the maintenance and application of the Holy Law of Islam. Later, when the Holy Law in all but personal and ritual matters was increasingly disregarded by Muslim governments, it could no longer serve as a touchstone of the just or unjust ruler; the term "justice" came rather to have the sense of balance, of equilibrium—that is, the maintenance of the social and political order, with each group, each element, in its proper place, giving what it must give and getting what it should get.

In either of these senses, the non-Muslim subjects had a certain place. If they seemed to be going beyond the place assigned to them, it was either, in the first sense of justice, a breach of the law, or, in the second sense, a disturbance of the social balance and consequently a danger to the social and political order. Here we may see a parallel in the Muslim attitude toward heresy, which differs very radically from the Christian attitude. In the history of the Christian churches, heresy has been a matter of profound concern. Heresy meant a deviation from correct belief as defined by authority, the deviation being recognized and defined as such by authority. In Islam there was less concern about the details of belief. What mattered was what people did—orthopraxy rather than orthodoxy—and Muslims were allowed on the whole to believe as they chose so long as they accepted the basic minimum, the unity of God and the apostolate of Muḥammad, and conformed to the social norms. Even heresies deviating very considerably from mainstream Islam were accorded tolerance. Heresy was persecuted only when it was seen to offer a substantial threat to the social or political order.[68]

Much the same considerations regulated Muslim attitudes toward the non-Muslim subjects. Trouble arose when Jews or Christians were seen to be getting too much wealth or too much power, that is to say, more than was thought proper or appropriate for them, and more particularly when they were enjoying them too visibly. The best-known example of this is the massacre of Jews in Granada in 1066, usually ascribed to a reaction among the Muslim population against a powerful and ostentatious Jewish vizier.[69] One could add a few other examples, more often directed against Christians than against Jews.

Another theme occurring in popular attacks on the non-Muslims is a charge of what one might call traffic with the enemy, that is to say, with the enemies of Islam. The first major case was at the time of the Crusades, when some Christian communities in Middle Eastern countries identified themselves with the Crusaders, and had to pay a price after the Crusaders had gone. Jews were of course not directly affected by this. They had no love for the Crusaders; quite the reverse. But they were sometimes also caught in the backlash, and were affected by the general feeling of resentment against non-Muslims who were seen—not without some reason—as unreliable subjects of a Muslim state at war with their coreligionists.

Another and more striking example occurred at the time of the Mongol invasions. The Crusaders had only succeeded in establishing some small states along the Syrian and Palestinian littoral; the Mongols conquered and dominated the heartlands of Islam and destroyed the caliphate, thus establishing a non-Muslim ascendancy over the major centers of Islam for the first time since the days of the Prophet. The Mongol rulers found Christians and Jews—local people knowing the languages and the countries but not themselves Muslims—very useful instruments, and appointed some of them to high office. Afterwards, when the Mongols were converted to Islam, became part of the Islamic world, and adopted Islamic attitudes, the Christians and Jews again had to pay for past collaboration with the pagan conquerors.

A more recent and in some ways parallel example is the role of the European empires in Islamic lands. Here again members of the minorities, Christians and to a lesser extent Jews, were in various ways useful and helpful to the imperial authorities. Some members of the minorities, and especially their upper classes, identified themselves with the European imperial powers, adopting their languages, their culture, and at times even their citizenship. After the end of the empires and the withdrawal of Europe, there was a reckoning to be paid by those who stayed behind.

One final item should be added to our typology of persecution, and this is the case where Muslim hostility to *dhimmīs* is instigated by outsiders, for reasons of their own. In the great days of Muslim power and civilization, such instigation was absent or ineffective, except for some earlier Christian influences on the Muslim perception of the Jew; but in the declining years of the Ottoman Empire it became a factor of some importance. The major *dhimmī* communities, the Greeks, the Armenians, the Arab Christians, and the Jews, were in many respects rivals, competing for a position in society complementary to that of the dominant Muslims. It was not uncommon for one minority to try and turn their Muslim masters against another. In particular, some of the standard themes of Christian European anti-Semitism were used against the Jewish communities of the Ottoman Empire by some of their Christian compatriots. In more recent times the countries of the Middle East have been a prime target for the successive leaders of world anti-Semitism; some of them have even at times aspired to that role themselves.

This raises the larger question of the development and transformation of Muslim attitudes toward the various subject minorities, against the background of internal and external changes, and in the larger perspective of fourteen centuries of Islamic history. In the early centuries of the caliphate we may speak of a move in the direction of greater tolerance. From the time of the Prophet to that of the first caliphs, and beyond that to the universal empire of the Umayyads and the Abbasids, there is an unmistakable increase in tolerance accorded to non-Muslims. From about the twelfth and thirteenth centuries onward, there is a noticeable move in the opposite direction.

In earlier times a good deal of easy social intercourse existed among Muslims, Christains, and Jews who, while professing different religions, formed a single society, in which personal friendships, business partnerships, intellectual discipleships, and other forms of shared activity were normal and, indeed, common. This cultural cooperation is attested in many ways. We have, for example, biographical dictionaries of famous physicians. These works, though written by Muslims, include Muslim, Christian, and Jewish physicians without distinction. From these large numbers of biographies it is even possible to construct a kind of prosopography of the medical profession—to trace the life curves of some hundreds of practitioners in the Islamic world. From these sources we get a very clear impression of a common effort. In hospitals and in private practiee, doctors of the three faiths worked together as partners or as assistants, reading each other's books and accepting one another as pupils. There was nothing resembling the kind of separation that was normal in Western Christendom at that time or in the Islamic world at a later time.

This kind of common endeavor in a shared field of learning was not limited to medicine and the sciences. It even included philosophy, wherein one might have expected differences of religion to make for separateness. An example may serve to illustrate this point. There is a chapter in one of the theological writings of the great Muslim theologian al-Ghazālī (1059-1111) that is almost identical to a chapter in a work by his near contemporary, the Jewish philosopher Bahye ibn Paquda. The connection between the two has puzzled many scholars. At one time it was assumed that Bahye must have taken the contents of the chapter from al-Ghazālī, since, while Bahye could read Arabic, al-Ghazālī could not have read the Hebrew script in which Bahye's work was written. When it was shown that there was no way in which Bahye could have seen or read al-Ghazālī's work, the problem seemed insoluble until the late Professor Baneth found the answer. An earlier text, previously unknown, was the common source of the relevant chapters in both al-Ghazālī and Bahye, and accounts for the striking resemblances between the two. What makes the case still more remarkable is that this earlier work was written by a Christian. We thus have a Christian who writes a theological treatise, presumably intended for Christian readers, which is then studied and, so to speak, borrowed by two subsequent theologians, one Muslim and the other Jewish, each writing a work of religious instruction for his own coreligionists. A society in which plagiarism is possible between theologians of three different religions has indeed achieved a high degree of tolerance and symbiosis.[70]

In the later Middle Ages such relationships begin to diminish. We find less and less of such sharing of intellectual, social, or commercial life, and see an increasing pattern of segregation and separation. There is more frequent and greater insistence on the enforcement of the restrictions of the *dhimma*. While in earlier times they were on the whole disregarded and only occasionally enforced, in later times they were more strictly applied and a relationship of humiliation, sometimes even of degradation, became the norm, especially in North Africa and in Iran and Central Asia.

Various explanations have been advanced as to why these changes took place. Professor S. D. Goitein ascribes them in the main to the disappearance of the bourgeois society of the classical Middle Ages and its replacement by a kind of military feudal order. In the bourgeois life of the cities, the merchant was a very significant figure, and international trade played an important part; religious differences did not matter all that much, while freedom of movement and cooperation mattered a great deal and were beneficial to all parties. Political decentralization and economic initiative both favored more tolerant relationships. With the decline of this bourgeois mercantile society and the establishment of regimes that were politically authoritarian and economically *dirigiste*, in which wealth was acquired less by trade than by taxation and other uses of the state apparatus, there was less inducement to tolerance, and greater scope, and even reward, for intolerance.

Another factor, certainly of major importance, was the threefold struggle waged by Sunni Islam during these centuries against Christendom, against Shi'ism, and against the Mongols. The bitter struggle in Spain, Sicily, and Syria-Palestine, which continued for more than two centuries between the Christian and Muslim worlds, together with the terrible examples of intolerance shown by Christian rulers to the Muslim peoples of the countries they conquered or reconquered in Spain, Syria, and Palestine, all led to a harshening of attitudes and a worsening of relations between Muslims and Christians. While Islam was still struggling to defend itself against Reconquest and Crusade from the west, it was suddenly attacked by a far deadlier enemy from the east—the pagan Mongol conquerors who came from east Asia and overran some of the heartlands of Islam. At the same time, while confronting Christendom in the west and heathendom in the east, Islam was riven at home by the major religious schism between Sunni and Shi'a, the latter often in radical and revolutionary forms. Between the tenth and thirteenth centuries the Sunni state was obliged to wage a long hard struggle to preserve what was perceived as Islamic orthodoxy and legitimacy against the seductive appeal of radical Shi'ite doctrines, the politico-military challenge of the Fatimid caliphate, and the terrorist menace of the Ismā'īlī assassins. In this threefold struggle against Christianity, paganism, and heresy, Muslims became more concerned for conformity, less tolerant of diversity. Although this was not directed primarily against the religious minorities, they were adversely affected by it.

A QUESTION of some importance is how far the Muslims, in their attitudes toward unbelievers, distinguished between Christians and Jews. In principle, as has been seen, the two major distinctions were theological, between monotheists and polytheists, and political, between unsubjugated enemies and subjugated *dhimmīs*. In general the Muslims show little interest in the subdivisions of the polytheists, and tend to look on the whole outside world as an undifferentiated whole, in accordance with the oft-cited dictum that *al-kufru millatun wāḥida*, unbelief is one religion.

They were, however, much more concerned with the differences between their own non-Muslim subjects, with whom they were obliged to deal in a number of ways. In the Middle East, North Africa, and Muslim Europe, these consisted overwhelmingly of Christians and Jews. They were known to the Muslims. The Prophet had dealings with both, and they figure prominently in the Qur'ān and in the traditions. They were familiar to the Muslims as compatriots, or more accurately as neighbors, sometimes as employees. Much information concerning their beliefs as well as their practices was made available to Muslims by new converts from these religions to Islam. Indeed, west of Iran and north of the Sahara, virtually all Muslims were descended from converted Christians or, to a much lesser extent, Jews. In most of these Muslim countries, one or the other of these religions, sometimes both, remained present.

Broadly speaking, Christians and Jews were treated in the same way. Sometimes we find the one better off, sometimes the other, but this was due to specific circumstances and not to general principles. The Qur'ān shows an unequivocal preference for Christians; the Muslim tradition, reflecting the circumstances of the Prophet's career, shows even more. In general, the portrayal of the Jew in *ḥadīth* is negative—less so in discussing his beliefs and practices, more so in reference to Jewish relations with the Prophet and Muslims. According to the great ninth-century Arab author al-Jāḥiẓ, the Muslim masses preferred Christians to Jews for a number of reasons. The most important, he notes, was that the Jews, unlike the Christians, had actively opposed the Prophet in Medina:

That struggle against them was prolonged, exhaustive, and it came increasingly into the open. Rancor built up, hatred doubled, and resentment was firmly established. The Christians, on the other hand, due to the fact that they lived far away both from the place where the Prophet—may Allah bless him and grant him peace—received his call and from the place to which he emigrated, did not undertake to slander Islam, nor did they have a chance to stir up plots, nor unite for war. This, therefore, is the first reason why the hearts of Muslims are hardened toward the Jews, but inclined toward the Christians.

In addition to this historical reason, due, as al-Jāḥiẓ observes to fortuitous circumstances, he adduces others: Christians occupy important positions as government officials, courtiers, physicians of the nobles, perfumers, and bankers, while Jews are normally dyers, tanners, cuppers, butchers, or tinkers, "so when the masses saw the Jews and Christians in this light, they imagined that the Jews' religion held the same place among the other religions as do their trades among other professions." Another reason for the popular Muslim preference is that the Christians, though ugly, are less ugly than the Jews, whose ugliness is accentuated by inbreeding:

> The reason that the Christians are less hideous—though they certainly are ugly—is that the Israelite marries only another Israelite, and all of their deformity is brought back among them and confined with them . . . they have, therefore, not been distinguished either for their intelligence, their physique, or their cleverness. As the reader certainly knows, the same is the case with horses, camels, asses, and pigeons when they are inbred.[71]

Al-Jāḥiẓ was famous as a humorist, satirist, and parodist and it is often difficult to know whether he is speaking in jest or in earnest. In any case, apart from the early religious literature, there is no evidence that Jews were viewed with greater hostility or accorded worse treatment than were Christians under Muslim rule. On the contrary, there are some indications that Christians were more open to suspicion than Jews. For most of the fourteen centuries of Islamic history, the major external enemy of Islam was Christendom. It was from the Byzantine emperors and other Christian rulers that the first

Muslim conquerors wrested Syria, Palestine, Egypt, North Africa, Sicily, and Spain. It was from Christian Europe that the Reconquest and the Crusades were launched to recover the lost territories, some of them for an interlude of time, some of them permanently. It was against Christian Europe again that the Turks launched the new wave of Islamic expansion that brought them twice as far as the walls of Vienna. And it was, finally, a new imperial counteroffensive from Christian Europe, both western and eastern, that brought the greater part of Muslim Asia and Africa under Christian rule for a while. With Christian *dhimmīs*, there was always the suspicion of at least sympathizing with the Christian enemy— a suspicion that was sometimes well founded. Jews were not subject to any such suspicion, and in certain situations—as, for example, in the Ottoman Empire in the fifteenth and sixteenth centuries—there was a marked preference for Jews in sensitive positions.

While the position of the Christian minorities under Muslim rule might be affected favorably or adversely by relations with the Christian powers beyond the frontier, this consideration did not apply to the Jews, except perhaps indirectly and consequentially. There were many Christian states, some friendly, some hostile, some weak and some powerful, and some indeed with Muslim subjects who could be used as hostages or for reprisals. The Jews had no such advantage or disadvantage— with one exception. For a few centuries in the early Middle Ages, the kingdom of the Khazars, a Turkic people who lived in the lands between the Don and Volga rivers, was converted to Judaism. As far as can be ascertained, the Khazar kingdom was governed by a relatively small dominant class of converts to Judaism, ruling over a larger population of heathens, Christians, and Muslims. How far the establishment, and later the disappearance, of a Jewish kingdom north of the lands of Islam affected the fate of the Jewish communities under Muslim rule and the attitude of Muslims toward them is difficult if not impossible to determine.

In general, Christians and Jews were accorded the same degree of tolerance; both were subject to the same disabilities and exposed to the same insecurities. And both were able to survive, often to participate, and sometimes to flourish in the states and societies founded by Muslims and governed by the laws of Islam.

In most respects the position of non-Muslims under traditional Islamic rule was very much easier than that of non-Christians or even of heretical Christians in medieval Europe, not to speak of some events in modern Europe or, for that matter, the modern Middle East. But their status was one of legal and social inferiority or, as we would say nowadays, of second-class citizenship. At the present time this expression conveys a formal condemnation and has become a catch phrase to denote unacceptable discrimination by a dominant group against other groups in the same society. But the phrase deserves a closer look. Second-class citizenship, though second-class, is a kind of citizenship. It involves some rights, though not all, and is surely better than no rights at all. It is certainly preferable to the kind of situation that prevails in many states at the present time, where the minorities, and for that matter even the majority, enjoy no real civil or human rights in spite of all the resplendent principles enshrined in the constitutions, but utterly without effect. A recognized status, albeit one of inferiority to the dominant group, which is established by law, recognized by tradition, and confirmed by popular assent, is not to be despised.

Under Muslim rule such a status was for long accepted with resignation by the Christians and with gratitude by the Jews. It ceased to be acceptable when the rising power of Christendom on the one hand and the radical ideas of the French Revolution on the other caused a wave of discontent among the Christian subjects of the Muslim states, an unwillingness to submit to the humiliations or even to the threat or possibility of humiliation, which existed in the old order. Just at the time when Christians were becoming less ready to accept these restraints, the Muslims—for some of the same reasons—were more convinced of their necessity. So long as the Muslim empires retained the reality or even the illusion of supremacy, they were prepared to tolerate the increasingly powerful hold of the minorities on the economic life. But with the change in the real relationship of economic and then of military power between Islam and Christendom in the eighteenth and nineteenth centuries, and still more with the belated Muslim awareness of the changes that had taken place, this situation of minority economic power became a source of concern, and ultimately of anger.

It is not uncommon in history for a relatively undeveloped economy to be stimulated by the commercial impact of another more active and more developed society. What is special to the case of the Middle East, in the age of European expansion, is that the agents and beneficiaries of the resulting economic changes were aliens on both sides. The outsiders were naturally Europeans, but even in the Middle East the principle actors were either foreigners or members of religious minorities seen and treated by the dominant society as marginal to itself. The new middle class—some historians use the term *comprador*—that evolved in the nineteenth and early twentieth centuries consisted largely of foreigners and of native Christians and some Jews, who as a result of this process became even less identified with their Muslim compatriots and even more with Europe. It was not until a comparatively late stage that a new Muslim bourgeoisie, not inhibited like its *dhimmī* predecessors by social separation from the ruling polity and the majority society, was able to have some social and political impact. It was of limited extent and duration, and in many countries has already given way to other elements.

The period of modernization from the late eighteenth century to the present time greatly strengthened the position of the non-Muslims in some ways, and seriously worsened it in others. Materially they did very well. As Christians they were more open to influences coming from the West, and therefore better able to make use of Western education and the many advantages it offered, especially important in an age of Western dominance. The role of foreigners and of members of minorities in financial matters may be illustrated by examples. In a document of 1912, forty private bankers are listed in Istanbul, not one of whom is a Turkish Muslim. Those who can be identified by their names include twelve Greeks, twelve Armenians, eight Jews, and five Levantines or Europeans. A list of thirty-four stockbrokers in Istanbul includes eighteen Greeks, six Jews, five Armenians, and not a single Turk.[72] Similar situations prevailed in the Ottoman provinces and, to a lesser extent, in North Africa and Iran.

The change was even more dramatic in those areas that, as a result of the imperial expansion of Europe at both ends, came under direct European rule. The maritime peoples of Western Europe advancing from the south and the Russians expanding overland from the north enclosed the Islamic heart-lands of the Middle East in gigantic pincers. In the territories they had acquired, the new imperial masters, like the Mongols centuries before, availed themselves of the skills and local knowledge of the non-Muslim populations of these lands. Not long after the Russian conquest of Armenia, Armenians appeared in the Russian service on the eastern frontier of Turkey, thereby posing challenges of different kinds to both the Turks and Armenians of the Ottoman Empire. Further south, in an example better known in the Western world, Bonaparte's expedition to Egypt drew extensively on the services of Copts and other Christians in its administration.

The sentiments of a Muslim observer at the time are vividly expressed in the writings of the Egyptian historian al-Jabartī, perhaps the last of the great Islamic historians in the classical mold. A member by background and education of the ulema class, al-Jabartī was no blind fanatic, no indiscriminate hater of things non-Muslim. He recognized some of the merits of French rule, and comments particularly on French commitment to justice, one of the qualities most esteemed in the Muslim scale of political values. He did not, however, appreciate their emancipation of the non-Muslim inhabitants of Egypt, in what amounted to a termination of *dhimma*. Al-Jabartī comments repeatedly and bitterly on the employment of Copts and other *dhimmīs* by the French. He was particularly offended by their wearing fine clothes, their bearing arms, contrary to old established usage, their exercising authority over the affairs and persons of the Muslims, and generally their acting in a way that seemed to him a reversal of the proper order of affairs as established by the law of God. Al-Jabartī was a fair-minded observer who found much to admire in the French and much to criticize in the Ottomans. Nevertheless, he warmly welcomed the return of Ottoman authority and with it the old order involving, in particular, the restoration of the *dhimma* and the restrictions it imposed on his Coptic compatriots.[73]

Al-Jabartī's was not the only negative Muslim reaction to the egalitarian ideas of the French Revolution. From 1798, when hostilities began between the French republic and the Ottoman Empire, Ottoman documents make frequent allusion to the "absurd and preposterous" ideas of equality among mankind.

Yet despite these objections and others like them, the new idea had struck roots, and in the course of the nineteenth century the concept of equal citizenship for men of different religions gradually gained strength. It drew support not only from the continuing and growing pressure of the European powers for reform within the empire, but also from a significant group of reformers among the Muslim Turks themselves who tried to bring their country into line with what they perceived as modern enlightenment. Finally, in the great reform *fermān* of February 1856, the age-old restrictions imposed on the non-Muslims were repealed and subjects of the Ottoman state, irrespective of religion, were formally declared to be equal.

The welcome accorded to this decree of emancipation was by no means uniformly enthusiastic—nor were the complaints entirely on the Muslim side. For the Muslims, of course, it meant the loss of the supremacy which they regarded as their right. But for Christians, too, or at least for the Christian leadership, it involved the loss of entrenched and recognized privileges. It also involved equalization downward as well as upward—a change not entirely to their taste.[74]

With the granting of legal equality, the poll tax was formally abolished and the non-Muslim subjects of the state were made eligible for the recently introduced compulsory military service. For a long time, however, they were not in fact called but were expected to pay a commutation tax, known as *bedel-i askeri*, military commutation, which replaced the now superseded *jizya*. It was levied and collected in much the same way. By the twentieth century, this form of discrimination was also abolished, and conscription was added to the privileges of citizenship and opened to non-Muslim subjects of the state.

Owing their favorable position largely to European support, the minorities relied heavily on European protection. Many acquired the status of protected persons, sometimes even the citizenship of various European states, and in the course of the nineteenth century several of the European powers established what were virtual protectorates over whole communities of the Sultan's non-Muslim subjects. At the same time their situation was complicated by other demands and aspirations—for independence from the Muslim state, for equality within the Muslim state. All these—foreign protection, domestic equality, national self-determination—were clearly incompatible with each other as well as with the basic assumptions of the *dhimma*. The resulting tensions culminated—but did not end—with the complete breakdown of the old order.

The ending of the classical Islamic system and the abrogation of the status it accorded the non-Muslims brought a considerable improvement in the formal and legal state of these communities in their respective countries. The actual working out of their emancipation, in an age of imperialist domination and nationalist revolt, of secular challenge and Islamic response, is a very different matter.

1. Torah scroll with case. Synagogue of Zaako, Iraqi Kurdistan.

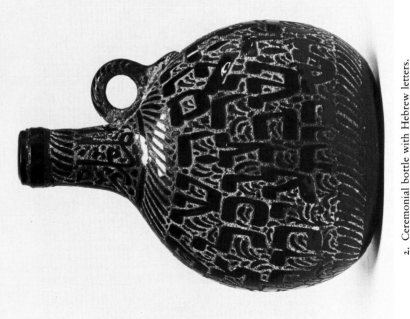

3. Sabbath lamp with Hebrew inscription.

2. Ceremonial bottle with Hebrew letters.

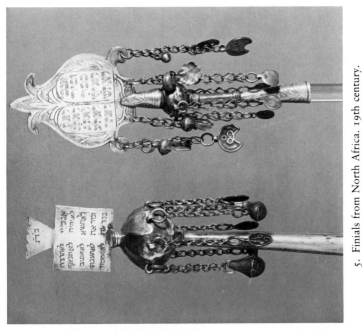

5. Finials from North Africa. 19th century.

4. Finials from Iran. 18th-19th centuries.

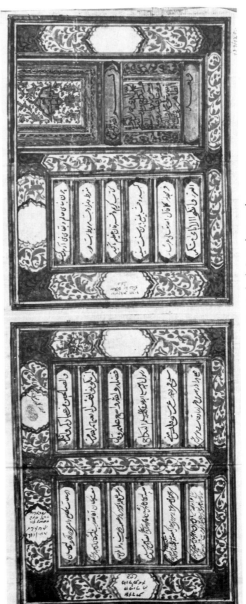

6. Ketubah (marriage contract). Meshed, Iran, late 19th century.

7. Ketubah. Isfahan, Iran, 1874.

8. Judaeo-Persian manuscript of a version of the Book of Exodus.
Illustrated by Nehemia ben Amshel of Tabriz, 1686.

9. Sacrifice scene from the Book of Exodus (see fig. 8).

10. Manuscript of sabbath blessings from Iranian Kurdistan, mid-19th century.

11. Jewish lady, from a Turkish manuscript of a book
on women. Istanbul, ca. 1793.

12. Bridegroom Ben Shlomo playing the *tar*. Iran, ca. 1846.

רחל דר חאל וסמה כשידן

13. Bride Rachel making up her eyes. Iran, ca. 1846.

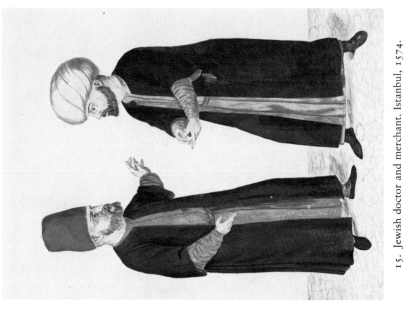

15. Jewish doctor and merchant. Istanbul, 1574.

14. Jewish woman and widow. Istanbul, 1574.

16. Jewish woman. Istanbul, 1714. Anonymous artist.

18. Jewish woman smoking a *chibouk*. Istanbul, 1768. By G. Rumpf.

17. Haham and widow. Istanbul, ca. 1850. By Amadeo, Count Preziosi.

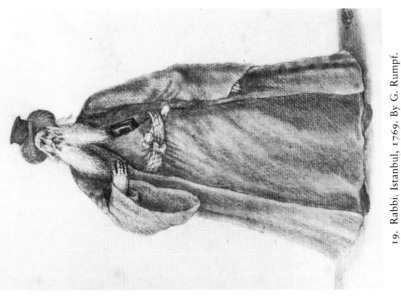

19. Rabbi. Istanbul, 1769. By G. Rumpf.

20. Jewish woman of the Seraglio. Istanbul, 1648.
By Georges de La Chappelle.

21. Jewish woman from the area of Akra, Kurdistan. Photographed in Israel.

TWO

The Judaeo-Islamic
Tradition[1]

FOR MOST of the Middle Ages the Jews of Islam
comprised the greater and more active part of the
Jewish people. The Jews who lived in Christian countries, that is in Europe, were a minority, and a relatively un-
important one at that. With few exceptions, whatever was
creative and significant in Jewish life happened in Islamic lands.
The Jewish communities of Europe formed a kind of cultural
dependency on the Jews of the far more advanced and sophisticated Islamic world, extending from Muslim Spain in
the west to Iraq, Iran, and Central Asia in the east.

In the later Middle Ages—the chronology is impossible to
establish with any precision—a major shift took place. In
numbers, the Jews of Islam diminished, both relatively and
absolutely, and the center of gravity of the Jewish world moved
from east to west, from Asia to Europe, from Islam to Christendom.

We have of course no population statistics, and can do no
more than guess at the numbers of Jews in Muslim countries.
But from the documents at our disposal, particularly from
about the year 900 C.E. onward, we can get an approximate
idea of the proportion of Jews to the general population.
Professor S. D. Goitein estimates that Jews constituted roughly
one percent of the population of Muslim countries, but that
they numbered many more in the cities, since they were mostly
an urban people with only a small and diminishing rural population.[2]

The Jews of the Islamic world also became a smaller proportion of the Jews as a whole. Having once been the overwhelming majority of the Jewish people, their numbers dwindled while those of the Jews of Christendom grew, until, finally,
the Jews of Islam became a minority of the Jewish people and

[margin note: see Goit. "Pol. Confl." on 10th– 11th cent mass migratns (E → W)]

[margin note: 1% of pop.]

the Jews of Christendom became the majority—within the context of Jewish life, even a dominant majority. Obviously, the main reasons for this shift must be sought in the changing relationship of Jews to the host societies of which they were a part. But that is not the whole story. The pace and modalities of change among the Jews do not conform entirely to the larger pattern, and certain aspects—at least of the change among the Jews—must be seen against the background of specifically Jewish events and trends. For this perspective a better understanding of the Judaeo-Islamic tradition, and of the Judaeo-Islamic symbiosis which gave rise to it, is a prerequisite.

The Jewish contribution to Islam, or more precisely the recognizably Jewish component in Islamic civilization, has been a favorite topic of Jewish scholarship since Abraham Geiger published, in 1833, his famous book *Was hat Mohammed aus dem Judenthume aufgenommen?*[3] (What did Muḥammad accept from Judaism?), in which he drew attention to certain biblical and rabbinical elements in early Islamic texts, with the obvious implication that these were Muslim borrowings from Jewish sources or, to put it in more familiar terms, Jewish contributions to Islam. This pioneer study was followed by many others, with some scholars even arguing that Muḥammad had had Jewish teachers or instructors who provided him with the rudiments of his religion. For a long time, such arguments passed unnoticed by Muslim scholarship. They did, however, evoke a certain reaction from rival claimants, from others who apparently also wished to claim credit for the advent of Islam and to argue that Muḥammad's formative influences had been not Jewish but Christian. Such views enjoyed particular favor with scholars whose background was in Protestant theology as, for example, the Scottish Arabist Richard Bell and the great Swedish scholar Tor Andrae, who was both a professor of comparative religion and a Lutheran bishop. Yet another view is that while Muḥammad may indeed have had either Jewish or Christian teachers, these were not rabbinical Jews or orthodox Christians, but followers of some outlandish sectarian group.

More recently there have been new approaches to the topic of alleged Jewish influences. While the Jewish origins of some Islamic ideas were originally adduced by Jewish, mostly rabbinic, scholars, in a kind of pride of ancestry, the same argument has been used by anti-Islamic polemicists, mainly Roman Catholic, whose purpose was not to glorify Judaism but to discredit Islam.[4] Most recently a work by two young scholars who might be described as post-Christian has presented the historical relationship between Judaism and Islam in an entirely new light, in which the share of Judaism in Islam is depicted as something vastly greater than a "contribution" or an "influence." This work, which depicts Islam as a kind of offshoot or aberration from Judaism, has aroused violent controversy.[5]

Hagarism

The whole problem of Jewish, or for that mattter of Christian or other extraneous influences on Islam is of course a problem for Jewish and other non-Muslim scholars. It is not a problem for Muslim scholars, for whom such a question simply cannot arise. As Muslims see it, Muḥammad is the Prophet of God, and the Qur'ān is divine in a sense both more literal and more precise than in the Jewish or Christian perception of the Old and New Testaments. According to what has become the accepted Sunni doctrine, the Qur'ān is eternal and uncreated, coexistent with God from eternity to eternity. The Qur'ānic text thus has a literal divine sanctity that has no parallel in the normal forms of Judaism or Christianity. To suggest borrowing or influence is therefore, from a Muslim point of view, a blasphemous absurdity. Does God borrow? Is God influenced? For a Muslim, Judaism, like Christianity, is a superseded predecessor of Islam. The Jewish and Christian scriptures were authentic divine revelations given to prophets sent by God. But they were neglected and corrupted by the Jews and Christians, and have been replaced by God's final and perfect revelation, which is the Qur'ān. If there are common elements or resemblances between the Bible and other Jewish and Christian writings and the Islamic dispensation, this is due to the common divine source. Where they differ,

Does God borrow?

Is God influenced?

the Jewish or Christian texts have been distorted by their unworthy custodians.

Some Jewish influence is mentioned by the early jurists and theologians of Islam, but where it is seen and recognized as such, it is perceived as a debasement or a dilution of the authentic message—as something like what in Christian history was called a Judaizing heresy. There is a whole body of early Islamic religious material that is neither part of the Qur'ān nor part of the accepted and authenticated *ḥadīth*, but that is used to supplement them. It consists of stories concerning the Prophets, narratives of various other kinds, and interpretations of these stories, many of them of midrashic origin, probably introduced and circulated by Jewish converts to Islam. This material is collectively known in Muslim literature as *Isrā'īliyyāt*, Israelite stuff or Israelitish fables. To begin with, this term, in Arabic usage, was purely descriptive. Never in any sense a term of praise, it was at first neutral and then came to have a distinctly negative connotation. In later times *Isrā'īliyyāt* became almost a synonym for superstitious nonsense, and was used, dismissively, to condemn stories, interpretations, and usages seen as not forming part of authentic Islam but as being due to Judaic and therefore unacceptable external influence.[6]

In general, when a Jewish influence or element is identified as such, it is for that reason rejected. If it is accepted as part of authentic Islam, then by definition it is not Jewish but divine in origin. If the Jews have something similar, then it is because they too were formerly the recipients of divine revelations.

There are, however, a few interesting cases in which it was not immediately clear whether a belief or a usage was of Jewish or divine inspiration and about which there was therefore some argument among the Muslim authorities. One such instance is the long debate among the doctors of the Holy Law on the sanctity of Jerusalem.[7] Is Jerusalem a holy city for Islam, or is it not? For some time now, it has come to be generally accepted by Muslims that Jerusalem is a holy city; indeed, most rank it third after Mecca and Medina. This was, however, by no means always accepted by Muslims, and in earlier times there was strong resistance among many theologians and jurists who regarded this notion as a Judaizing error—as one more among many attempts by Jewish converts to infiltrate Jewish ideas or practices into Islam. A story told by the great ninth-century historian Ṭabarī, describing a visit by the caliph ʿUmar to the newly conquered city of Jerusalem, illustrates this point:

> When ʿUmar came ... to Aelia[8] ... he said, "Bring me Kaʿb."
>
> Kaʿb was brought to him, and ʿUmar asked him, "Where do you think we should put the place of prayer?"
>
> "By the Rock," answered Kaʿb.
>
> "By God, Kaʿb," said ʿUmar, "you are following after Judaism. I saw you take off your sandals."
>
> "I wanted to feel the touch of it with my bare feet," said Kaʿb.
>
> "I saw you," said ʿUmar. "But no ... we were not commanded concerning the Rock, but we were commanded concerning the Kaʿba [in Mecca]."[9]

Kaʿb al-Aḥbār[10] was a well-known Jewish convert to Islam and an important figure often cited in connection with what are seen as Judaizing insertions into true Islamic doctrine. The point of the story clearly is that the sanctity of Jerusalem is a Jewish, not a Muslim, belief, that Kaʿb was at fault in maintaining it despite his conversion, and that only Mecca is the direction of prayer and the place of pilgrimage for Muslims.

The story is almost certainly an invention, probably reflecting the controversies of the following decades. There are other stories of this type, the purport of which is that to venerate Jerusalem as a holy city is a sign of Jewish influence and therefore bad. This was a view that did not prevail, and it was in time forgotten. After some vicissitudes, the principle was generally adopted that Jerusalem was indeed a holy city of Islam. The loss and recapture of the city during the Crusades and the obvious enormous importance attached to it by the Christians no doubt had some impact, too, as did the great controversies among the European powers over the holy places in Jerusalem during the late Ottoman period. By now the Islamic sanctity of Jerusalem, whatever its origin, is firmly established.

Another example is the establishment of Friday as the Muslim sabbath, clearly a reflection of the Jewish Saturday and the Christian Sunday.[11] As the Christians distanced themselves from their Jewish predecessors by moving the sabbath from Saturday to Sunday, so too did the Muslims distance themselves from both their predecessors by choosing Friday. But they differed also in another important respect. Not only did they choose a different day of the week; they also changed the whole conception of the nature of the sabbath. The Muslim "sabbath" is primarily a day of public prayer, as is indicated by the Arabic name given to Friday, *yawm al-jum'a* (the day of gathering). In classical times, Friday was not a day of rest, and the idea that it should be treated as such, though often put forward, was condemned by most Muslim authorities as a blameworthy imitation of the practices of the Jews and Christians. In time, the attractions of the day of rest prevailed over theological doubts concerning its origins, and by the present day most Muslim states have adopted what is now the universal practice and instituted a weekly day of rest.

For the early period of Islamic history, in the seventh and the greater part of the eighth century, the historian of the Judaeo-Islamic tradition is mainly concerned with identifying Jewish elements in Islam, with what might be called Jewish influences or Jewish contributions. This is in itself by no means an easy task. Despite many stories told of Jewish converts and their (mostly harmful) influence, there is little hard information. The only evidence on early Islam is that in the Qur'ān and the Islamic traditions and, as is well known, the interpretation and evaluation of these traditions, even their dating and authenticity, raise many problems. There is also the question of how far the Jewish component in Islam came directly from Jewish sources, and how far it was mediated via Christianity. The Christian element in early Islam is no less than the Jewish, and possibly greater, and the Christian component in itself incapsulates certain Jewish elements that had already become part of Christianity. The task of the historian is further complicated by the activities in or near Arabia of Judaeo-Christian groups and other Jewish and Christian sectaries about whose beliefs and practices we are poorly informed.

During the late eighth century a new complexity was added. By this time, the traffic in influence was no longer one way. The Jews were no longer bystanders, perhaps assistants, at the birth of a new religion, but were one component among many in a diverse and pluralistic civilization. In this situation, parallels and resemblances between Jewish and Muslim beliefs and practices may well be due to Muslim influences on Judaism and not merely—as earlier scholars believed—to Jewish influences on Islam.

A few examples may serve to illustrate the different kinds of problems the scholar encounters.

Muslim law lays down that during the fast of Ramaḍān the obligation to fast applies only during the daytime. During the night, from sunset to dawn, it is permitted to eat and drink. The fast begins again at daybreak, "when a white thread can be distinguished from a black thread" (Qur'ān, II,187). Abraham Geiger[12] first drew attention to the resemblance between this mandate and the dictum in the Talmud defining daybreak, for the purposes of the Shemaʿ prayer, as the time when one can distinguish between blue and white or, according to another opinion, between blue and green. The Jerusalem Talmud is a little more specific and refers to the "fringes" that contain a blue thread and are used when reciting the Shemaʿ. In this case, as in the case of Jerusalem, the chronology is not in doubt. Both Mishna and Gemara, both of Babylon and of Jerusalem, were completed before the advent of Islam. The resemblance between the two is close enough at least to suggest a connection; even the difference—black and white instead of blue and white or blue and green—could be an intentional distancing, like the adoption of Sunday and later Friday instead of Saturday as a day of public prayer. For the Muslim believer, the Talmudic passages represent distorted relics of some lost earlier revelation, reiterated in its complete and final form in the Qur'ān. For the comparativist the choice is between Jewish influence and common origin.

cf
Halperin

Sometimes the Islamic version of a Jewish theme or story is transformed and adapted, to carry a different message or to meet different circumstances. An example of this is the story of Korah, who rebelled against the authority of Moses and was duly swallowed up in the earth, along with all his people. In the Jewish versions of this story, both Biblical and Aggadic, Korah's offense is that he questions and even rebels against the authority of the Torah and of its upholders, variously named as Moses, the priests, or the rabbis. In some of the Aggadic versions Korah appears as Pharaoh's treasurer and a man of immense wealth. It is this aspect that predominates in the Muslim versions, where Qārūn, as he is named in the Qur'ān, becomes the prototype of the arrogance of wealth. He possesses immense riches and is marked by avarice and ostentation, unrelieved by charity or good works. The message of his fall, when he, his palace, and his treasures are swallowed up in the earth, is that wealth and the power it confers in this world are fleeting and insignificant. Only God has true power; only God's recompense has true value.

Qārūn:
prototype
of
arrogance
of
wealth

Other Biblical and rabbinical themes—for example, the stories of Elijah and of the curse of Ham—also have significantly different Islamic analogues. By medieval times, even Jewish discussions of some of these themes were sometimes influenced by Islamic versions that had become known to Jews.[13]

Jews
of
Arabia

THERE were Jews in Arabia at the time of the advent of Islam. They were few in number, and apart from the role that they played or that the Muslim historiographic tradition ascribes to them in the circumstances of the Prophet's career, they were of no great importance in Jewish history and are virtually unknown to Jewish historiography.[14] Of far greater significance were the large and active Jewish communities in Southwest Asia and North Africa—countries into which the Arabs came in a great wave of conquest in the seventh and eighth centuries, and which constituted the core of the Islamic caliphate.

Among the Jews of the Middle East at that time were two important divisions, one cultural, the other political, the two not wholly coinciding. Culturally, there was a major cleavage between the Aramaic-speaking Jews and the Hellenized Jews. Most of those who lived in the Fertile Crescent spoke Aramaic, and had a culture expressed in that language. Specifically Jewish forms of Aramaic served as the media of both the Babylonian and Jerusalem Talmuds, as well as of many other, mostly religious writings. The second group consisted of the Jews of Alexandria and other cities in the eastern provinces of the Roman Empire who had adopted the Greek language and had become part of the Hellenistic civilization of the time.

Besides this cultural division, there was also a political division between the Jews of the Roman Empire, or later the Byzantine Empire, on the one hand, and the Jews of the Persian Empire on the other. The former included all the Mediterranean lands; the latter, besides the plateau of Iran, ruled over Iraq, where indeed the Sasanid emperors had their capital, at Ctesiphon. The ancient and learned Jewish communities of Babylonia and their brothers in Palestine and Syria were thus subjects of two empires, between which there was perpetual rivalry and frequent war.

Arabia, where the Islamic faith was born, belonged to neither empire. But both Rome and Persia were active in the peninsula, which at times was the arena of commercial and diplomatic as well as military clashes between the two. During the sixth century, that is to say, on the eve of Muḥammad's mission, Arabian Jews played an obscure but possibly important role in this imperial competition.[15]

The Arab conquests and the creation of the Islamic caliphate brought together the eastern and western halves of the Middle East for the first time since the death of Alexander the Great. The Persian Empire was overthrown and its territories absorbed in their entirety. The Byzantine Empire remained standing, but was reduced to Anatolia and southeastern Europe. Syria, Palestine, Egypt, and North Africa were conquered, and their Jewish communities, now joined to those of Iraq and Iran, formed the overwhelming majority and also the most advanced and active part of the Jewish people.

In these communities of southwest Asia and northern Africa, united under Islamic rule, a number of important changes took place. The first was the process of unification itself, the merging of the very disparate and diverse groups that were now joined together under one rule. Jews from the shores of the Atlantic Ocean to the borders of India and China formed one society, for a while subject to one state. And even when that state, for a variety of reasons, broke up into many small states, the cultural, social, and to some extent economic unity of the society was maintained, with a remarkable degree of personal and physical mobility between countries as far apart as Iran and Morocco or Spain and the Yemen. Right through the Middle Ages there was active commercial and cultural intercommunication between the far-flung regions of this vast Islamic world and consequently also between its Jewish communities.

One of the major changes that took place in Jewish life in these countries was the process of Arabization, meaning primarily but not exclusively the replacement of the older languages by Arabic. Aramaic died out as a spoken language, surviving—apart from a few remote and isolated communities—only in juridical and liturgical use. Greek was forgotten, and Latin had hardly been adopted by Jews. Hebrew of course remained, but its use was limited. It was above all a religious language, used in the liturgy of the synagogue and in poetry, sometimes more generally in belles lettres. But for most purposes Hebrew and all the other languages formerly used by Jews were replaced by Arabic, which became the language of science and philosophy, of government and commerce, even the language of Jewish theology when such a discipline began to develop under Islamic influence. Yehuda ha-Levi composed poetry and Maimonides wrote on Jewish law in Hebrew, but when they wished to expound a philosophy both used Arabic, which possessed the necessary linguistic resources. Arabic reigned everywhere except in the easternmost parts of the Islamic Empire, in Iran and beyond. Even there, Arabic was for a while the dominant language, though apparently among Persian Jews, as among other Persians, it did not become the spoken language. In Iran and points east, Persian was still spoken and later, in a new form, recovered its literary status. West of Iran, Arabic became the language not only of literature and government but also of everyday speech. The Jews adopted Arabic and made it their own as they have done with only a few other languages in their history. This was in striking contrast to the situation in medieval Christendom, where the Jews made very limited use of Greek and virtually none of Latin.

Jewish history shows <u>two contrasting patterns</u> of cultural relations between Jews and their neighbors. In one the Jews are <u>culturally integrated</u> into the society in which they live, using the same language and to a large extent sharing the same cultural values as the surrounding majority. This is the situation in modern Western Europe and America. The other pattern is one in which the Jews are <u>linguistically and therefore culturally separated</u>, using either Hebrew or, more commonly, some other language they brought from elsewhere and transformed into a Jewish language used exclusively by Jews. Such was the Judaeo-Spanish of the Sephardic Jews in the Ottoman Empire or the Judaeo-German (Yiddish) of the Ashkenazi Jews in the Polish kingdom and the Russian Empire. Such too, at an earlier date, were the Judaeo-Aramaic dialects used in the Fertile Crescent and beyond. These two situations produce different types of Jewish life and of course a different relationship between the Jewish minority and the dominant majority.

The medieval symbiosis of Jews and Arabs is in this respect <u>far closer to the pattern of modern Western Europe and America and very different from the situation in the Roman, Ottoman, and Russian empires</u>. As Professor Goitein has pointed out, this symbiosis produced something that was not merely a Jewish culture in Arabic. It was a Judaeo-Arabic, or one might even say a Judaeo-Islamic, culture. There were some minor differences in language. The Jews, like the Christians, developed their own specific dialects of Arabic with distinctive

[margin annotations: patterns ① separated integrated ② separated; SYMBIOSIS NB; SYMBIOSIS]

lexical and phonetic characteristics.[16] For some purposes the Jews wrote Arabic in the Hebrew script while Christians sometimes wrote Arabic in the Syriac script. In Middle Eastern religions, based on revealed scriptures and expressed in written liturgies, there is an intimate association between script and cult, script and faith. But the resulting differences in Muslim, Christian, and Jewish Arabic were in medieval times comparatively minor. What was far more important was the sharing of the language and of the cultural values expressed in it—the whole cultural frame of reference that made possible a degree of communication, indeed of cooperation, that is comparatively rare in the history of the Jewish diaspora.

The process of the acculturation of the Jews in the Arab Islamic world goes beyond the point of Arabization, a term that is perhaps too narrowly linguistic, and might better be designated as Islamization. This does not necessarily mean conversion to Islam, though there were of course many Jewish converts, some of whom who played a role of great significance. What is intended here is not the adoption of the Islamic religion but assimilation to Islamic modes of thought and patterns of behavior—in a word, a Judaeo-Islamic tradition parallel to the Judaeo-Christian tradition of which we are accustomed to speak in the modern world.

We have already noted some of the problems of the interrelation between Judaism and Islam, and the influences either may have exerted on the other. It is often difficult and sometimes impossible to say of one or another practice or idea, which is the earlier and which is the later, and which therefore inspired or influenced the other. It is safer for the time being to use a neutral formulation, and to speak of a series of remarkable resemblances between developments in Judaism and parallel developments in Islam. In some matters, the simple facts of chronology indicate beyond reasonable doubt which is the source, which is the recipient of influence. In others the line of development is more difficult to determine.

The late Rabbi Ignaz Maibaum, a reform rabbi in London, was once involved in a polemic with some of his orthodox rabbinic colleagues in the columns of a Jewish weekly paper.

At one point, an orthodox rabbi remarked in a letter that reform rabbis are merely "Jewish clergymen," a term that was clearly intended to convey that they had departed from the authentic Jewish tradition and were imitating the ways of Christian priests and ministers. Maibaum replied that if reform rabbis could be described as Jewish "clergymen," orthodox rabbis could equally well be described as Jewish ulema.

orthodox as ulema

ʿālim

The meaning of the counteraccusation is clear enough. There are indeed certain resemblances between the position of the ulema in Jewish life and that of the rabbinate in orthodox Jewish communities. Neither the ʿalim (the singular of ulema) nor the rabbi is an ordained priest; neither has any sacerdotal office. Neither Judaism nor Islam has sacraments, altars, ordination, or priestly mediation. There is no religious office that an ʿalim or a rabbi can perform that any ordinary adult male believer, possessing the necessary knowledge, cannot perform equally well. Both are professional men of religion, but neither is in any sense a priest. They acquire their status through knowledge, through learning, and through recognition, which becomes a form of certification—the semikha of the rabbi closely resembling the ijāza a new ʿalim receives from his teacher. In all these respects as well as some others, there are striking resemblances in training, qualification, and function between the orthodox rabbi and the Sunni Muslim ʿalim. (The Shiʿite mullah is somewhat different.) So striking a resemblance, underlined by the difference between their common status and that of the priesthood in Christianity and some other religions, clearly argues for some historical connection.

semikha/ ijāza

The resemblance extends beyond the doctors of the law and may be seen even in the law itself—another point in which Judaism and Islam resemble one another and differ from Christianity. The two religions have much in common in their conception of the law, its scope, the range of topics that the law embraces, and the place accorded to the law in everyday personal, public, and private life. Both agree substantially on the divine source and dual nature of the law, written and oral, in revelation and tradition. The Jewish notion of halakha and the Islamic notion of *sharīʿa*—both words mean "path" or "way"—are surely closely related. Since the *halakha* both as a term and as a corpus of law, originated some centuries earlier than the beginnings of the *sharīʿa*, it would seem that in this case the initial influence was from Judaism to Islam, and not vice versa. But even here, in the subsequent development of both legal systems, there are clearly mutual influences.[17]

FIQH

The vocabulary of *fiqh*, Muslim jurisprudence, owes much to rabbinical precedents. But the subsequent development and discussion of rabbinic law also owes a great deal to the categories, the formulations, even the terminology of the Muslim jurists.

teshuvot
fatwa

An obvious parallel is in the practice of responsa—the rabbinical *teshuvot*, the Islamic *fatwā*. The earliest extant examples of the two are roughly contemporary, but here we may find a common source in the *responsa prudentium* of the Roman jurists, which are very much earlier than either and probably underlie both.

Kalam

In the literature of philosophy and even of theology one may say without hesitation that the influence flowed from Islam to Judaism and not the other way around. The notion of a theology, of a formulation of religious belief in the form of philosophical principles, was alien to the Jews of Biblical and Talmudic times. The emergence of a Jewish theology took place amost entirely in Islamic lands. It was the work of theologians who used both the concepts and the vocabulary (either in Arabic or calqued into Hebrew) of Muslim *kalām*.[18] This illustrates another important influence—the lexical impact of Arabic on Hebrew. Arabic and Hebrew are of course cognate languages, with a large stock of common roots. The borrowing or imitation of lexical material from the one to the other was therefore easy. Educated Jews in the lands of Islam in medieval times were thoroughly familiar with both languages. A very large part of the philosophical and scientific vocabulary of medieval Hebrew, much of which has passed into modern Hebrew, was formed by calque or loan translation from Arabic. To cite but one example: the Hebrew *murkav*, compound, is clearly a loan translation from the Arabic *murakkab*. There are many other similar formations.

This raises the larger question of Arabic influence on Hebrew philology. Jews, studying Hebrew to achieve a better understanding of the Hebrew Bible, followed many of the procedures devised by Muslims examining Arabic for the parallel purpose of studying the sacred text of the Qur'ān. The origins, growth, and development of grammar and lexicography, the desire and the effort to establish an authentic text, are remarkably similar in the two religions, and the question inevitably arises whether there was a connection between the activities of the Masoretes and their concern for fixing the text of the Hebrew Bible, and the parallel and probably earlier Muslim effort to establish an authoritative text of the Qur'ān.

Muslim influences on Judaism went beyond the world of thought and scholarship and even affected the ritual and worship of the synagogue. Dr. Naftali Wieder published some years ago a remarkable study on Islamic influences in Jewish worship. This is, incidentally, one of the few Hebrew works of scholarship translated into Arabic.[19]

In literature and the arts, the Muslim influence on the Jews is enormous, and it is almost entirely one way. Hebrew poetry, in the medieval golden age, follows very closely on the prosody and technique of Arabic poetry and indeed on its whole system of symbol and allusion. Though written in a non-Islamic language and script, medieval Hebrew poetry and much of the prose literature belong to the same cultural world as Arabic and the other literatures of Islam. Islamic influence on Hebrew poetry is not limited to the Jews of the Islamic world; it even spread through Spain into Provence. In the visual arts, Judaism and Islam share certain common attitudes concerning the representation of human and even animal figures, and both were affected by the resulting direction of artistic expression.[20] There are striking resemblances between Islamic art and Jewish works of art produced not only in Islamic countries but, as with poetry, also in Christian Europe, where, for example, Jewish book illumination on the one hand and Jewish synagogue architecture on the other show recognizable Islamic influences.

A comparison between the Jews of Christendom and the Jews of Islam shows to what extent the Jewish minorities followed the mores and adopted the norms of the dominant communities, even in matters of intimate personal and religious significance. An obvious example is the law of marriage. One of the clearest and most striking differences between Christian and Islamic usage is that while Islam permits polygamy and concubinage, Christianity bans both. In the Christian world the Jews adopted and practiced monogamy to the point of making it a rule of law; in the Muslim world most Jewish communities practiced, or at least permitted, polygamy and concubinage until almost the present day.[21]

Another very striking distinction is in the perception of martyrdom and the circumstances in which it becomes a duty. There is a Judaeo-Christian tradition of martyrdom—and this is one case where one may legitimately use that rather overworked expression "Judaeo-Christian"—according to which the believer must be prepared to lay down his life rather than renounce his religious beliefs. Jews still honor the ancient Jewish martyrs: Hannah and her sons, Rabbi Akiva and his companions, and many others. The same tradition was maintained by the Christians, and also, with no lack of opportunity, by the Jews in Christian countries. Christianity was a religion that both made and provided martyrs.

In the Islamic world both the Muslims and their subjects, with perhaps the partial exception of the Shīʿa, took a rather more relaxed view. In a verse already quoted, the Qurʾān lays down that "there is no constraint in religion," which was interpreted to mean that people cannot be or should not be forced to change their religions, unless of course they are heathens or idolaters, in which case they deserve no consideration. But there were few if any heathens or idolaters in the central lands of Islam, where the main tradition was formed and from which the communal historic memory derives. For Christians and Jews under Muslim rule, the question of forced conversion and therefore of martyrdom rarely arose. For the Muslims themselves, it did not arise until centuries later.

Islam does, however, possess the notion of martyrdom, which

is indeed connoted by a word with the same meaning. The Islamic term for martyr is *shahīd*, from an Arabic root meaning "to witness," and thus corresponds to the Greek *martyros*. The normal Arabic word for a witness in the legal sense is *shahīd*, from the same root. But a Muslim *shahīd* is something quite different from a Jewish or Christian martyr. The *shahīd* is one who dies in battle, fighting in the holy war for Islam. Since holy war is a religious duty incumbent on the believers, those who fulfill that duty and are killed in doing so are considered martyrs in the technical Islamic sense of the word, and qualify for the rewards of martyrdom. The Judaeo-Christian notion of martyrdom—to suffer and testify for one's faith rather than renounce it—is not unknown to Islam. The fate of the Medina Jewish tribe of the Banū Qurayẓa, who accepted death rather than abjure their faith, is part of the semi-sacred biography of the Prophet, and is related with respect, at times bordering on admiration.[22] But this was not seen as an example for Muslims to follow—if for no other reason, because in the early formative centuries of Islamic history the question did not arise and Muslims were not put to the test. On the rare occasions when Muslims were subject to religious constraint, it was within rather than from outside the faith, and arose from attempts by one or another school of Muslim doctrine to impose its views on the rest. In such a situation it was natural to take a more lenient view of compliance, and the doctrine arose and was widely accepted that it was permissible to conceal one's true beliefs so long as one preserved them in one's own heart and mind—that it was reasonable to accommodate to the prevailing doctrines in order to survive, so that in due course, when circumstances were more favorable, one might resume and proclaim one's true faith.[23] Once this principle was adopted, it was capable of extension. Centuries later, with the Muslim retreat from Spain and Italy, Muslims confronted a new and far greater threat to their beliefs—not just the pressure of a rival Muslim doctrine, but the determined persecution of a competing religion. Some chose martyrdom or exile. Others practiced accommodation, and for as long as it was possible they preserved their own religion in secret.

This response to persecution is of course familiar in Jewish history, and is known as marranism, the practice of the Spanish and Portuguese Marranos, who affected conversion to Catholicism but preserved their Jewish faith and to some extent even worshiped in secret until they came to another time, or more commonly another place, where it was possible to revert openly to their own faith. Significantly, the phenomenon of marranism in Jewish history is virtually limited to countries of Islamic civilization or influence. The outstanding examples are the Jews of Spain and Portugal after the expulsion. Other instances are attested in Islamic lands from North Africa to Iran and Central Asia. It is almost completely unknown among the Jews of Christendom, who suffered incomparably greater persecutions, and yet—in curious accord with their persecutors—chose death or exile rather than submission.

Some medieval Jewish authors, among them the great Maimonides, even tried to provide a theoretical justification for this contrast and argued on theological grounds that while a Jew must suffer torture and death rather than pronounce a Christian creed, he may affect conversion to Islam in order to survive. The significant difference was that while the Jews recognized Islam as a strict monotheism of the same kind as their own, they had some doubts, which they shared with the Muslims, about Christianity. For one who believed neither statement, it was a lesser perjury to testify that Muḥammad was the Prophet of God than to testify that Jesus was the Son of God. These distinctions, while no doubt based on an imperfect understanding of Christian doctrine, were nevertheless important in shaping interfaith attitudes.

Another issue on which Judaism and Islam were closer to each other than either of them to Christianity was the matter of dietary laws. Muslim dietary laws are not as strict as those imposed by Rabbinic law. The loosening of some of these restrictions is specifically indicated in the Qur'ān, and indeed, willingness to eat camel's flesh was sometimes used as a test

dietary laws

of the sincerity of a Jewish convert, rather in the way that eating pork was imposed on Jewish converts to Christianity. The Muslims, however, shared the Jewish prohibition of the pig and some lesser abominations. More important, they shared the notion—unknown to Christianity—that some foods were permitted, others forbidden by divine law. This could even have practical consequences. Muslims were permitted by most religious authorities to eat Jewish meat[24]—a matter of some importance when traveling abroad in countries where there were resident Jewish communities but no Muslims. Jews for their part, while not permitted to eat Muslim meat, nevertheless had far greater affinity with the general Muslim attitude. The important exception was Shīʿa Islam, which, by its insistence on ritual purity and on the polluting effect of contact with a *dhimmī* rejected as unclean any food prepared or even touched by a Jew, let alone admit the lawfulness of Jewish meat.

If we compare the Muslim attitude to Jews and treatment of Jews in medieval times with the position of Jews among their Christian neighbors in medieval Europe, we see some striking contrasts. Even the hostilities of the two majority communities differ considerably. In Islamic society hostility to the Jew is non-theological. It is not related to any specific Islamic doctrine, nor to any specific circumstance in Islamic sacred history.[25] For Muslims, it is not part of the birth pangs of their religion, as it is for Christians. It is rather the usual attitude of the dominant to the subordinate, of the majority to the minority, without that additional theological and therefore psychological dimension that gives Christian anti-Semitism its unique and special character.

compared w/ Xian Europe

Partly because of the non-ideological nature of the hostility directed against Jews, partly also because the Jewish minorities in Islamic lands, unlike those of Christendom, were one among many minorities in a diverse and pluralistic society, they were far less noticeable. This was on the whole an advantage.

In general Muslim polemicists pay little attention to the relatively insignificant Jews. Insofar as they deign to discuss the superseded religions, they are far more concerned with the

Christians who, as the bearers of a competing proselytizing religion and the masters of a rival universal empire, offered a serious alternative and therefore a potential threat to the Muslim dispensation and the Islamic oecumene. The Jews offered no political threat to the Islamic world order, no religious challenge to the Islamic faith; nor, like the Christians, did they compete with the Muslims for the adherence of the still unconverted heathens. Despite the condemnation of Jews and Judaism in the Qur'ān, and in both commentary and *ḥadīth*, anti-Jewish polemic was rare, and when it appeared it was almost always the work of Jewish converts to Islam justifying their own change of faith, and providing their new coreligionists with facts and arguments to use against their old.

Much the same may be said about Christian converts, who, because of their greater numbers and importance, had a far greater impact. Among the notions and attitudes brought by Christian converts into Islam was a certain hostility toward Jews, which sometimes influenced Muslim writings on this subject. Professor Moshe Perlmann, who has made an extensive study of this literature, observes that:

> It would seem that to a very great, decisive measure, Islamic polemic directed against Jews and Judaism originated from and was fed by Christian sources, partly pre-Islamic, flowing into the Islamic milieu with the mass conversion of Christians. These arguments were in turn partly rooted in the anti-Jewish lore of antiquity, and were refurbished by Jewish converts. There was a stock of arguments for Islam and against the older faiths, a stock supplied by Jewish and Christian converts to Islam.[26]

Where specific references to Jews and Judaism occur in Muslim religious writings, they are usually rather negative. Given the predominantly hostile presentation of the Jew in both Qur'ān and *ḥadīth*, and the mainly Christian source of a good deal of the information about Jews that was subsequently acquired, this is hardly surprising.

There are exceptions. Thus, the tenth-century Baghdadi the-

ologian al-Bāqillānī, in a work stating the Muslim case against
other religions and philosophies, includes a discussion of Judaism. His treatment of Jewish scriptures and beliefs is brief
but well informed. It is also free from invective, and is on the
contrary courteous, even respectful, in tone.[27] At a time when
theological differences within and between religions usually
aroused strong passions, expressed in strong language, such
moderation is remarkable. What is perhaps more remarkable
is that in classical times there is only one serious attack on
Judaism written by a major author that has come down to
us. This is a treatise by the scholar, heresiologist and litterateur
Ibn Ḥazm (994-1064), a dominant figure in the intellectual
history of Muslim Spain, known both for a charming little
book on courtly and poetic love and a major treatise on the
religions of the world. The latter shows his harsh and intolerant attitude not only toward non-Muslim religions but even
toward those forms of Islam that differed from his own. In
addition, Ibn Ḥazm wrote an anti-Jewish tract, refuting a
pamphlet allegedly written by Samuel Ibn Nagrella, in which
he attacked Islam. Ibn Ḥazm had not seen Samuel's tract, if
indeed it ever existed, and therefore refuted it on the basis of
a previous Muslim refutation. The book is extremely hostile
in content and in tone and was certainly not unrelated to Ibn
Ḥazm's resentment of Samuel Ibn Nagrella (993-1056), who
enjoyed a remarkably successful career as a statesman and
general in the service of a Muslim ruler, and as a scholar,
poet, and communal leader among the Jews. It is difficult to
say how much impact Ibn Ḥazm's diatribe had on medieval
Muslim opinion. It is surely significant that it is the only
known book of its kind.[28]

In Ibn Ḥazm's major treatise on religions, he devotes more
space to Judaism than to Christianity. In this disproportion—
due certainly to the special circumstances of southern Spain
in his time—he is virtually alone. Most writers devote far more
attention to the Christians not only, as already pointed out,
because of their numbers and importance, but also because,
as an established part of the bureaucracy and intelligentsia of

Middle Eastern cities, they were better known and more familiar to Muslim scholars.

Where we find a more positive attitude among Muslim authors discussing Jews and Judaism, it is the context sometimes of rationalist or even skeptical thought, sometimes of Sufi mysticism. For both the skeptic and the mystic, the difference between religions was of no great importance. For the one they were all equally false, for the other almost equally true.[29] More generally, among the urban middle class in times and places of high civilization, a more tolerant and liberal attitude prevailed and is expressed in the literary sources. The spread of rationalist relativism and mystical pantheism both undoubtedly contributed to this result.

All this helped to create, in earlier though not later Islamic times, a kind of symbiosis between Jews and their neighbors that has no parallel in the Western world between the Hellenistic and modern ages. Jews and Muslims had extensive and intimate contacts that involved social as well as intellectual association—cooperation, commingling, even personal friendship. With the exception of certain mystical poets who insist on the oneness of all religions, there was no inclination on the Muslim side to concede equality; but there was nevertheless an attitude of live and let live, and even a certain respect for the possessors and transmitters of older cultures and revelations.

Thus, for example, in eleventh-century Toledo a Muslim qāḍī, in a book on the "Categories of Nations," enumerated the eight nations that have contributed to the growth of science and scholarship among mankind. They are: the Indians, Persians, Chaldees, Greeks, Romans (a term that includes the Byzantines and Eastern Christians generally), Egyptians (meaning the ancient Egyptians), Arabs (including Muslims in general), and Jews. The Jews are thus in good company, and the chapter devoted to them is courteous in tone and well informed in content. In early times, the qāḍī notes, the Jews were not distinguished in philosophy but were concerned mainly with the study of the Holy Law and the lives of the Prophets. In this latter subject they were the best informed of all and

were thus a major source of information for Muslim scholars. Israel was the cradle of prophecy, and it was among this people that the apostolate first appeared. The majority of the prophets, he notes, were Jews. The remainder of the chapter is devoted to Jewish scientists and scholars in the Islamic lands, ending with the author's own contemporaries in Muslim Spain.[30] Athough this admiring account of Jewish achievement is virtually unique in classical Islamic literature, there are discussions of Jewish religious beliefs and sectarian divisions, and also of chronology and calendars, topics that seem to have interested Muslim scholars.

This interest was no doubt awakened by the Qur'anic references to Biblical persons and events, some of which thus found their way into classical Islamic historiography. The ancient Jewish heroes and prophets were, so to speak, given right of entry into Islam through the Qur'ān, and some Muslim scholars went so far as to seek fuller information from other, including Jewish, sources, to supplement the brief and sometimes cryptic Qur'anic allusions. Such a search, involving the study of abrogated scriptures and superseded religions, required some intellectual daring, and there were therefore few who undertook it. Enough did so, however, to introduce a modicum of Biblical and rabbinical information to the corpus of Islamic learning.[31]

While the earlier universal histories usually included some account of the prophets before Muḥammad, it is not until the late Middle Ages that we find connected accounts of Jewish history. Two works are especially important among the larger universal histories produced by Arabic and Persian authors in the later Middle Ages. Rashīd al-Dīn (1247-1318), himself a Jew converted to Islam, included in his universal history an account of "the history of the children of Israel" based on the Old Testament and supplemented, for the post-Biblical period, by unspecified apocryphal materials. Unlike most other Muslim writers on ancient Israelite history, Rashīd al-Dīn does not close his account with the destruction of the Second Temple in A.D. 70, but alludes briefly to the revolt of Bar Kokhba and its suppression: "Then came Hadrian and destroyed this

place and took the people with all their possessions captive."
He ends his narrative with an enumeration of the Byzantine
and Roman emperors who held sway over Palestine until the
Arab conquest.[32] Another major Islamic historian, Ibn Khaldūn (1332-1406), also includes an account of the children of
Israel in his survey of universal history; it is derived from an
Arabic translation, made by a Yemenite Jew, of the Hebrew
chronicle of Josippon, itself loosely based on the writings of
Josephus.[33] Some of the manuscripts of the chronicle of Rashīd
al-Dīn contain illustrations, purporting to depict episodes in
the history of the ancient Israelites. Pictorial representations
of Jews, as of other specific ethnic or religious elements, are
extremely rare.

In general, however, the Jews receive little attention from
Muslim authors, whether historians or theologians, and if
positive comments are rare, so too are attacks.

WHILE the Jews of Islam were not subject to occupational
restrictions such as we find in Europe, there was a tendency,
for a variety of reasons, for Jews to favor some occupations
and avoid others. There were obvious barriers to a military
or bureaucratic career; talented and educated Jews therefore
found other professions, in which they sometimes played an
important though never a preponderant role. There is an old
Arab saying that the Jew rises to greatness with either the
medicine bottle or the moneybag in his hand. This expresses
a generally verifiable historic truth, that the two ways to success open to an ambitious Jew were either through the practice
of medicine or the handling of money.

The advantages of these two professions are obvious. With
respect to money, the Muslims had a whole series of prohi-
bitions and inhibitions regarding the handling of money and
precious metals, seen as dangerous to their immortal souls. A
result of this feeling was that in the Muslim world these matters were left largely to Christians and Jews. Rulers in need
of ready cash often had recourse to the services of *dhimmī*
bankers, able to make use in turn of their own networks of
coreligionist colleagues scattered throughout the far-flung Is-

lamic dominions. The ability to provide money at short notice and in large quantities was an excellent way of gaining access and favor at court.

The practice of medicine also had its benefits. When men are very sick, the desire to get the best medical treatment is likely to overcome even the strongest religious prejudices. In medieval Islam, as in some other times and places, Jewish physicians, dependent not on public appointment but on private practice, were able to go as far as their talents would take them. Their access to other languages and therefore to other bodies of medical literature sometimes gave them an advantage over their Muslim colleagues. A successful medical practitioner might include high officials and even rulers among his patients. Through the close and immediate access to the center of power that this gave him, he could achieve some advantage for the Jewish community to which he belonged and of course for himself, his family, and his friends. Occasionally we find Jewish physicians playing a political role of some importance, though this is rare in medieval times and usually at some stage requires conversion to Islam before the practitioner can exploit his position to the full.

In a society governed by personal autocratic rule, access to the ruler was an important, often the only, avenue to positions of power and influence. But this kind of power, like the authority from which it derived, was always precarious. It could be ended abruptly and painfully by the death or ousting of the ruler, by the loss of favor of the favorite, or by a simple change in political circumstances. Such a fall, after such a rise, could often be disastrous for the family and community of the incumbent, who rose and fell with him.

If medicine and money were the two routes by which a Jew could attain political power, there were other ways of earning a livelihood. The Jewish poor seem on the whole to have consisted of small artisans and craftsmen; the Jewish rich were merchants, and in the earlier period formed an important component in the merchant community of the Islamic Empire.

If in general Jews tended to gravitate toward trades that for one reason or another were regarded with disfavor by Muslims, there were other "sensitive" occupations, to use Professor Goitein's word, that Jews found it safer to avoid.[34] In the wide range of Jewish industrial and commercial activities reflected in the Geniza documents from medieval Egypt, there are significant gaps. The most notable are those connected with food, transportation, and war. Jews do not appear as dealers in the major cereals, such as wheat, barley, and rice, nor are they concerned with raising or selling cattle for food. They had nothing to do with the trade in camels, horses, and other riding and pack animals. They did not buy or sell arms, except to a limited extent for their own guards. Nor, in these documents, is there any reference to Jewish participation in the slave trade, though Jews played some part in this traffic in other times and places. We can only guess at the reasons for these exclusions, which are by no means universal in Islamic history. Goitein's suggestion that these trades are "sensitive," in a strategic sense, may well be the answer. It is surely significant that while Jews did not trade with Christian Europe in these commodities, they were well represented in the trade with India, where no major religious or military conflict existed.

Slave trade
(Lewis is wrong here: see Ashtor on Radhanites)

CONVERSION
↓

THERE was one way in which the Jew could always overcome any and all of these difficulties, and that was by conversion to Islam.

In the course of the centuries during which Jewish communities lived under Muslim rule, considerable numbers of Jews, for one reason or another, embraced Islam. Our information about such conversions is, in general, scanty. Jewish writers preferred not to dwell on so painful a subject, while Muslim authors deemed it hardly worthy of mention. For the Muslims, unlike the Christians, the conversion of the Jews to their faith had no special theological significance. It was merely a part—a relatively small part—of the inevitable spread of the true faith among mankind.

Such information as we have is concerned for the most part with three situations: the conversion of named and prominent

CONVERSION

individuals, which awakens some echo in the historical and biographical literature; conversions that give rise to legal disputes in matters of personal status, and thus leave some record; and finally, the comparatively few occasions when, either by constraint or attraction, large numbers of Jews, sincerely or otherwise, adopt the dominant faith.

three kinds recorded

The first such wave of conversion seems to have occurred in the early years of Islam. To some Jews at the time, the advent of the Prophet in Arabia and the creation of a new world power that overthrew the might of both Rome and Persia and wrested Jerusalem and the holy land from the heavy hand of Byzantium seemed to presage the imminent fulfillment of the Jewish prophecies and the coming of the Messianic age. Fragments of Jewish apocalyptic and other writings of the time give some indication of the fervor and expectation aroused by the early Arab victories. A *piyyūṭ* (liturgical poem), probably composed after the first Arab victories in Palestine but before the capture of either Jerusalem or the Roman provincial capital, Caesarea, may serve as an example:

On that day when the Messiah, son of David, will come
To a downtrodden people

These signs will be seen in the world, and will be brought
    forth:
Earth and heaven will wither,
And the sun and the moon will be blemished,
And the dwellers in the Land will be struck silent.

The king of the West and the king of the East
Will be ground against one another,
And the armies of the king of the West will hold firm in
    the Land.

And a king will go forth from the land of Yoqtan
And his armies will seize the Land,
The dwellers of the world will be judged
And the heavens will rain dust on the earth,
And winds will spread in the Land.

Gog and Magog will incite one another
And kindle fear in the hearts of the Gentiles.
And Israel will be freed of all their sins
And will no more be kept far from the house of prayer
Blessings and consolations will be showered on them,
And they will be engraved in the Book of Life.
The Kings from the land of Edom will be no more
And the people of Antioch will rebel and make peace
And Ma'uziya and Samaria will be consoled
And Acre and Galilee will be shown mercy.
Edomites and Ishmael will fight in the valley of Acre
Till the horses sink in the blood and panic.
Gaza and her daughters will be stoned
And Ascalon and Ashdod will be terror-stricken.[35]

The mood of exaltation passed as it became clear that the empire of the caliphs, though representing a considerable improvement from the Jewish point of view on what had gone before, was still not the fulfillment of Jewish Messianic dreams. Many Jews were converted to Islam and identified themselves with the new faith and dispensation; the remainder gradually adjusted themselves to a new existence under Muslim rule, and in time evolved a new symbiosis with the Muslim Arab rulers.

Jewish Messianic expectations of Islam did not entirely die out and reappeared from time to time in syncretistic Messianic movements led by Jewish claimants to the title of Messiah. One such was a certain Abū ʿĪsā of Isfahan, a Jewish false Messiah of the early eighth century, who, while claiming to be the Jewish Messiah, was prepared to recognize the authenticity and validity of both Christianity and Islam—for Christians and Muslims.[36]

Such movements became increasingly rare. In the later centuries the most usual reason for large-scale or mass conversion was compulsion or repression. Sometimes a Muslim ruler, in defiance of both Muslim law and tradition, decreed and enforced the compulsory Islamization of his Jewish subjects, who responded with conversion, marranism, or emigration. Forced conversion of this kind was comparatively rare; more common, especially in North Africa and in Iran, was a situation in which the Jews, subject to increasing humiliation and degradation and without hope of relief, sought escape from their problems by joining the majority. This means of escape was always there and always easy, and what surprises us is not its occurrence but its rarity. The poet and philosopher Yehuda Ha-Levi, in his *Kuzari*, speaks with pride of "prominent men amongst us who could escape this degradation by a word spoken lightly, become free men, and turn against their oppressors, but do not do so out of devotion to their faith."[37]

Apart from such occasions, our information about conversion refers to the acts of individuals. For a Muslim, it was natural to assume that a new recruit to his faith was attracted by its self-evident truth—indeed, the term for a new Muslim is *muhtadī*, literally, one who has found his way to the right path. For the convert's former coreligionists, who saw him as an apostate or renegade, it was equally natural to look for baser motives. The nonreligious reasons that might impel a Jew to adopt Islam are listed by the thirteenth-century Jewish philosopher Ibn Kammūna: "He is moved by fear or ambition; he is liable to a heavy tax, or wishes to escape from humiliation, or is taken prisoner, falls in love with a Muslim woman, or some other motives like these."[38]

Ibn Kammūna's list seems to cover most cases where conversion cannot be ascribed to religious belief. Fear—of persecution or even discrimination—must have led to individual as well as group conversions. Ambition was clearly the motive of many who, in the course of a successful career in the service of a ruler reached the ceiling of their posssible advancement as members of a minority faith. Some were content to stop at that point; others, by conversion, broke through the ceiling to reach greater, and more dangerous, heights. Sometimes conversion was necessary not only to advance further but even to survive at the point already reached, and was seen as the only way to escape the envy and hostility aroused by past successes. Conversion as an alternative to punishment—as a way to set aside a sentence of death, imprisonment, or lesser penalties—is a common feature of criminal procedure. And marriage, in medieval as in modern societies, may be the most common single cause of change of religion. Under Muslim law, a Muslim man may marry a Christian or Jewish woman. She is not required to become a Muslim, but her children must be brought up as such. A non-Muslim man, however, may in no circumstances marry a Muslim woman. The penalty for such a marriage, or any sexual relationship, is death. Only by conversion to Islam can a non-Muslim escape the consequences of such a relationship in the past, or make one possible in the future.

The individuals whose conversion, for one reason or another, is known and documented, provide examples of all of these motivations, as well as of conversion through religious conviction. A few representative cases may serve as illustrations.

Ka⁺b

Certainly the most famous among Muslims of all Jewish converts to Islam was a Yemenite Jew known as Kaʿb al-Aḥbār, Kaʿb of the Aḥbār, who was probably converted in about 638.[39] He is said to have arrived in Medina during the reign of the caliph ʿUmar I, and to have accompanied him to Jerusalem in 636. The name Kaʿb may represent the Hebrew Jacob (Yaʿqov) or, more likely, Aqiva; Aḥbār is the plural of Ḥabr or Ḥibr, from the Hebrew Ḥaver. This was used as a title for scholars, below the rank of rabbi, in the Palestinian Jewish academies. Nothing appears to be known of Kaʿb from Jewish sources, but he figures prominently in Islamic literature as an authoritative relater of traditions. He died in Syria between 652 and 656. According to Gibb, a gravestone bearing his name is still extant in Damascus. In general, the Muslim tradition presents Kaʿb in a favorable light. He is credited with wisdom and knowledge, the latter including both Biblical scholarship and old Yemenite tradition. In addition to what he knew as a learned Jew and as a Yemeni, he is also cited as an authority for the life and times of the caliph ʿUmar, with whom he was on intimate terms.

While the historical figure of Kaʿb is so overgrown with myth and legend as to be barely distinguishable, there is enough to show that his image had a negative as well as a positive side in Muslim perceptions. His frequent use of Biblical and rabbinical material in interpreting and elaborating Muslim doctrine brought charges of trying to infiltrate Jewish elements into Islam. Politically, his strong support for the caliph ʿUthmān in the struggle leading up to the first civil war in Islam earned him the reprobation of ʿUthmān's enemies and accusers. One of them, the radical ascetic Abū Dharr who is now enjoying a new popularity as a precursor of Arab socialism, is even reported to have set upon Kaʿb and flogged him for this offense. The theme of Kaʿb as a false convert trying to undermine and destroy Islam from within is of comparatively minor importance in classical Islamic literature, though it has enjoyed some recent revival. Kaʿb is usually highly regarded, and is frequently quoted as a source by major narrators of Muslim tradition.

Another early narrator much cited in Muslim literature is Wahb ibn Munabbih, born in Ṣanʿāʾ in the Yemen in about 654 or 655. According to some Muslim traditions he was either by birth or by ancestry a member of the People of the Book (*Ahl al-Kitāb*); others are more specific and describe him as a Jew. The evidence is conflicting. He is named as an authority for both Christian and Jewish material and is even credited with a work entitled *Kitāb al-Isrāʾīliyyāt*, the book of Israelitish material. While this seems dubious, he is in any case often cited as a source of *Isrāʾīliyyāt* stories and interpretations. Known for his pious and ascetic way of life, he nevertheless managed to fall foul of authority, and died in 728 or 732 after a flogging administered by order of the governor of the Yemen.[40]

Many early converts from Judaism were undoubtedly inspired by genuine religious conviction, and they or their sons or grandsons, drawing on their previous Jewish learning, made a substantial contribution to the religion and community they had joined. Even those, at a later date, whose conversion was not wholly religious in origin sometimes rendered some service to Islam. One well-known figure was Yaʿqūb ibn Killis (930-991), a Baghdadi Jew who settled first in Palestine and then in Egypt, where he entered the public service and rose to high

CONVERTS: ① Ibn Killis
② Abul Barakat
③ Samawal al. Magh.
④ Ishaq b. Abr. b. Ezra

98 · CHAPTER 2

rank under the rule of Kāfūr. According to an early account, Ibn Killis was told by Kāfūr that if he became a Muslim he could be vizier, whereupon in 967 he adopted Islam and undertook a course of religious instruction in his new faith. At some stage he seems to have espoused both the Fatimid cause and its Ismāʿīlī doctrine. Fleeing from Egypt to North Africa, he entered the service of the Fatimid caliph al-Muʿizz (952-975) and returned with him to Egypt, where he was placed in charge of the state finances. He achieved his greatest power under the second Fatimid caliph in Egypt, al-ʿAzīz (975-996). The Muslim historians and biographers speak very highly of his accomplishments and his services to the state. Some authors even describe him as a specialist in Ismāʿīlī jurisprudence and the author of a treatise on Ismāʿīlī law, which is, however, unknown to the Ismāʿīlī bibliographical tradition.[41] Although the sincerity of his conversion is not generally questioned, he was accused of favoring his former coreligionists. Such accusations are commonplace when *dhimmīs* or even former *dhimmīs* hold positions of power. Often, they are not without foundation.

Ibn Killis is almost the classical example of the convert whose conversion was a necessary, and in his case also an acceptable, step in his *cursus honorum*. Another famous convert whose conversion was somehow, though rather differently, related to his career was the philosopher Abu'l-Barakāt Hibatallāh Ibn Malka al-Baghdādī, known as Awḥad al-Zamān, "the unique one of his time" (ca. 1077-1164). A native of the region of Mosul, Abu'l-Barakāt, like so many other Jews, reached greatness through the practice of medicine, serving as physician both to the Abbasid caliphs in Baghdad and to the Seljuq sultans. According to his biographers, his relations with his royal patrons and courtly rivals were often difficult, and it was because of these, it would appear, that he decided, late in life, to embrace Islam. Various reasons for this conversion, derived no doubt from conflicting rumors heard at court, are given in the sources. One version ascribes his change of faith to wounded pride; another to fear of the consequences when a wife of the sultan died under his treat-

Baghdadi

ment; a third alleges that he abjured his faith in order to save his life when he was taken prisoner in a battle between the armies of the caliph and of the sultan. Some idea of the situation of *dhimmī* physicians at court can be gathered from an incident related in the biography of his professional rival at court, the Christian physican Ibn al-Tilmīdh, known as Amīn al-Dawla. According to this story the Christian lampooned the Jew in a verse in which he remarked that his stupidity was manifest and that he was outranked by a dog. A Muslim colleague then dismissed the pretensions of both the Christian and the Jew:

Abu'l-Ḥasan the doctor and his rival
Abu'l-Barakāt are engaged in a feud
The one in his modesty rises to the Pleiades
The other in his haughtiness sinks to the depths.[42]

One of Abu'l-Barakāt's pupils was a certain Isḥāq, the son of the famous Hebrew poet Abraham ibn Ezra and the son-in-law of the even more famous Yehuda Ha-Levi. In 1140 he traveled with his father-in-law from Spain to Egypt, where they parted company. Isḥāq went to Baghdad and became a disciple of Abu'l-Barakāt, for whom he composed a panegyric in Hebrew. At some stage, for what reason is not known, he embraced Islam. At a later stage he apparently decided to return to Judaism and, since apostasy is a capital offense under Islamic law, he emigrated to a Christian country for this purpose. Away from the comforts of civilization, he became ill and died.[43]

Another of Abu'l-Barakāt's pupils was a certain Samaw'al (Samuel) al-Maghribī, a Jew of North African origin who acquired some fame as a scholar, physician, and mathematician. Like his master Abu'l-Barakāt and his fellow student Isḥāq ibn Abraham ibn Ezra, Samuel made the decision to convert from Judaism to Islam. But while Abu'l-Barakāt was converted toward the end of his life and had nothing to say about it, and while Isḥāq later regretted his conversion and returned to his previous religion, Samuel became and remained a convinced Muslim who is chiefly remembered for his polemics against Judaism and the Jews.[44]

apostasy sometimes permitted

Occasional exceptions were made to the rule that the penalty for apostasy was death. A famous case was that of Maimonides, who was forcibly converted to Islam in his birthplace in Spain and reverted to Judaism when he was able to escape to the east. One day, while at the height of his power and fame in Cairo, he was recognized by a Muslim fellow countryman who knew of his earlier conversion and denounced him as an apostate from Islam, demanding the penalty of death. Fortunately for Maimoides, the case was heard by the qāḍī al-Fāḍil, his friend and patron. The qāḍī ruled that since Maimonides' conversion to Islam in Cordova had been obtained by force, it was not legally or religiously valid, and his reversion to Judaism did not therefore constitute apostasy.[45]

Not all detected apostates were as fortunate. Like the Spanish Marranos who fled from Christian Spain to Muslim Turkey or Morocco in order to revert to Judaism, so under Muslim rule Jewish converts who changed their minds had to leave the lands of Islam and travel to Christendom. Apparently neither Muslims nor Christians objected to Jews abjuring the rival religion.

Rashid al-Din

Sometimes even conversion did not end the troubles of a former Jew. One such case was the famous Rashīd al-Dīn Fażlallāh, a Persian Jew by birth, and according to an early source the son of a Jewish apothecary in Tabrīz. As usual, his avenue to fame and power was the practice of medicine, but it is not as a physician that he is chiefly remembered. At the court of the Mongol Il-Khāns in Iran he revealed great talent and won respect as an administrator and, indeed, a statesman; while at the same time, his immense universal history, which he planned and edited and in great part wrote, ranks him among the foremost historians of Islam. Like many Jewish courtiers and officials, at some stage in his career he found it expedient to adopt Islam; like not a few of them he appears, at the time of his change of religion or subsequently, to have undergone a genuine conversion. In his action and benefactions, as well as in his writings, there is ample evidence of an authentic commitment to the Islamic faith.

His commitment did not, however, save him from suspicion during his lifetime and insult after his death. On one occasion, in 1312, he had a narrow escape when his enemies produced a forged letter purporting to be written by him and instigating another physician to poison the Il-Khan. Rashīd al-Dīn was able to prove the letter a fake and expose the plot, and thus he continued for a while in favor. Significantly, the alleged poisoner was a Jew, and the forged letter written in the Hebrew script. A few years later, in 1318, he was again accused by his rivals of having poisoned the Il-Khan's father and predecessor. This time the accusers achieved their purpose. Under interrogation, Rashīd al-Dīn admitted that, against the advice of the Il-Khan's physicians, he had prescribed a purgative, which worsened instead of remedying his disorder. Though more than seventy years old, he was put to death by mutilation and decapitation. All his goods and estates were confiscated, while the quarter in Tabrīz that he had founded and endowed, and which bore his name, was looted by the mob. Even the *waqfs*, or pious foundations for Islamic religious purposes, established by him were deemed invalid and their assets seized. Several early sources relate that after his execution his severed head was taken to Tabrīz and paraded around the city for several days amid cries of "This is the head of the Jew who abused the name of God; may God's curse be upon him!" Almost a century later another ruler, Mīrānshāh, the demented son of the great Tamerlane, renewed the attack on Rashīd al-Dīn. His tomb was destroyed, and his bones were exhumed and reburied in the Jewish cemetery.[46]

In the central lands, however, converts were usually welcomed and well treated, and they disappeared rapidly into the main body of Muslims. It was only rarely that Muslims of Jewish birth—still more rarely of Jewish ancestry—were stigmatized or penalized as such. In Iran and North Africa, in contrast, the memory of Jewish ancestry was retained for many generations, both by the descendants of the converts and, more especially, by their neighbors.[47] Significantly, both were countries where forced conversion was practiced.

Humiliation

For those who remained Jews, there was a dark as well as a bright side to life as a *dhimmī* under the rule of Islam. "Humiliation and wretchedness were stamped upon them and they were visited with wrath from God" says the Qur'ān (II,61), speaking of the Jews. From time to time Muslim rulers, and more often Muslim populations, felt it necessary to restore this condition if the Jews seemed to be escaping from it. In general, what they had to fear was not violence, not persecution, not expulsion, but minor harassment, petty humiliation, taunts and insults, and of course chronic insecurity. In the age of the Crusades and after, there was a notable deterioration in the position of the Jews, as of other religious minorities. The physician and philosopher Maimonides, whose writings on science in Arabic and on Jewish religious learning in both Arabic and Hebrew are among the greatest achievements of the Arab-Jewish symbiosis, had himself been a victim of the new intolerance. It was from personal experience as well as religious concern and learning that he was able to send a letter of advice to the Jews of Yemen in 1172, when they too faced the problem of forced conversion. There is a striking contrast between Maimonides' letter to his Hebrew translator in Europe in which he speaks of the richness of the Arabic language and the superiority of the Arab sciences, and his letter to the persecuted Jews of the Yemen, in which he complains bitterly of the wretched state of the Jews under Muslim rule: "You know, my brethren, that on account of our sins God has cast us into the midst of this people, the nation of Ishmael, who persecute us severely, and who devise ways to harm us and to debase us. . . . No nation has ever done more harm to Israel. None has matched it in debasing and humiliating us. None has been able to reduce us as they have."[48] These strictures, no doubt written under the impact of his own memories of Spain and Morocco revived by the recent news from southern Arabia, cannot be accepted as an accurate general picture. Maimonides' own position, his pride and his success as a court physician and communal leader in Cairo,

RMBM's forced conversion

attest the contrary. But his observations certainly contain a proportion of truth.

Some indication of Muslim perceptions of Jews and Judaism may be gathered from the ways in which these appear in certain common themes of Muslim discourse. One, frequently encountered in classical times, is the attribution of a Jewish origin or ancestry in order to discredit an individual, a group, a custom, or an idea. An example cited by Goldziher indicates that this practice goes back to early Arab times. In a passage he quotes, two rival poets of the Arab tribe of Awf challenged each other's right to trace his descent from this tribe. One of them, to discredit the other, accused him of being of Jewish descent. A similar charge was made against the philologist Abu 'Ubayda by his enemies, and by Abu 'Ubayda himself against an Umayyad governor whom he wished to denigrate.[49]

These and other similar examples amount to little more than social snobbery—the game, widely practiced in many societies, of asserting and impugning pedigrees. More serious is the recurring tendency to attribute subversive and extremist doctrines to Jewish origins or instigation. Thus, for example, the emergence of the Shi'a and hence of schism within Islam, and more particularly the appearance of the exaggerated exaltation of 'Ali and the later imams, is attributed to the demonic figure of 'Abdallah ibn Saba, allegedly a Yemenite Jew converted to Islam. In the Sunni tradition, he is the instigator of Shi'ism; in the Shi'ite tradition, he sometimes appears as the originator of extreme doctrines of the type that were reprobated by the moderate Twelver Shi'a. Modern critical scholarship has successively cast doubt on 'Abdallah ibn Saba's role, his Jewishness, and even his historicity.[50]

Another example is the ninth-century Mu'tazili Ibn al-Rawandi, who is blamed for some of the more extreme ideas propounded by or on behalf of the early Abbasids. He is also credited with having been one of the leading proponents of free-thought and materialism in this period. There are different versions about Ibn al-Rawandi's background; in some of them he is said to have been of Jewish origin.[51]

A third and more famous example is 'Abdallah ibn Maymūn al-Qaddāḥ, who figures in anti-Ismāʿīlī and anti-Fatimid polemical writings as the founder of the Ismāʿīlī faith and the ancestor of the Fatimid caliphs. ʿAbdallāh ibn Maymūn is a shadowy figure, and again there are different versions of his biography. In several of them he is said to have been of Jewish birth, with the implication that Ismāʿilism was a Judaizing heresy and the Fatimids were usurpers of Jewish extraction.[52]

Needless to say, there is no serious evidence for any of these assertions. Nevertheless, the tendency to see Jewish involvement in subversive ideas and seditious actions—familiar in other times and places—persisted for some time among the Muslims, too. A striking example is the dangerous dervish revolt that in the early fifteenth century almost destroyed the nascent Ottoman state. The leader of the dervishes, who was accused by the historiographic tradition of preaching inter-denominationalism and communism, was the famous qāḍī of Simavna, Bedreddin. Associated with him was a certain Torlak Hu Kemal, said by some to have been a convert from Judaism and to have played a particularly evil role.[53]

In modern times this line of argument is switched from religious to political subversion. Thus, conservative opponents of the Young Turks, particularly in the Arab provinces of the Ottoman Empire, made much of their alleged Jewish connections—though, it should be noted, this particular accusation appears to have originated in Christian Europe. More recently, Jews were accused of being responsible for spreading socialist and related ideas in the Islamic world. These accusations ceased when socialism changed its status from a menace to a merit and was added to the official designations of most states and political parties. It was only the enemies of socialism who ascribed it to Jewish instigation, and they are now silent, or at least cautious.

As well as the demiurgic subversive, the Jew also appears in Muslim folklore in another role—as the ultimate example of the humble and downtrodden. A figure of speech common in Muslim writings is to state a fact or proposition in a grotesque and exaggerated form—not, as in the Western *reductio ad absurdum*, in order to prove it false, but for the opposite purpose: to show that even when pushed to an improbable extreme it remains true. The Jew, like the black, is sometimes used for this purpose. One little story, told about many different Muslim rulers to illustrate their concern for justice and respect for the law, may serve as an example. In the Ottoman form, it is related that when Sultan Süleyman the Magnificent was preparing to build the great Süleymaniye mosque, his plans were impeded by an obstinate Jew who owned a small piece of land on the intended site and refused all offers to buy it from him. The sultan was urged by his advisers to confiscate, or at least compulsorily to purchase, the land from the recalcitrant infidel; but he refused to do so, since this would be contrary to the law of God. The same story is told by Sunnis of the caliph ʿUmar, by Shiʿites of the caliph ʿAlī, and no doubt of many other rulers, and is a standard myth depicting the just ruler. The same theme sometimes occurs in a more explicitly historical context. Thus the emir Zangi, who ruled in Mesopotamia and northern Syria in the twelfth century, is praised by historians for his piety and his restoration of Islamic legal norms; as an example, "Even if the plaintiff was a Jew and the accused his own son, he would still do justice to the plaintiff."[54] Goitein's inference from this that "an unprotected member of a second-class community had little chance normally that his case would be properly heard" seems reasonable for that and perhaps some other times and places. It was not, however, true of the Ottoman Empire, where the evidence of judicial records makes it clear that Jews could and frequently did have recourse to the qāḍī's court, and that they could, on occasion, sue Muslims and win.[55]

SOMETIMES Jews even resorted to the qāḍīs' courts for the adjudication of disputes among themselves. Normally, however, they were ruled by their own Jewish courts, where rabbinical judges dispensed justice in accordance with *halakhic* law. This was part—perhaps the most significant part—of the whole apparatus of quasi-autonomy, whereby the Jewish community, like other religious communities subject to the Muslim state, was in large measure responsible for the conduct of its

autonomous communal controls

own internal affairs, and even, at certain periods, for the assessment and collection of taxes, which were then remitted to the state authorities. This system of communal autonomies was a natural extension of the practice of the pre-Islamic empires; it flourished in a society in which religion was the ultimate determinant of a man's identity and the dominant force shaping his way of life. The *dhimma* was an arrangement—whether pact or grant—conceded to the community, not the individual; the *dhimmī* had a status and a role only as a member of a community recognized as possessing those attributes. This pattern of social organization gave great authority, sometimes even power, to the leaders of the community, especially when these were recognized or accredited by the Muslim state. The exilarch—Resh Galuta, Prince of the Captivity—of Abbasid Baghdad held an office that had existed since Sasanid times, and he was often a figure of some significance at the caliphal capital. The emergence of similar communal leaders in other Muslim capitals weakened his position. In the later Middle Ages, with the strengthening of state authority and the weakening of autonomous institutions generally, the office of Chief of the Jews lost its importance.

The simplified and idealized nineteenth-century accounts of the history of the Jews in Spain present a black and white picture of Christian intolerance and Muslim tolerance, with the Jews fleeing from the one to the other. It was not always so. During the centuries when both Muslim and Christian states existed in the Iberian peninsula, there were times and places, as in Maimonides' own birthplace, when it was the Muslims who persecuted and the Christians who offered refuge. In North Africa on the one hand and in Iran and Central Asia on the other, the pattern of Jewish life from the later Middle Ages was one of increasing poverty, misery, and degradation. Only in the central lands of the Middle East, under the rule of Mamluk sultans and far more under the rule of the Ottoman Empire, were Jews able to preserve some status and dignity, and even to enter on a new age of efflorescence.

THREE

The Late Medieval
and Early Modern Periods

FOR SOME time now it has been the practice of Western historians to divide history, for convenience of discussion, into three periods designated ancient, medieval, and modern, each of which may be further subdivided into early and late or into even smaller subunits. This classification is derived from the study of European history, and strictly speaking is only appropriate to the consideration of European topics. It has, however, become acceptable to use these categories also in discussing the history of other civilizations, which may have developed at a different pace, with a different rhythm, and in response to different pressures and impulses. Even in the Islamic lands of the Middle East and North Africa, it is now usual for historians to write the history of their own countries and societies in this European terminology. Writers in Arabic, Persian, and Turkish have devised the necessary equivalent terms in their own languages, including renderings of such previously unknown concepts as Middle Ages and medieval.

The use of categories derived from one civilization to classify the phenomena and developments of another is always hazardous, often ambiguous, and sometimes downright misleading. When, for example, does the "medieval" history of Islam, or for that matter of India or of China, begin? When does it end? Does the medieval history of Islam mean the events that occurred during those centuries which in Europe are known as medieval? Or does it mean the period during which Islamic society shared certain distinguishing characteristics, certain specific qualities, with the European society known as medieval? When does the medieval history of Islam end— when modern history begins in Europe, or when modernization transforms the Middle East? Even the formulation of these questions presupposes certain assumptions about Islamic history, especially that the most important determining factors, the chief motors of change, are the same as those of Europe, or at least close enough to make such analogies meaningful.

To designate a chapter in the history of the Islamic Middle East and North Africa with the terms "late medieval and early modern" may thus perhaps require some apology, certainly some explanation. The terms are used here because they are part of a universally accepted terminology, current now even in the Middle East and North Africa, and may therefore serve to convey, in a few words, an approximate idea of what is intended. It may, however, be useful to devote a moment or two to the periodization of Middle Eastern history in the era that began with the advent of Islam in the seventh century and has continued to the present day. The whole question of periodization in Islamic history is still at a very rudimentary stage of discussion; this indeed may be a major reason for the common acceptance of the European categories. A preliminary and tentative periodization—a convenience for the historian, not an attempt to discern innate patterns in Middle Eastern history—must suffice for the time being.

Perhaps the simplest and most immediately intelligible way of dividing Middle Eastern history in the Islamic period is in terms of invasions. There have been many of these, but three in particular had an enormous, in many respects a decisive, influence on the events that followed. The first was the invasion of the Arab Muslims in the seventh and eighth centuries, which brought a new religion, Islam; a new language, Arabic; and created a new political structure, the caliphate. These changes initiated a new political, social, and cultural order in the Middle East, to a high degree consistent within itself, and significantly different from what went before.

The next major transformation begins with the invasion of the Middle East by the steppe peoples from the north and northeast, starting with the migration of the Turks in the tenth and eleventh centuries, and culminating in the great Mongol conquests of the thirteenth, which destroyed the Islamic cal-

iphate and inaugurated a new age. Politically, it was dominated by the Mongols and the Turks, and governed by the
long-lasting and elaborately administered kingdoms and empires which they created. Culturally, it was expressed mainly
in Persian and in various Turkish languages. Religiously, it
remained Muslim, but with a new kind of Islam, more struc-
tured, more hierarchic, more concerned with order and with
orthodoxy.[1]

This period, too, ends with yet another invasion, this time
from Europe. The kingdoms of Islam had tried several times
to conquer Europe—the Arabs in Spain and Sicily, the Islamized Tatars of the Golden Horde in Russia, the Ottoman Turks
in southeastern Europe, twice reaching as far as the walls of
Vienna. All three attempts to dominate Europe failed, and as
the Europeans expelled the invaders and conquerors, they
themselves, in turn, began to follow their former masters into
their own homelands. The Spaniards and the Portuguese, and
later the other maritime peoples of Western Europe, pursued
the Moors to Morocco and then, sailing around Africa, carried
their war against the Muslims to south Asia and the southern
approaches to the Middle East. The Austrians and Hungari-
ans, recovering from their defeats, began to push the Ottomans back through the Balkans toward Constantinople. The
Russians, having freed Moscow from the "Tatar yoke," em-
barked on a vast series of conquests that took them southward
to the Black Sea, the Caucasus, and the Caspian and thus to
the northern approaches of the Middle Eastern heartlands of
Islam.

The period with which we are concerned here is the second—the period, that is to say, that begins with the coming
of the steppe peoples and ends with the coming of the Europeans, at which point we may plausibly speak of the modern
history of the Middle East or of the Islamic lands.

Chronologically, this middle period begins in about the thirteenth century, when the rule of the Mongol khans was extended to most of southwest Asia and when the Ayyubid
dynasty, founded by Saladin, gave way to the sultanate of the
Mamluks who ruled in Egypt from the mid-thirteenth century

to the early sixteenth. The ending of this period is more difficult to date with any precision, since the processes of European expansion and the resulting changes affected different parts of the Middle East and North Africa at different times—for some beginning as early as the seventeenth century, for others delayed until the nineteenth or even the twentieth.

During the earlier part of this period, there were six major centers of power in the world of Islam, all but one of them dominated by Turkish dynasties and armies. These centers were India, Central Asia, Iran, Turkey, Egypt with Syria, and North Africa. In the sixteenth century the number was reduced by a considerable expansion of the power of the Ottomans who, already controlling Anatolia and much of southeastern Europe, destroyed the Mamluk sultanate and incorporated its territories—Egypt, Syria, Palestine, and parts of Arabia, into the Ottoman Empire. This was followed by the extension of Ottoman suzerainty over North Africa, to include the countries that are now called Libya, Tunisia, and Algeria. Only Morocco, still ruled by Arab dynasties, remained beyond the reach of Ottoman power. In 1534, in one of a long series of wars fought between the Ottomans and the shāhs of Iran, Iraq was finally wrested from the Persians and incorporated into the Ottoman realm.

The Ottoman Empire reached its apogee in the sixteenth and early seventeenth centuries when it struggled with the Hapsburg Empire for the control of central Europe. In this struggle, the Turks were at first victorious, were held for a century and a half, and then were slowly but decisively defeated. The second unsuccessful Turkish siege of Vienna in 1683 was followed three years later by the loss of Buda, that is, Budapest, which had been the seat of a Turkish pasha since 1541. At the end of the seventeenth century, after the victories of the Austrians and their allies, the Ottoman Empire, for the first time in its history, was compelled by a victorious enemy to sign a peace treaty as a defeated power. Meanwhile a new and still more dangerous enemy was threatening the Ottomans—the rising and expanding power of Russia, growing southward and eastward largely at Turkish expense. By 1783

LATE MEDIEVAL, EARLY MODERN PERIODS • 111

the Russians were able to annex the Crimea, which for centuries had been a Turkish and Muslim land. From the conquered Crimea the Russians spread eastward and westward along the northern shore of the Black Sea, and threatened the Turks at both ends of it. The city of Odessa was founded in 1795 on the site of a Tatar village.

Iran and Central Asia were for some time dominated by Islamized successor states of the great Mongol Khans—some of them ruled by descendants of the line of Jenghiz Khan, others by Mongols and Tatars of other lineage. In Central Asia these dynasties continued to reign until they were conquered and absorbed by the Russian Empire in the nineteenth century. In Iran proper they were overthrown and supplanted by a new dynasty, that of the Safavids, which gained power at the beginning of the sixteenth century and laid the foundations of the modern realm of Iran. In Muslim India, where various Turkish dynasties had held sway since the first Turkish incursions in the eleventh century, another line of Turco-Mongol rulers, descendants of the redoubtable Tamerlane or Timur Lang, ruled most of the subcontinent until they were supplanted by the British. They are sometimes known as the Great Moguls.

At first, there were two major Jewish groups in the Islamic world, one Iranic, the other Arabic. The first consisted of the Persian-speaking Jewish communities of Iran, with its cultural extension eastward into the territories that now form the republics of Afghanistan and of Soviet Central Asia. In all of these there were Jewish communities of Persian language and culture. Even in India, which at this time formed part of the Perso-Islamic world, we find some indications, on a very much smaller scale, of a Jewish presence. Until the sixteenth century, the Persian-speaking Jews formed a single community. It was split into two by the establishment of the Shi'ite Safavid monarchy, which separated Iran from Sunni Central Asia. The latter in turn was split in the eighteenth century by the rise of new and warring powers, forming the states of Bukhara and Afghanistan. These three Jewish communities seem to have had little contact with the outside world or even with each other.

West of Iran, from Iraq all the way to Morocco, were the numerous Arabic-speaking Jewish communities that in earlier times had been the creators and custodians of the Judaeo-Islamic tradition.

Besides these two main groups there was a third, differing from both of them, and at first relatively small and insignificant. This consisted of the Jews of the former Byzantine Empire, still found in Asia Minor and in southeastern Europe. These had never been either under Arab or Persian rule, and had never adopted either the Arabic or Persian language. Most of them appear to have been Greek-speaking; some, in those former Byzantine territories in Asia Minor that were now governed by Turkish emirates, began, in some measure, to adopt the Turkish language. This adoption never seems to have gone very far, however, and Turkish-speakers remained a small minority of the Jews in the Turkish lands. In time both Turkish-speakers and Greek-speakers among the Jewish communities in these areas were swamped by the influx of European Jews from the late fifteenth century.[2]

The Arabic-speaking Jewish communities may be subdivided politically, according to the states to which they were subject. Iraq had once been a major center, both in antiquity and in the Islamic Middle Ages. It had now lost much of its importance. No longer the seat of a great empire nor even of an independent power, it had become an outlying and often disputed province of the other empires. In the earlier centuries it was for the most part ruled from Iran; then, after a period of struggle, it was finally incorporated into the Ottoman Empire. It still remained a border area, however, threatened at first by the rival Islamic power in Iran, and later by the advance of the maritime powers of Europe from the Persian Gulf. The circumstances of Iraq in these centuries did not permit either the Jews or anyone else to flourish.

Syria and Palestine during this period were also dominated from elsewhere—at first by the Mamluk sultans in Egypt, and later from Turkey. During the Mamluk period, Egypt was for a while a center of some importance, and so too, though to a much lesser extent, was Syria. With the incorporation of both regions in the Ottoman Empire, the main center of activity inevitably shifted to the new capital, and these countries shrank into provincial insignificance. West of Egypt, all the regions of North Africa had Jewish communities, the largest of which were in Morocco and—on a much smaller scale— in Tunisia. To this enumeration of the Arabic-speaking Jews one should add the Yemen in the southwestern corner of Arabia. This was a remote and isolated Jewish community, cut off from most other centers, but enjoying a rich and varied cultural life of its own.

Of all these Jewish communities, the most important by far came to be that of the Ottoman Empire. It owed its importance to two major developments—one general, one Jewish. The general factor was of course the rise and expansion of the Ottoman Empire itself, which conferred a new and greater importance on all those communities that formed a part of it. The specifically Jewish factor was the great immigration of Jews from Europe, especially though not exclusively from Spain, Portugal, and Italy, which revived the dwindling Jewries of the Levant with a fresh infusion of numbers, knowledge, wealth, and—perhaps most important of all, at least in the short run— gave them an opening to the world of Europe, then beginning its rise to world hegemony.

In the course of its expansion the Ottoman state acquired, by one means or another, a considerable number of Jewish subjects, who constituted a large and ramified community, with wide regional and social variation. The student of Jewish history under Islam, looking both at the sources of information and the scholarly work accomplished, cannot but be struck by the contrast between the classical and Ottoman periods— the latter field of study offering such greater opportunity, showing such smaller accomplishment. For virtually all the pre-Ottoman communities, the source material available is sadly limited. Jewish historiography is sparse and slight. Rabbinical responsa survive, but in very small numbers, and only from a few places. Jewish literature is rich, but the historical material it provides is incidental and often insubstantial. The general Muslim historiographic and other literature contains many references to Jews, but the information provided is episodic and fragmentary, and its value is mainly in illuminating the general cultural and social background. There are no archives; only the Geniza provides a body of significant contemporary documentation. The great work of S. D. Goitein on the Jews of medieval Egypt, based largely on Geniza material, shows how much can be learned from even this kind of documentation, and how much is permanently unknowable without it. And even the Geniza is a random collection of waste paper, very different from a genuine archive in which documents are still preserved in their original series and sequence.

A student of Ottoman-Jewish history is far better placed in every respect. The sources at his disposal may be divided into three main groups—the Jewish, European, and Ottoman, in Turkish, Arabic, and other languages. The most important of the Jewish sources are the rabbinical responsa, which have come down to us in great quantity from various Ottoman cities and notably from such centers as Salonika, Istanbul, and Izmir.[3] These are very rich and informative and shed a flood of light on social and economic history. Sometimes the responsa even contain some details about the course of events, though from their nature this does not amount to a great deal. In general the historiographic poverty of the earlier period continues into Ottoman times, though there is some slight improvement. It may seem strange that the scholars of this community—so active in other respects—should have shown so little interest either in their own history or in the history of the country in which they lived.[4] The only books in Hebrew dealing with Ottoman history or even with Ottoman Jewish history were written outside the Ottoman Empire. One of them was composed in Crete, at a time when the island was still a possession of the Venetian republic and therefore within intellectual reach of the European Renaissance; the other was written by a French-born Jew in Italy.[5] The composition of these two books reflects the impact on Jews of the new scholarship of Europe rather than anything that arose within either the Ottoman or Jewish worlds.

In addition to literary sources, there are Jewish records of various kinds—communal and synagogue records, not only in the Ottoman and former Ottoman territories, but also in Europe. The congregation of Spanish and Portuguese Jews in London, for example, kept two series of documents relevant to the East. One, entitled, in Portuguese, *Cautivos*, deals with the ransoming of captives taken prisoner by Muslim corsairs or Christian pirates and privateers in the Mediterranean; the other, called *Terra Santa*, is concerned with requests for money from indigent and distressed persons coming from the holy land—a term sometimes taken to include the whole of geographical Syria. These files, though limited in scope, give some insight into at least one aspect of Jewish life in the Levant.[6] Similar documentation may well exist in the archives of other European Jewish communities, especially in Italy, which had connections with their coreligionists in the East. The archives of international Jewish organizations, as also those of the Ottoman Jewish communities, do not become important until the nineteenth century.

Far richer than Jewish documentary sources are those of the various European countries that had dealings of one kind or another with the Ottoman Empire. These include diplomatic and consular reports, which exist in virtually every state in Europe, as well as the records of the trading companies and chambers of commerce that operated extensively in the Ottoman domains. These European governmental and commercial archives are on the whole well preserved and fairly well studied. The European merchants and their diplomatic and consular protectors often had occasion to deal with Ottoman Jews in various capacities, and their reports contain a great deal of useful information.[7]

These sources can be supplemented by a fairly rich travel literature. In the course of the centuries, considerable numbers of travelers from Christian Europe visited Turkey and the adjoining lands—pilgrims and missionaries, traders and diplomats, spies and military officers, archeologists and scholars, and, toward the end of our period, gentlemen travelers and later even lady travelers in search of new sights and new experiences—the vanguard of the modern army of tourists. These travelers often have something interesting to say about individual Jews and even about Jewish communities in the cities through which they passed, and though their comments often throw more light on themselves and their countries of origin than on the countries and peoples that they describe, they nevertheless have much to offer. They are, in general, more informative than the Jewish travelers from Europe. Apart from the numerous pilgrims and settlers who have left us descriptions of Jerusalem and the holy land, Jewish travel literature is rather meager and uninformative before the nineteenth century, when European Jews in greater numbers felt the desire and found the opportunity to travel.[8]

Until recently, scholarly studies on Ottoman Jewish history were based almost exclusively on these two groups of sources, the Jewish and the European. The result was that Ottoman Jewish communities were often presented as if they were living in a vacuum, with an almost total disregard of the larger societies and polities of which they were a part. This usually resulted in a serious distortion of perspective. To take a single example: it is impossible to evaluate the position of the Jews as a minority in the Ottoman lands, without at the same time considering the parallel positions of the Christian minorities. The Jewish minority is not, as in much of Europe, unique, but is, so to speak, one of a class of phenomena, and its position is not intelligible without reference to others in the same class. And, needless to say, in order to understand Ottoman Jewish history it is useful to know something about the Ottoman state and society—a point that might seem self-evident but has frequently been overlooked by scholars working in this field.

This knowledge of course requires the study of the Turkish sources, which, for the purposes of Jewish history, has barely begun. References to Jews in Turkish chronicles and other literary materials are comparatively few.[9] The historians of the Ottoman Empire did not regard the affairs of the *dhim-*

mīs—Jews and others—as very important, and they therefore devote little attention to them. In general, references to Jews in the Ottoman chronicles occur only in connection with the deeds or misdeeds of occasional named individuals or, even more rarely, when there is some public incident or disorder in which Jews are concerned, either as perpetrators or as victims.

If, however, the literary sources are few, the archives are of enormous richness and value. Archival collections are still preserved in many provincial capitals both in the present republic of Turkey and in some of the former Ottoman provinces, as, for example, in Damascus, Aleppo, Jerusalem, Cairo, Sofia, and no doubt other cities. Most important of all are the former imperial archives in Istanbul, which contain, on current estimates, some 60,000 bound registers and letterbooks, and between fourteen and fifteen million documents. These records, needless to say, are extraordinarily informative for every aspect of life in the Ottoman Empire, especially in its great days, but also to no small extent during the centuries of decline.

Of particular relevance to the study of Jewish history is the *Defter-i Hakani*, sometimes known as the *Tapu*, the imperial survey of land, population, and revenue. For each *sanjak* or province, from Buda to Basra, there is a register, often a series of registers, in which the population is enumerated, city by city and village by village, and within each city quarter by quarter, community by community, street by street, and house by house. The *Tapu* series alone contains an estimated fifteen hundred volumes in the Istanbul archives alone as well as others in Ankara and elsewhere. This series does not include Egypt or the other African territories of the empire, nor was it extended to the Arabian peninsula. There are only a few registers for the three *sanjaks* of Iraq—that is, of Mosul, Baghdad, and Basra—and a rather larger number for the provinces into which Syria and Palestine were divided. For the Anatolian and European *sanjaks* the number of registers is very much greater and surveys were renewed at more frequent intervals.[10]

From these it is possible to tabulate the Jewish communities in almost all the European and Asian provinces of the Ottoman Empire—where they lived, in what quarters or communities they were organized, and what their numbers were, usually with a list of names of adult male Jews. In those areas where registers were renewed at intervals, it is possible not only to tabulate distribution but also to observe change over a period of time. A Turkish scholar, the late Professor Ömer Lûtfi Barkan, prepared statistics of the religious distribution of the inhabitants of the principal cities of the Ottoman Empire, according to the surveys completed between 1520 and 1530.[11] (See table.) The figures are for households. More recently, Mark Epstein listed population statistics for all the Jewish communities in the European and Asian provinces of the empire, based on the same series of registers, but extending over a longer period.[12]

Even for the history of the Jews of Iran, the best statistical evidence dates from the comparatively short period when parts of western Iran, the provinces of Azerbaijan, Hamadān, and

Religious composition of the population of the main towns of the Ottoman Empire, 1520-1530

Towns	Muslim Households	Christian Households	Jewish Households	Total Households
Istanbul	9,517	5,162	1,647	16,326
Bursa	6,165	69	117	6,351
Edirne	3,338	522	201	4,061
Ankara	2,399	277	28	2,704
Athens	11	2,286	—	2,297
Tokat	818	701	—	1,519
Konya	1,092	22	—	1,114
Sivas	261	750	—	11
Sarajevo	1,024	—	—	1,024
Monastir	640	171	34	845
Skopje	630	200	12	842
Sofia	471	238	—	709
Salonika	1,229	989	2,645	4,863
Siroz	671	357	65	1,093
Trikala	301	343	181	825
Larissa	693	75	—	768
Nicopolis	468	775	—	1,343

NB!

Kermānshāh, were incorporated into the Ottoman Empire and made the subject of similar survey registers. The registers give the following figures:

Tabrīz	54 Jewish households	
Hamadān	132 " "	
Kermānshāh	53 " "	

The first is dated A.H. 1140 = 1727 C.E. The second and third are undated, but were compiled during the reign of Ahmed III (1703-1730).[13]

While the *Tapu* series is of the most obvious immediate value, much useful information about Jewish life and activities can be obtained from other series of registers and documents in the Ottoman archives, including some devoted specifically to the affairs of the non-Muslim communities. One series is of special importance for Jewish and, indeed, for general history. This is the *Sijill* registers, containing the records of the office of the qāḍī. The qāḍī of an Ottoman provincial city was not only the chief judicial authority; he also exercised a wide range of administrative and even fiscal functions, and the qāḍī's registers, often extremely detailed, offer to the researcher a day-by-day picture of events. In principle, a series of *Sijill* registers should exist in every city that was the seat of an Ottoman qāḍī. In fact, considerable numbers have come to light, and are only just beginning to yield results. The studies of Amnon Cohen on the *Sijill* registers for Jerusalem have shown how much these can offer for Jewish history.[14] Similar researches on other series will no doubt yield comparable results.

For a long time the study of Ottoman Jewish history, such as it was, was left to premodern scholars who wrote prescientific history, supplemented by occasional rabbinical studies based on one or another collection of responsa, often used without any reference, even the most perfunctory, to the Ottoman background and documentation. From these premodern efforts there is a quantum jump to more recent work, notably by Uriel Heyd and a few others who have worked on Turkish archival and literary sources.[15]

SIJILL
(of
Qadi)

AFTER this excursus on the documentation of Ottoman Jewish history, we can now turn to the composition of the Ottoman Jewish communities. These may be considered in successive layers, and in chronological sequence. The first and oldest are those known as the Romaniot Jews—the native Greek-speaking Jews whom the Turks found on the spot when they conquered the original provinces out of which the Ottoman state was formed. These were the communities in western Asia Minor, in the Byzantine capital of Constantinople, in Greece, and in some of the Balkan cities. In Jewish ritual and liturgy they followed the *Minhag* Romania, that is, the custom of the Byzantine Empire. Their language was and had for long been Greek, and they had lived in that area for a very long time.

The second layer consisted of early immigrants from Europe, chiefly Ashkenazi Jews coming from Germany and even from France. There is mention of such immigrants at the beginning of the fifteenth century; some may have come even earlier. They were, however, dwarfed into insignificance by the massive immigration of Sephardic Jews from southern Europe, from the end of the fifteenth century, following the edicts of expulsion against the Jews of Spain in 1492 and of Portugal in 1496. From this time they began to arrive in the Ottoman domains in ever-increasing numbers. As well as in Istanbul, the capital, sizable Sephardic Jewish communities appeared in Salonika, Izmir (Smyrna), Edirne (Adrianople), and other cities in Anatolia and the Balkan peninsula. Edirne had been the capital of the Ottoman Empire before the capture of Constantinople, and already had a Jewish community at that time. The Ottoman survey registers enable us to plot in some detail the numbers, distribution, and even the provenance of these communities. In cities where Jews were present in any numbers, the separate communities are listed by name, with the names of their adult male inhabitants. In Hebrew sources these communities are known as *kehillot*; in the Turkish registers they are designated by the term *jema'at*, commonly used of newly arrived groups.

After the conquest of the Fertile Crescent and Egypt, and

the extension of Ottoman suzerainty in North Africa, the Ottoman Empire also acquired a large population of Arabic-speaking Jews. These are usually designated in the Ottoman records as *musta'riba*, a word meaning Arabized and apparently used by Ottoman officials to distinguish between the Arabic-speaking Jews of Syria, Iraq, and Egypt and the Greek, Turkish, or Spanish-speaking Jews who were more familiar to them. There were in addition some very much smaller groups of Kurdish speakers and Aramaic speakers in remote areas. These are of considerable philological and historical interest, but are numerically insignificant.

The acquisition by the Ottomans of growing numbers of Jewish subjects was speeded by two methods, conquest and immigration. The first of these was shared with many other communities that became Ottoman subjects through the expansion of the Ottoman armies and the extension of Ottoman power. The second element was almost entirely limited to Jews, who thus had the distinction of being, so to speak, the only Ottoman subjects by their own free choice. For centuries Jews in great numbers continued to travel from various parts of Christian Europe into the Ottoman lands, attracted by the reports they had heard about the greater tolerance and greater opportunity offered by the Ottoman government.

These migrations were not, however, always entirely voluntary. Sometimes the registers list groups of Jews in one or another city who are designated as *sürgün*.[16] This Turkish word means exile or deportation, or simply compulsory transfer from one place to another. The *sürgün* was a method much used by the Ottoman state; it could be applied to an individual or a family, or to a group of individuals or families, to a nomadic tribe, to whole populations, sometimes even to whole districts. The use of *sürgün* was of two kinds. Sometimes, less commonly, it was penal; that is to say, a person or a group of persons was exiled or forcibly relocated for some offense they had committed. More frequently, *sürgün* was imposed for reasons of state policy, because it was believed that the interests of the empire would be served by transferring certain populations from one place to another.

This practice was by no means limited to Jews but was commonly applied to many elements in the empire, Muslim and Christian as well as Jewish. Sometimes the motive appears to be economic, as for example when the *sürgün* were agricultural colonists or pastoral nomads. Sometimes it was strategic, as when populations of questionable loyalty were transferred away from border districts and replaced by elements that were both martial and faithful. Jews were not infrequently included in such compulsory transfers to some new destination.

Such a movement is reported after the conquest of Constantinople in 1453, when large numbers of Jews were settled by imperial order, in what now became the Ottoman capital of Istanbul. They were brought from Ottoman provincial cities in both Anatolia and the Balkan peninsula where, as we can see from the Ottoman cadastral registers, many cities were almost denuded of their Jewish inhabitants.[17] A hundred or so families of prosperous Genoese Jews, living in Pera at the time of conquest, were apparently also moved at this time across the Golden Horn to the old city of Istanbul. The purpose, it would seem, was to introduce to the city an economically active but politically reliable population. In this way it was possible to encourage the development of the city without leaving a dangerously large role in economic affairs to possibly disaffected Christian merchants. A Turkish census report of 1477 shows that Istanbul at that time possessed a population of 1,647 Jewish households, forming 11 percent of the total.[18] These numbers increased considerably after the arrival of the Iberian and Italian Jews, as is indicated by later estimates. A Turkish register dated 1535 lists 8,070 Jewish households in the capital. By the last years of the fifteenth century the German pilgrim Arnold von Harff puts the Jews of Istanbul at 36,000; a Spanish traveler in the mid-sixteenth century estimates them at 10,000 households; while an English merchant who visited Istanbul in 1594 speaks of "Jues in and near about the citie, at least 150,000." This figure does not include women.[19] At the turn of the fifteenth-sixteenth centuries, the same policy was applied in Salonika, which had been conquered by the Ottomans in 1430. There had been a Jewish community in Salonika in the Middle Ages, but when the city passed under Venetian rule most of the Jews left.[20] If any remained, they were probably included in the transfers to Constantinople. The first extant Ottoman survey register of Salonika, compiled in 1478, shows large numbers of Greek Christians, small numbers of Catholic Christians, and some Muslims, but no Jews. Subsequent registers show a rapid increase in the Jewish population of the city. A register of 1519 lists twenty-four Jewish communities, most of them bearing the names of cities or countries in southern Europe, and together forming more than half the total population of 4,073 households. By 1613 the communities have increased to twenty-five, with a list of 5,163 names—2,933 households and 2,230 bachelors. By this time they formed 68 percent of the inhabitants of the city.[21] We know from other sources that the Ottoman authorities were anxious to settle Jewish populations in newly conquered Christian cities. The Jews were sometimes persuaded, sometimes compelled to go there.

[margin annotation: Salonika 68% Jewish in 1613]

The Turkish conquests of Rhodes in 1523 and of Cyprus in 1571 were both followed by imperial orders to settle Jews in the newly acquired provinces. The case of Cyprus is interesting in that it happens to be well documented. The Ottoman records for the period immediately following the conquest contain a number of deportation orders for the transfer of populations to Cyprus. They include Turkish peasants, to be sent to the island so that the countryside should not be exclusively Greek and Christian but partly Turkish and Muslim. There were orders to transfer Turcoman tribes—Turkish pastoral nomads—from Anatolia, so that stockraising and the supply of animals for food and transport should be safely in Muslim hands. And from about 1576 onward, we find orders to send Jews to Cyprus. Thus an order of that year addressed to the governor of the *sanjak* of Safed in Palestine instructs him to send "1000 rich and prosperous Jews . . . with their property and effects and with their families" to Cyprus. A little later, an order dated 1577 speaks of "500 Jewish families from the rich and wealthy among the Jews in Safed" to be transferred to Cyprus. Another document, addressed to the governor general of Cyprus, informs him that these Jews are arriving and instructs him to make arrangements for their settlement. An interesting phrase occurs at the beginning of the order: "In the interests of the said Island my noble command has been written . . . to conscribe and send 500 families from the Jews of Safed." The purpose was to serve "the interests of the said island," meaning of course the interests of the Ottoman state in the said island. The governor of Safed was warned that he was to send rich and not poor Jews: "In the course of conscribing and registering the prescribed number of Jews, if anyone receives protection or if any are removed from the register and instead of them others are taken so that in their place not rich but poor Jews are conscribed, your excuses will not be accepted. . . ." The governor was further warned that he would not merely be dismissed but would also be severely punished. All this gives an interesting insight into the purposes and modalities of the transfer.

The Jews of Safed were not in fact sent. They had influential friends in Istanbul who, by means that unfortunately if unsurprisingly are not recorded in the archives, were able to persuade the authorities to drop this proposal. However, the governor general of Cyprus, who appparently was very anxious to acquire some Jews, got partial satisfaction in an order of 1579, in which he was authorized to retain and resettle a consignment of Jews whom he had intercepted on their way from Salonika to Safed.[22]

Jews were needed for this policy of strategic settlement. If the established communities in the empire were unwilling to move, and the supplement provided by voluntary immigration was insufficient, more Jews could be obtained by right of conquest.

After the Turkish conquest of Belgrade in 1521 and of Buda in 1524, thousands of Jews and Christians were transferred from those places and resettled in Ottoman cities—in Edirne, Izmir, Salonika, and Istanbul. In the words of an Ottoman chronicler of the conquest of Buda: "Among the infidel rayahs and Jews who were given quarter, some thousands, of those who had requested it, were put on ships with their families and children and sent as *sürgün* to the realm of Islam. They settled some families in the Yedikule district [in Istanbul]; of the Jews, they sent some to Salonika and the rest to other places."²³

This story is also related independently by the European Jewish chronicler Joseph ha-Kohen, who confirms that the Jewish transferees were volunteers and that they were sent on ships, presumably down the Danube.²⁴ Communities of "Jews from Buda," or of "*sürgün* from Buda," duly appear in the Ottoman survey registers of Salonika, Edirne, Istanbul, and other cities. There are reports of similar transfers in the seventeenth century when the Ottomans raided parts of Poland. According to a contemporary observer, the little town of Kirk Kilise, between Istanbul and Edirne, was "almost entirely possessed by Jews, transplanted thither from Podolia by Sultan Mahomet, by whom the same corrupt German is still spoken as in Poland."²⁵ In the survey records of Istanbul and some other cities that enumerate the Jewish communities and list their members, there are usually separate lists of those who were compulsorily transferred and those who came of their own accord. The former were known as *sürgün*; the latter as *kendi gelen*, literally "coming oneself." The *sürgün* came mainly from regions occupied or even raided by the Ottoman forces; they included many localities in Anatolia, in Greece and the Balkans, and even in central Europe. The *kendi gelen* consisted of voluntary immigrants from European Christian countries, most of them from Spain, Portugal, and Italy, but some also from Germany and Hungary. Such patterns of settlement can be seen in several Ottoman cities, in both Europe and southwest Asia.

The history of Jewish communal organization in the Ottoman Empire presents some problems. In the nineteenth century, as part of the great Ottoman reforms, the famous *millet* system, developed in the main for the governance of the Greek and Armenian communities, was extended in similar form to the Jews. According to this system, as interpreted at that time, each of the religious communities of the empire was organized

millet

internally, subject to its own laws in matters of religion and personal status, administered under the authority of its own religious chief. The Jews were recognized as a *millet* under the authority of the *hahambashi*, the chief rabbi, established and recognized by Ottoman imperial decree, with roughly the same status, rights, and duties as the ecclesiastical heads of the Greek and Armenian churches. A kind of historical mythology developed to which both Turks and Jews contributed. According to this version, the *hahambashi* dated back to the time of Mehmed the Conqueror: when he conquered the city of Constantinople in 1453, he recognized its chief rabbi, Rabbi Moses Kapsali, and thus instituted the Ottoman office of *hahambashi*, with authority over all the Jews of the empire.

This story is almost certainly untrue. It was common Ottoman practice to project into the past any reform thought to be expedient to establish in the present, and we can be reasonably sure that in this as in many other cases it was without historical foundation. The evidence of the Turkish records, confirming the evidence of the rabbinical responsa, gives us a somewhat different picture. The Ottoman documents amply confirm that the Jewish communities of the empire lived in *kehillot*, each *kehilla* living in its own quarter, grouped around its own synagogue, and subject to its own *haham*, or rabbi. This was in accord with the general pattern of Ottoman urban organization. The effective unit of the Ottoman city was not the city as such, but the quarter or ward, called *mahalle*, consisting of a community, usually religiously defined and organized around its place of worship, mosque, church, or synagogue, under the leadership of its *imām* or priest or *haham*. The Jewish *kehillot* was normally named after their places of origin. Thus the *kehillot of the* city of Edirne are named Catalan, Portugal, Germany, Spain, Apulia, Toledo, Aragon, Sicily, Italy, Buda; those of Salonika include Spain, Sicily, Maghrib, Lisbon, Italy, Otranto, Catalan, Aragon, Apulia, Provençal, Castilian, Evora of Portugal, German, Calabria, Saragossa of Aragon, Corfu; those of Istanbul include most of these as well as many Balkan and Anatolian names. Hungarian (Majar) and German (Alaman) communities are listed

Kehillot

in Edirne, Istanbul, Safed, and elsewhere. Some of the *kehillot* have Hebrew names. The probability is that since these show no territorial provenance, they were indigenous—most likely the native Greek-speaking Jews.

There is frequent evidence of splits in these communities. For example, the Catalan communities both in Salonika and Edirne split at a certain point into two groups, henceforth known as "old Catalan" and "new Catalan." This is not an infrequent occurrence. We do not always know the reason for the split, but often it appears to be between those who came early and those who came later—a point that has always been of great significance in Jewish communal life.

Before long a major split seems to have developed between the European, predominantly Spanish, immigrants, and the native Greek-speaking Jews. The term commonly used by the Sephardic immigrants for the native Jews, when writing in Hebrew, was *toshavim*. In Hebrew usage, it will be recalled, *toshav* is often associated with *ger*. This word might fairly be translated as "natives," with perhaps the same nuance. In Spanish, they were referred to as Griegos, Greeks. It would seem that neither term is intended as a compliment. The Griegos for their part sometimes speak of their newly arrived coreligionists from Spain as *megorashim*, those who have been driven out. This again does not sound exactly like an expression of compassion.

There is no real evidence from the fifteenth or sixteenth century of any such office as a chief rabbinate of the Ottoman Empire, that is to say, of the existence of a chief rabbi with jurisdiction extending throughout the Ottoman lands. In this respect the pattern of organization of Jews in the Ottoman Empire seems to have been rather more like modern America than like modern Europe. We are told on fairly good evidence that after the Turkish conquest of Constantinople, the conqueror Sultan Mehmed II confirmed the existing Byzantine rabbi, Moshe Kapsali, in his office. But it is virtually certain that this office was as chief rabbi of the city, not as chief rabbi of the empire. In late Byzantine times these two were virtually the same, since the empire had been reduced to the city. But there was a great deal more of the Ottoman Empire, and nothing shows that Kapsali had any jurisdiction outside the newly conquered capital, nor over Jewish communities in the older Ottoman lands.²⁶

After Kapsali's death he was succeeded by another Romaniot Jew, Rabbi Eliyahu Mizrahi, whose jurisdiction was presumably similarly limited. In return for this privilege, the Jewish community was required to pay a special tax known as the *rav akçesi*, the rabbi's asper. After the death of Eliyahu Mizrahi in 1526, disagreements between the two major groups made it impossible for them to agree on a chief rabbi, even of Istanbul, until 1834, when one was imposed on them by the Ottoman sultan. A responsum of the Salonika rabbi, Samuel de Medina (1506-1589), briefly describes the situation:

> This second tax is called in the language of the Ishmaelites *rav akçesi*, because in return for it the Jews were permitted to have a chief rabbi by royal patent. It is not known whether the king imposed this on the Jews as one of his own royal statutes, or whether the Jews asked the king to let them have the said rabbi, and in return took it upon themselves to pay this second tax. And in any case the matter of the said rabbi only lasted, because of our many sins, for a very short time, while the matter of the second tax still drags upon us, "till the Lord look down and behold" (Lamentations III,50).²⁷

The *rav akçesi* was indeed imposed throughout Ottoman Asia Minor and Europe though not, apparently, in the Arab provinces. Its collection, with the amounts received, is recorded in the fiscal and survey registers. This was presumably related to the numerous provincial rabbis who exercised authority over the Ottoman Jews, each in his own city or community.

Evidence about religious and cultural life among the Ottoman Jews after the sixteenth century is meager, and it is difficult to resist the conclusion that the paucity of evidence reflects the poverty of life. At the beginning of the period, rabbinical learning was of great importance, and there is a large, rich, and valuable literature of responsa. There was also an active mystical movement, and a considerable cabalistic literature. But none of this lasted much beyond the sixteenth century, after which Jewish literature, whether in Hebrew or in the Judaeo-Spanish vernacular, is of limited appeal. As already noted, there is virtually no historiography within the empire. There is some Hebrew poetry, but later judgment has not found it worth recalling except for the Damascene poet Israel Najara (d. 1628), whose religious verses had a considerable influence on liturgical poetry—the only kind that flourished—in the Middle Eastern communities. Better known is the Judaeo-Spanish literature, partly oral and partly committed to writing. Even here the part of the Judaeo-Spanish literature of the Ottoman Empire that has received most attention is what the immigrants brought with them from Spain. There are, for example, medieval Spanish romances, some of them lost in Spain or preserved only in fragmentary form, which survive in fuller and better versions, through oral transmission, among the Ottoman Jews. Some original literature was added to the Spanish heritage, but it has so far not been adequately studied.

The cultural contribution of the Ottoman Jews to Turkish life—that is, to the cultural life of the Ottoman Empire—was somewhat circumscribed. It was in the main limited to three areas—medicine, the performing arts, and printing. The Jews brought with them an important body of medical knowledge from Europe. By the time of their arrival the positions of the Islamic and Christian worlds in the medical and other sciences had been reversed, and the science and practice of medicine were now on a far higher level in Europe than in the Middle East. This fact was recognized by highly placed patients who, whatever their religious convictions, preferred to be treated by the disciples of Paracelsus rather than by the followers of Avicenna. Avicenna in his time had represented the peak of medical achievement, but some centuries had passed since then, during which there had been major advances in medical knowledge and practice in Europe. Muslim physicians, at that time for the most part still following the old books and rules, were no longer the superiors, nor even the equals, of their European colleagues.

   The prominence of Jews in the medical profession in Turkey did not begin with the arrival of the Sephardim from Spain and Portugal, but is well attested during the fifteenth century. A Jew from Italy, Giacomo of Gaeta, served as personal physician to Sultan Mehmed II the Conqueror and rose to a position of eminence. At some stage in his career he became a Muslim and a vizier, and ended his days as Yakub Pasha.[28] He left two families, one Jewish, the other Muslim. By the sixteenth century there were so many Jewish physicians at the Ottoman court that the records of the palace establishment show two separate corps of physicians, one of Muslims, the other of Jews.[29] It may be assumed that the first treated their patients according to the rules of Galen and Avicenna, the latter according to the European practice of the time. Some of these Jewish practitioners, by virtue of their personal access to the sultans and to the viziers, were able at times to exercise influence on matters of high state policy. In the sixteenth century and, infrequently, later, Jews sometimes appear as informal advisers on matters of foreign policy, and were occasionally sent to European capitals as interpreters to Ottoman envoys or even, rarely, as envoys themselves.

   Besides treating patients, these refugee Jewish doctors from Europe also produced some medical literature, translating medical books into Turkish and even writing a few original works, including what must be one of the earliest treatises on dentistry.[30] But this did not last much beyond the sixteenth century, when the Jews of Turkey lost contact with the Europe from which they had come. The second and third generations of Sephardic Jews, born and educated in the Middle East, were no wiser and no more skilled than their neighbors. The Jewish physicians at the Ottoman court became fewer and rarer, and were in time replaced by Western-educated Ottoman Greeks. These were able to do what the Jews had never done—to stabilize and even institutionalize the influence their medical practice gave them over Ottoman foreign relations. The first and second holders of the new office of chief dragoman of the empire were both Italian-trained Ottoman Greek physicians. Thereafter that office remained entirely in Greek hands, until the outbreak of the Greek war of independence in 1821.

A second important Jewish contribution was in the performing arts. The Jews had brought with them the art of the theater, previously virtually unknown in the empire, and for some time theatrical performances in the major Turkish centers were mainly the work of Jews. They appear to have trained some successors, mostly gypsies. The Jews were in due course outclassed and outshone by Armenians, who became the leading performers until the emergence of the modern Turkish theater.[31]

A third Jewish contribution to Ottoman life that we may count as cultural was the introduction of printing. This too was something Jews had brought from Europe. Jews began printing in Istanbul, Salonika, and elsewhere before the end of the fifteenth century. But they were permitted to print by the Turkish authorities only on the strict understanding that they did not print in Arabic characters. To print in Turkish or Arabic would defile the holy script—and of course infringe the vested interests of the scribes and calligraphers. Jewish printers were authorized to print in either Hebrew or Latin characters, and thus offered no threat to either prejudice or interest. It was not until the eighteenth century that the first Turkish printing press was set up to print in Turkish. At that time recourse was had to the services of Jewish printers, since they, together with some Greeks and Armenians who had also begun to print in their own languages, were the only skilled printers available in Istanbul.[32]

The Jewish contribution appears far more important when we turn our attention from cultural to economic life. Here Jews achieved prominence in a number of fields. Their initial success is not difficult to understand. When they arrived in Turkey they had useful things to offer—knowledge of Europe, of its languages, and of the conditions prevailing there. In these qualifications and in the services they were able to render they had few rivals or competitors. It is therefore not surprising that Jews were employed in considerable numbers in tasks where these skills and this knowledge were of value.

From the late fifteenth century both Ottoman and European documents show Jews engaged in commerce, and playing an important, at times even a predominant, role in the textile trade, particularly in woolen cloths. In addition to serving as middlemen between European, local, and Eastern merchants, they also seem to have been the pioneers of an Ottoman textile industry. The records for Salonika and Safed, two important centers of textile manufacture, indicate that these were entirely Jewish in their origins and largely Jewish in their operations. A third textile manufacturing center, in Istanbul, also seems to have been at least partly Jewish.

In the fifteenth and sixteenth centuries Jews were strongly established as traders and manufacturers, and some of them attained great wealth. It was no doubt because of their financial resources that they were able, in this period, to play an important role in the farming of taxes. Even before the arrival of the mass immigration from Europe, there were Jewish tax collectors, tax inspectors, and tax intendants, as well as tax farmers. They were particularly active in the ports. A high proportion, perhaps even a majority, of the tax farmers and employees of the imperial Ottoman customs service were Jews, starting from the intendant of customs of a whole province to the lowly functionary who handled luggage. We find a similar pattern in Egypt and other more distant provinces, where Jews played a prominent role as intendants, more frequently as farmers, of the customs revenues. In later times, however, there was less scope for economic enterprise in general, and for Jewish enterprise in particular. In this period, the surest way to make money was neither through commerce nor through industry but through access to the financial activities of the state. The Jewish role in the Ottoman customs thus gave Jews a certain advantage, and enabled small but significant numbers to acquire wealth and the kind of power that wealth can give. But both wealth and power were always precarious, and from time to time we hear of the disastrous fall of one or another high Jewish dignitary. This usually meant the spoliation and death of the person concerned, and often also of his associates and dependents.

So important was the Jewish element in the customs service that many of the customs receipts, collected by Venetian merchants trading in the Levant and still preserved in boxes in the Venetian state archives, are in Hebrew writing. This will not surprise us if we will recall that a customs receipt was originally given so that it might be shown if necessary to another customs officer. It is only comparatively recently that such a receipt has acquired other functions and purposes.

Jews were also employed in the mints—on the technical side, concerned with striking coins, on the administrative side, and on the financial side. Sometimes individual Jews exercised authority on larger matters affecting the currency—its distribution, its control, and on occasion its recall.

At a relatively early date, Jewish merchants from Salonika established a special relationship with the corps of janissaries. The janissaries employed a functionary who had the title of *ocak bazırganı*, merchant of the corps, and acted as a kind of private enterprise quartermaster. His task was to arrange supplies for the corps of janissaries, and, like so many things in the Ottoman Empire, this office and function became hereditary. Specifically, it became the hereditary possession of a small group of Jewish families in Istanbul and Salonika, an arrangement that continued until the destruction of the janissaries in 1826. A large proportion of the uniforms worn by the janissaries were supplied by the Jewish textile manufacturers of Salonika. On the evidence of Ottoman account books, the amount of woolen cloth delivered to the government purchasing agent in Salonika rose from 96,000 ells (61,280 meters) at the beginning of the sixteenth century to 280,000 ells (178,733 meters) by the end of the century.[33]

This relationship between the Jews and the janissaries was not limited to Istanbul and Salonika. The pattern is repeated in a number of provincial cities where there were similar understandings between janissary quartermasters and Jewish merchants and financiers.

Of special importance in the Ottoman provinces were the

"men of business" of the pashas. A pasha appointed to the governorship of a province, on leaving Istanbul to take up his appointment, would normally have with him a "man of business" to handle his affairs, these being beneath the notice and often beyond the competence of any self-respecting pasha. Some of these "men of business" who accompanied the pashas to their provinces were Sephardic Jews. Nuclei of Spanish-speaking Jews from the capital emerged in places such as Damascus, Cairo, and Baghdad. They had come in the first instance in the suite of the Ottoman pashas who were sent to govern these cities, and joined the small groups of local Jews who were employed in government service.

Later, when the governorship of the provinces tended to become autonomous or even hereditary, Jewish merchants and financiers sometimes fulfilled similar functions as "men of business" for local rulers, pashas and others. The famous Farhi family of Damascus, for example, rose to prominence in the eighteenth century as financial advisers to the various autonomous rulers of Syria. Jews also served on occasion as middlemen or local representatives for European merchants. But this was restricted. The more usual pattern was that local Christians served the Europeans, while Jews served the Turks.

"art of war"

Another contribution the Jewish newcomers from Europe may have brought to their new masters was in the arts of war. Neither the Turkish nor the Jewish sources have much to say about this, and on the face of it one would not expect the Jews—a very unmilitary element in Renaissance Europe—to have much to offer. They seem, however, to have possessed some skills in weaponry and related technology, and contemporary European Christian travelers speak with bitterness of the gain to Turkey, and the consequent injury to Christendom, resulting from such a transfer of technology. Thus the well-known traveler Nicholas de Nicolay who visited Turkey in 1551, writes of the Marranos "not long since banished and driven from Spain and Portugal, who, to the great detriment and damage of Christendom, have taught the Turk several inventions, artifices and machines of war, such as how to make artillery, arquebuses, gunpowder, cannonballs and other weapons."[34]

A Spanish visitor, writing a few years later, says much the same thing: "Here at Constantinople are many Jews, descendants of those whom the Catholic King Don Ferdinand ordered to be driven forth of Spain, and would that it had pleased God that they be drowned in the sea in coming hither! For they taught our enemies the most of what they know of the villanies of war, such as the use of brass ordnance and of firelocks."[35] These and similar statements by other travelers, some of whom accuse the Jews of instructing the Turks in the mounting of field ordnance, probably exaggerate the Jewish contribution to an art in which the Turks were already highly proficient, and no doubt reflect the views of anxious as well as hostile observers. However, the Jewish role in the transfer of knowledge in weaponry, as in printing and medicine, may have been of some significance.

A question of obvious importance concerns the Turkish attitude toward the Jews. How did the Turks regard their Jews? How did they see the place of Jews in the life of the Ottoman Empire? Jewish reports on Turkish behavior and Turkish attitudes are almost uniformly favorable. Perhaps the earliest statement on this subject is the famous Edirne letter, probably written some time in the first half of the fifteenth century by a writer who describes himself as a French Jew born in Germany and settled in Edirne. In this letter he invites his coreligionists to leave the torments they are enduring in Christendom and to seek safety and prosperity in Turkey:

I have heard of the afflictions, more bitter than death, that have befallen our brethren in Germany—of the tyrannical laws, the compulsory baptisms and the banishments, which are of daily occurrence. I am told that when they flee from one place a yet harder fate befalls them in another . . . on all sides I learn of anguish of soul and torment of body; of daily exactions levied by merciless oppressors. The clergy and the monks, false priests that they are, rise up against the unhappy people of God . . . for this reason they have made a law that every Jew found upon a Christian ship bound for the East shall be flung into the sea. Alas! How evil are the people of God in Germany entreated; how sad is their strength departed! They are driven hither and thither, and they are pursued even unto death. . . . Brothers and teachers, friends and acquaintances! I, Isaac Zarfati, though I spring from a French stock, yet I was born in Germany, and sat there at the feet of my esteemed teachers. I proclaim to you that Turkey is a land wherein nothing is lacking, and where, if you will, all shall yet be well with you. The way to the Holy Land lies open to you through Turkey. Is it not better for you to live under Muslims than under Christians? Here every man may dwell at peace under his own vine and fig tree. Here you are allowed to wear the most precious garments. In Christendom, on the contrary, you dare not even venture to clothe your children in red or in blue, according to our taste, without exposing them to the insult of beaten black and blue, or kicked green and red, and therefore are ye condemned to go about meanly clad in sad colored raiment . . . and now, seeing all these things, O Israel, wherefore sleepest thou? Arise! And leave this accursed land forever![36]

More than a century later Samuel Usque, a Portuguese Jew who wrote a famous book called *The Consolation for the Tribulations of Israel*, expresses a similar view. Usque sets forth these consolations in two categories, the one human, the other divine. Among the human consolations the "most signal is great Turkey, a broad and spacious sea which God opened with the rod of His mercy as He opened the Red Sea at the time of the exodus . . . here the gates of liberty are always open for the observance of Judaism."[37] This must have come as a considerable surprise to a traveler from sixteenth-century Portugal.

Certainly, great numbers of Jews from Europe found a refuge from persecution in Turkey, and a few of them, in the fifteenth and still more in the sixteenth centuries, rose to greatness. Among such were the famous Doña Gracia Mendes and her nephew João Miques, better known as Don Joseph Nasi. Portuguese Marranos, they established an international banking and trading house that for a while, in the third quarter of the sixteenth century, played a role of some importance in the affairs of the empire. It was thanks to the influence of such figures that the sultans were on occasion willing to extend their protection not only to Jews in their own realms, but even to their Jewish subjects and protégés abroad. A noteworthy example was the Ancona incident of 1556. This seaport, which formed part of the states of the church, was an important center of the eastern trade, and had attracted a number of former Marranos who now openly reverted to Judaism. Pope Paul IV, who reorganized the Inquisition and gave it a new militancy, found this intolerable. The Jews were arrested, their property seized, and their lives declared forfeit unless they repented and returned to Christianity. Only the direct intervention of Sultan Süleyman secured a reprieve[38]—and then only for those who had come from Turkey and could thus claim Turkish protection. The remaining accused, who had never left Christendom and who refused to recant, were duly burned at the stake.

The Turkish attitude, though generally tolerant, was not quite as warm and welcoming as depicted in some of these more enthusiastic commendations. Turkish documents of the late sixteenth, seventeenth, and eighteenth centuries show that from time to time resentment grew among the Muslim populace and ulema at what was perceived as the excessive freedom or opportunity enjoyed by the non-Muslim communities, and occasionally the sultans found it necessary or expedient to renew or reassert the restrictions imposed by Holy Law on the *dhimmīs*, including the Jews. Thus we find orders reminding the *dhimmīs* that they are not permitted to ride horses or own slaves or sell wine, or instructing them to demolish places of worship that had been built without proper authority.[39] Even the latitude in dress, mentioned by the letter writer from Edirne as one of the attractions of Turkey, gave way to a stricter enforcement of Sharīʿa rules, especially in the provinces. But it was still half-hearted and intermittent, at least for a while and in the capital. An English traveler, in a letter from Istanbul dated 30 March 1600, remarks that "it is proclaimed about the city that neither Jewe nor Greeke shall wear garment or chackchiers [*çakşir*, a kind of trousers] of fine cloth; but this, I thinke, will not longe be observed." About a century later, a French visitor to the city found a somewhat different situation: ". . . the Subjects of the Grand Signior, Christians or Jews, have them [their slippers] either red, violet, or black. This Order is so well establish'd, and observ'd with such Exactnesss, that one may know what Religion any one is of by the Feet and the Head."[40]

Sometimes these waves of hostility to the *dhimmīs* were caused by political developments—attack or invasion by European powers, rebellion or subversion by the Christian subject populations. Sometimes they arose from trivial local incidents, as, for example, arguments over the occupation by non-Muslims of government-owned houses, with government approval, at the time of the resettlement of the city by Mehmed the Conqueror. However, these troubles seem to have affected Christians far more than Jews. Even when the Turkish attitude toward Jews was negative, it was on the whole contemptuous rather than hostile, and it does not seem to have caused any noticeable inconvenience to Jews until the seventeenth century and after.

One reason for Jewish well-being under Ottoman rule is that Jews were seen as a useful and productive element and were used as an instrument of imperial policy. Most textbooks of Jewish history contain an account of how, when the Jews of Spain were driven from their homes, the Turkish sultan graciously permitted them to take refuge in Turkey. "Graciously permitted" is perhaps not quite the right expression. The Jews were not just permitted to settle in the Ottoman lands; they were encouraged, assisted, and sometimes compelled. The methods used to direct Jewish settlers to particular places varied from forced deportations to tax remissions in selected places. As already noted, the *sürgün* system was frequently used to settle Jews in places where it was thought desirable, in the imperial interest, for them to be. The Ottomans did not merely admit Jewish refugees. They often provided transport for them and decided where they should go.

The Ottomans had quite definite and specific reasons for these actions. Broadly speaking, the Jews in the Ottoman Empire in the fifteenth and sixteenth centuries, and to some extent after that, were complementary to the Turks and not in competition with them. The Turkish ruling elites retained the professions of government, religion, and war as their preserve. They were also indirectly engaged in a number of economic enterprises, notably in sea transportation, agricultural reclamation, and trade by commenda. There were, however, other things, mainly economic, which they did not wish to do, or were not able to do, or perhaps, most importantly, regarded as beneath them to do. In later Ottoman times the Jews developed a sort of symbiotic relationship with the Turks, who needed the services they were able to provide and preferred them to their competitors. These competitors were mostly Christians—at first Greeks and Italians, later joined by Arabic-speaking Christians from the Levant, and finally, to an increasing extent, by Armenians.

From the Turkish point of view the Jews, particularly those coming from Europe, offered several advantages. Some of them brought much-needed capital, which helped to alleviate the chronic financial straits of the Ottoman government. They brought useful knowledge of Europe. Printing and medicine have already been mentioned as cultural contributions. To these we may perhaps add gunnery and navigation, important for the conduct of war on both land and sea. Because of their knowledge of European affairs and their relative freedom from European commitments, Jews for a while played a part of some importance in the foreign relations of the Ottoman Empire as advisers on dealings with European powers. They were an economically productive, revenue-producing element in the population. Furthermore, they had, from the Turkish viewpoint, the great advantage of not being Christian and therefore not being suspect of treasonable sympathies with the major enemy of the Ottomans, which of course meant European Christendom.

A French Capuchin traveler in Turkey, writing in 1681, gives us some idea of how the position of the Jews in Turkey struck a Christian European visitor:

> They [the Jews] are so skillful and hardworking that they make themselves necessary to everybody. There is no considerable family among the Turks and the foreign merchants which does not have a Jew in its service, whether to value merchandise and assess its quality, to serve as interpreter, or to give advice on everything that happens. They can say precisely and in detail all that is available in the city, who has what, its quality and quantity, whether it is for sale or barter, so much so that it is only from them that one can obtain enlightenment on trade. The other eastern nationalities like the Greeks, the Armenians, etc. do not have this talent and cannot equal their skills; this forces the merchants to make use of them, however great their aversion to them.[41]

BUT
DECLINE
↓

The decline in position of the Ottoman Jews may be measured by comparing this passage with another, from a nineteenth-century author, Ubicini:

> Little by little, however, the taste for study and letters was lost among the Jews of Turkey. When the Greeks, following their example, began to study the languages of Europe, the fear of being supplanted by them, instead of stimulating their ardor, struck them with a kind of apathy, and they saw themselves gradually dispossessed of their positions as interpreters and other lucrative functions which they had occupied at the Sublime Porte and in the chanceries. Later even the humbler jobs which they had retained, whether in the customs or finances of the Empire or in the households of the pashas, were taken from them by the Armenians. While the other communities, Christian and Muslim, familiarized themselves more and more with the languages and affairs of Europe, they continued to remain stationary, and, with apparent indifference, saw their riches pass into the hands of their rivals.

But there was some consolation. The same author goes on:

> However, if the Jews have degenerated intellectually, if by
> their own fault they have placed themselves in the lowest
> rank of the nations subject to the Porte, they compensate
> for this inferiority by economic and moral virtues which
> place them well above the Christians. No community is as
> well administered as theirs. One rarely hears that a Jew had
> apostasized. Their morals are strict, never any scandal among
> them. Not even any abuses, except perhaps those engen-
> dered by the absolute omnipotence of the rabbis ... the
> disorders and scandals so common among the Greeks and
> Armenians, simony, extortion, drunkenness, fraud, theft and
> murder are unknown among the Jews.

The compliments are not unmixed, however. He goes on
to speak of the effects of early marriage and a high birth rate
and complains very much of their dirty habits, which he says
are "worse among the Jews of Turkey than among those of
other countries, except perhaps Polish Jews."[42]

Ubicini's picture of the abject and degraded condition of
the Ottoman Jews, and the contempt, even contumely, with
which they were regarded, is amply confirmed by other European travelers of the early and mid-nineteenth century. In
a sense, the contrast between these reports and those of six-
teenth- and seventeenth-century European visitors to Turkey
reflects the change, not so much in Ottoman conditions as in
European expectations. To visitors from Renaissance Europe,
especially from the German lands and the Iberian peninsula,
the measure of freedom enjoyed by the Ottoman Jews and
the degree of affluence attained by them must have seemed
very great and indeed excessive. Visitors from nineteenth-century Europe, on the other hand—from almost anywhere outside the Russian Empire—had a different standard for the
treatment of religious and ethnic minorities, and were often
shocked to find that the Ottoman treatment of Jews and other
minority groups fell somewhat below the newly established
standards of the West. But even allowing for these changes
in perception on the part of European observers, there can be

no doubt that between the luster of the sixteenth century and
the degradation of the early nineteenth, the Jews of the Ottoman Empire had fallen on bad days.

To some extent this was a result of the weakening of the
Ottoman Empire, and indeed of the Islamic world as a whole,
both in relative military and political power, and in cultural
creativity. But the decline of the Jews of the Middle East
cannot be wholly explained in terms of the changes in Islamic
cultural patterns and the waning of Ottoman strength. Jewish
decline was more extensive and more rapid within the Islamic
world than that of the Muslims themselves, still more so than
that of the other non-Muslim minorities under Muslim rule.
One may well ask why.

The signs are clear enough—the growing segregation, the
dwindling tolerance, the diminished participation, the worsening poverty, both material and intellectual, of the Jewish
communities under Muslim rule. Seen in perspective, the Ottomans, in their days of greatness, halted and for a while
reversed a process that had begun before their advent. There
was a time when, thanks on the one hand to Ottoman policies
toward the Jews and on the other to the revitalizing effects
of immigration, new skills and new knowledge were injected
into the Ottoman Jewish community—skills and knowledge
that were also invaluable to the Ottoman state. But the interlude was comparatively brief, and after it the decline was
resumed as part of the decline of the Ottomans themselves,
but much faster.

It is to the specifically Jewish causes of this process that we
may address ourselves. Some of these causes can be readily
identified. One is certainly the drying up of immigration from
Europe. During the fifteenth and sixteenth centuries there had
been a massive influx of European Jews, which can be clearly
documented from the Ottoman archives and the effects of
which were manifest in every aspect of Jewish life, and some
aspects even of Ottoman life. The Jewish communities of the
Ottoman Empire in the fifteenth and sixteenth centuries owed
their eminence and prosperity to their contacts with Europe,
and to the advantages and usefulness with which these con-

tacts endowed them. When immigration from Europe ceased and contact with Europe was lost, the skills that had previously served the Jews and their Turkish masters faded, and Jews ceased to have anything special or useful to offer. Jews still spoke Spanish in the Turkish lands, but they wrote it in Hebrew letters and forgot the Latin script. Their language was no longer Spanish but Judaeo-Spanish, and it no longer served as a link with Christendom. By the early seventeenth century, a Jewish informant, writing to the English consul in Aleppo, addressed him in Judaeo-Spanish, that is, in Spanish in Hebrew letters, presumably in the expectation that the consul would have his own Jew to read it to him.[43] The fact that at this time a Jewish merchant was simply not capable of addressing the English consul in a Western language or even in a script he could read shows how great a change had occurred in the course of the previous century, and how wide a gap had been opened. This skill, the knowledge of a Western language and the resulting contact with Europe, was vital to the role played by the non-Muslim communities in the Ottoman Empire.

To make matters worse, as Ubicini indicates, the decline of the Jews was paralleled by the rise in the empire of other minorities who were acquiring the skills the Jews had lost. The Ottomans needed helpers with Western connections. At first they relied on people coming from Europe, some renegades and adventurers, and considerable numbers of Jewish and other refugees. When the flow from Europe ceased, they found substitutes among their own subjects. The movement of Jews from Europe to Turkey was replaced by a movement of Ottoman Christians from Turkey to Europe. Increasingly, the Greeks and later other Ottoman Christians sent their sons to Europe to be educated, and thus acquired the same kinds of skills and connections as the Jews had previously possessed and had now lost. Christians, in their competition with Jews for the service of the Ottomans, had many advantages: that of numbers—there were far more of them than there were of Jews; that of education, in that they sent their children to Christian schools and often to European universities, while the Jews did not; and that of patronage both from their churches, which the Jews lacked, and from Christian Europe, which naturally tended to favor Ottoman Christians at the expense of Jews.

After the death of the financier Joseph Nasi in 1579, no other Jew ever attained to such lofty, and dangerous, heights in the Ottoman state. For a while a few Jews could still play some part, most of them followers of two professions. There were Jewish physicians who advised their exalted patients on their policies as well as on their health; there was the succession of remarkable Jewish women, known by the Greek title *kira*, lady, who served as purveyors of goods and services to the imperial harem and were thus able, for a while, to wield considerable though indirect influence. By the turn of the seventeenth century both groups disappeared. The Jewish doctors were replaced by medically better qualified and politically more adept Greeks; the last of the kiras perished, with her sons, in a bloodbath at the hands of the mutinous soldiery.[44]

For a while Jews continued to play a role in commerce, and were, for example, able to share in the benefits of the transfer of trade from Venice, which had usually been restrictive toward them, to Livorno, which followed a more open commercial policy. Indeed, some Livornese Jews settled in the Ottoman lands, and thus to some extent restored the personal link with Europe that the Ottoman Jews had once enjoyed and subsequently lost.[45]

But the times were against them. The Jewish share of the international trade of the empire dwindled in the seventeenth century and virtually came to an end in the eighteenth. Fewer and worse-situated than their Christian fellow subjects, the Jews now had to endure the consequences of the rising power of Christendom. The Christians had many friends in Europe; the Jews had few. The Christians had ships; the Jews had none. And above all, the Christians could count on the support, the Jews on the ill will, of the European traders, and by this time it was the preferences of European Christians rather than of Muslim Turks that counted.

Two cases, both from Egypt, may serve as illustrations of

Fall of (17th + 18th cent.) Egypt, tax officials

LATE MEDIEVAL, EARLY MODERN PERIODS · 145

the changes that were taking place. In 1697 a Jew of Alexandria, named Yāsif al-Yahūdī in the Arabic chronicles and Leon Zaphir in European documents, was summoned to Istanbul where he submitted a plan of financial and fiscal measures to deal with the deteriorating situation in Egypt. Yāsif, who held an important position as customs director of Alexandria and intendant of the mint, proposed a new currency to replace the debased coins in circulation, and a package of taxes and customs dues. His proposals were accepted by the sultan's government; but they aroused so much opposition when he tried to apply them on his return to Egypt that the Ottoman governor, himself threatened with deposition by the mutinous garrison, was reluctantly obliged to surrender him to the mutineers. Yāsif was first imprisoned, then murdered in prison, and his body was dragged through the streets and publicly burned amid general rejoicing.[46]

Yāsif suffered his fate as a tax collector, not as a Jew, and the position of the community as a whole was not, it would seem, affected. The fall of another Jewish tax official seventy years later produced very different results. In 1768 Isḥāq al-Yahūdī, head of the customs of Bulaq, the river port of Cairo, was arrested, fined 40,000 gold pieces, and put to death. This case differs in three important respects from the earlier one. There was no immediate public censure; the arrest and execution were not in response to popular demand, but by order of the ruler; and, most important, the fall of Isḥāq inaugurated a decisive change for the worse in the position of the Jews in Egypt.[47]

In eighteenth-century Egypt, as in other similar societies, the service of the state was the surest avenue to economic self-betterment. Through their position in the customs, the mint, and the tax farms, Jews in the Ottoman lands retained a foothold in international trade, usually as intermediaries, sometimes as principals. Many earned a livelihood; a few became very rich, and were even able to act as bankers, lending money to foreign merchants as well as government offices and officials.

The fall of Isḥāq al-Yahūdī marked the end of all this in

Egypt. A few months after his death he was replaced—not as previously by another Jew, but by a Syrian Catholic, and before long members of this community supplanted the Jews throughout the Egyptian customs administration. The Syrian Catholics, not long previously installed in Egypt, were already challenging the Jews for control of these profitable offices. Allying themselves with the French, by now the most important European trading power in Egypt, they were able to secure effective protection and immunities. Some of the Jews were associated with the declining power of Venice; most were Ottoman subjects.

The loss of their foothold in government led to a rapid decline of the Jewish community. The French consul in Alexandria reported that the loss of the customs "had completely ruined the Jewish nation," and the post of third dragoman to the French consulate, hitherto assigned to a Jew in recognition of Jewish influence in the administration, was now and henceforth given to a Christian.

What happened in Egypt was paralleled in other provinces of the empire, where local Christians, with European support, replaced the Jews. The English Levant Company, for example, banned Jews both as members at home and as dragomans in the Levant;[48] other Western traders were little better disposed. The Jews had usually served as agents or intermediaries to the Ottoman officials; the Christians worked for the foreign merchants and envoys. The decline of the Jews and the rise of the Christians accurately reflect the changing distribution of power.

Perhaps the most important single cause of Jewish apathy was the career of Shabbatai Ṣevi (1626-1678) and its aftermath.[49] The false Messiah of Izmir had led an extraordinary Messianic movement among the Jews of the Ottoman Empire. He aroused immense hopes and ended his career in failure and humiliation. Given the choice by the Turkish authorities between martyrdom and conversion, the Messiah chose conversion, and ended his days as a minor functionary in the sultan's palace. Some of his more passionate followers saw even this as part of his mission, and voluntarily followed him into Islam. They preserved their own beliefs and rituals in secret, and still exist as a separate group to the present day. They are known as *dönme*, a Turkish word meaning convert.[50] But most of Shabbatai Ṣevi's followers turned away from him after his conversion.

The Shabbatai Ṣevi affair had a destructive impact on the Jewish communities of the Ottoman Empire. It left them a double legacy: on the one hand, discouragement verging on despair; on the other, an unprecedented reenforcement of rabbinical power. The Jews had no church, but in the rabbinate they had a kind of ecclesiastical authority, without the compensating advantages of structure and patronage.

In the meantime, the attitude of the Turks themselves was becoming more negative, and sometimes even hostile. In a time of weakness and retreat, the Muslim majority became suspicious and less tolerant. There were many signs of change for the worse, not only for Jews but for the minorities generally. There was growing fanaticism leading to a harshening of conditions for non-Muslims, a stricter enforcement of the restrictions imposed by Holy Law on the *dhimmīs*, and an increasing tendency to regional and social segregation. However, open persecution and violence remained infrequent. When there were attacks against Jews, they were almost always instigated by Christians, and were due to rivalries between the competing *dhimmī* communities rather than to any pressure of hostility from the Ottoman state or the Muslim majority. An example is the occasional appearance of the blood libel. While accusations were rare, they had been of sufficient importance for Sultan Mehmed the Conqueror to issue an imperial decree that such cases should not be tried by governors and judges but be brought before the Imperial Divan in Istanbul, where, presumably, the high officers of state would be less subject to bigotry and superstition and less open to local pressures. A revival of these accusations during the reign of Süleyman the Magnificent (1520-1566) brought a new *fermān*, repeating and confirming the earlier one and making the same requirement. Similar orders were issued by several later sultans in the sixteenth and seventeenth centuries.[51] It was not, however, until the nineteenth century that such accusations became common and constituted a serious problem for the Ottoman Jews. By this time, the European and Christian origin of these charges is beyond doubt.

OUTSIDE the provinces and dependencies of the Ottoman Empire, there were two major Islamic political centers in which Jews survived in any numbers. These were Morocco and Iran. In both of them the position of Jews was substantially worse than in the Ottoman lands. The Jewish community in Morocco was old, deep-rooted and numerous, and like the Jewish communities of the Ottoman Empire it had been reenforced and revitalized by the arrival of refugees from Spain and Portugal. But the Jews of Morocco, as compared with their co-religionists under the Ottomans, suffered from two major disadvantages. One of them was the shattering experience of Almohad persecution and repression, which had left them in a state of material degradation and intellectul impoverishment from which they never fully recovered. The other was their position as the only religious minority in an otherwise entirely Muslim land. In Egypt, Syria, Iraq, Turkey, even in Iran, there were other non-Muslim communities, mostly larger and more prominent than the Jews. These helped to create a more pluralistic and therefore more tolerant society; and even when things went badly, these others shared the brunt of Muslim resentment. Indeed, because of their greater numbers and prominence, they were often its primary victims. In Morocco, Christianity died out as a result of the Almohad persecutions, and the Jews remained as the only minority, disturbing an otherwise uniformly Muslim society. In this respect, their position was similar to that of the Jews of medieval Christendom, and different from that of Jewish communities in the eastern Islamic lands. These same circumstances exposed them to the same dangers and often the same misfortunes.

After the decline and fall of the Almohads, the Moroccan Jews began to restore their religious and communal life in the various cities of Morocco. Numerically, the Moroccan Jews were of considerable importance. They were certainly the largest Jewish community in North Africa, and probably the largest single Jewish community in the Islamic world. Moroccan rulers after the fall of the Almohads were not notably ill-disposed. The popular mood, however, remained hostile and often made life difficult for Jews. Under the Marinid dynasty, during the thirteenth, fourteenth, and early fifteenth centuries, we still find Jews at court and serving in various official capacities. As Norman Stillman has noted, the Jews had certain advantages from the point of view of the ruler.[52] As a marginal group in Moroccan society, they had no power base and no hope of independent political action. As an unpopular religious minority, they could count on no sympathy or support from the general population. They could thus serve the ruler in the same way as the various groups of slaves, eunuchs, and other marginal and deracinated groups had served Muslim sovereigns in both east and west. Their vulnerability and unpopularity were demonstrated by the need, felt by both the rulers and the Jews themselves, to place them in Jewish quarters, known as *mellāḥ*. This was originally done not as a punishment or humiliation, but for their own protection against the hostile populace. That did not, of course, make it any more welcome nor any easier to endure. The *mellāḥ* of Fez was founded in 1438 on the model of the earlier *juderias* of Spain, situated near the royal residence and offering royal protection. The *mellāḥs* established in other towns by later rulers were more definitely intended to isolate and penalize rather than to defend or protect their inhabitants. The protection was not always effective. A major pogrom took place in 1465, when the inhabitants of the *mellāḥ* in Fez were almost wiped out in the course of a rebellion that eventually deposed the Marinid dynasty.[53]

In the late fifteenth and sixteenth centuries the Jewish communities of Morocco began to recover from these upheavals, and were strengthened by the arrival of refugees from Spain and Portugal. Like the Sephardic immigrants in Turkey, these were soon able to establish a cultural, economic, and communal hegemony over the native Jews, whom they seem to have regarded as their inferiors. Just as the Sephardim in Turkey referred to the native Greek-speaking Jews as *toshavim* (natives) or Griegos (Greeks), so the Sephardim in Morocco spoke of the native Moorish Jews as *forasteros* (strangers) or Berberiscos (Berbers, North Africans). The Sephardim in Morocco were also able to render to their Moorish masters the same kind of service as their compatriots in the east. We find them employed as commercial and diplomatic intermediaries, helping the sultans in their dealings with various European countries. Some of them entered the service of the Moroccan sovereigns as skilled craftsmen and technicians, possessing both civilian and military skills. Within the Jewish community the Sephardim, in Morocco as in Turkey, established a paramountcy that survived until modern times.

The general treatment of Jews was in many ways worse than in the Ottoman east. The institution of the *mellāḥ*, the enclosed Jewish quarter, has already been noted. It has no parallel in the Ottoman lands. Jews were subject to severe restrictions when moving outside the *mellāḥ*; for example, they were not permitted to wear normal shoes but had to indicate their identity by going barefoot or wearing distinguishing footgear.[54] In Fez they were required to wear sandals made of straw. In general, the discriminatory restrictions laid down in the *dhimma* were far more strictly applied in Morocco than elsewhere. Indeed, the Moroccans devoted considerable thought to this topic, as is indicated by the body of juridical literature dealing with it, and introduced a number of humiliating restrictions unknown in the east. The long struggle against the Portuguese and the Spaniards gave a special intensity to religious sentiment among the Muslims and worsened the condition of the only sizable resident non-Muslim community. During the centuries that followed, Jewish life in Morocco was on the whole unpleasant. European visitors, mostly Christian, are almost unanimous in presenting a picture of what Stillman has aptly called "the highly ritualized degradation of the Jews in the major towns and cities."[55]

The Jews of Iran were not the only non-Muslim community in that country. There were also Armenian Christians, and a small remnant of followers of the ancient Zoroastrian faith.

The Jews were the most visible, however, and the only minority community that was represented all over Iran. The attitude of the Muslim majority toward them was in general hostile. If the severe Mālikī doctrines of the Moroccans led them to adopt a harsher attitude toward their Jewish subjects than did the Turks and Arabs of the Middle East, the Persians adhered to an even stricter standard, that of the renascent and militant Twelver Shīʿa. For these, the Jews were not merely infidels, to be despised and humiliated as such; they were ritually unclean—people whose very touch brought pollution. Even before the accession of the Safavids and the establishment of Shiʿism as the state religion at the beginning of the sixteenth century, the Jews of Iran had been going through hard times. The Mongol Khans had made use of them during their period of domination; but when the Mongols themselves were converted to Islam and began to adopt the attitudes and mores of their Muslim subjects, they shared their hostility against the former servants of their pagan forebears. As so often happened, the ending or transformation of alien domination was followed by a wave of hatred and vengeance against those who had served it. After the greatness some individual Jews had attained under the Mongols, who incidentally had abolished the *dhimma* altogether, the reaction was all the more severe. A number of Jews were executed and their community endured hard times.[56]

We have little information about the fate of the Jews in Iran in the period immediately preceding the rise of the Safavids.[57] Their accession, and the creation of a powerful, unified, and prosperous realm in Iran, brought some incidental benefit to the Jews, as to other inhabitants of the country. Their position, however, was often difficult and always precarious. Unlike the sultans of Turkey and even of Morocco, the shāhs of Iran of the Safavid and the succeeding dynasties were usually unwilling to allow any place to Jews at their courts or in any positions of power or influence. On the contrary, they were at times reluctant to allow them even to survive. Cases of forced conversion to Islam are very rare in Islamic history. Apart from one or two in Morocco and in the Yemen, most of them occurred in Iran. The enlightened shāh ʿAbbās I (1588-1629) was for a while an exception, and allowed Jews, Armenians, and other Christians to settle in his capital, Isfahan. But even he changed his attitude toward the end of his reign. The discriminatory rules were strictly enforced, and in 1656 all Jews were summarily expelled from Isfahan on the grounds of their ritual impurity, and they were compelled to embrace Islam.

Later, possibly because of the loss of fiscal revenues, this order of forced conversion was withdrawn. According to a seventeenth-century Persian Jew who wrote a rhymed chronicle of these events, the Muslims of Yazd, in response to the gold-backed pleas of their Jewish fellow citizens, sent a delegation of notables to Isfahan to intercede with the shāh. Pointing out that the departure of the Jews would greatly inconvenience the Muslims, they argued that forced conversion was worthless: "You may wash a negro 200 times; you will still look in vain for any sign of whiteness."[58] The French traveler Jean de Thevenot reports a similar argument for allowing the Jews to revert to their faith: "They found that what external professions so ever they made of Mahometanism, they still practised Judaism; so that there was a necessity of suffering them to be again bad Jews, since they could not make good Musulmans of them."[59] In 1661 a new edict permitted Jews to revert openly to Judaism on condition that they paid the arrears of poll tax and wore the Jewish patch on their outer garments.[60] Similar measures were taken against Christians and Zoroastrians, who had also been expelled from the city. In 1658 the pope appealed to the shāh on behalf of the Christians; no one appealed for the Jews.

The rule of Nādir Shāh (1736-1747), a Sunni Muslim, brought an interval of greater tolerance and even permitted the formation of a new Jewish community in the Shiʿite holy city of Meshed, perhaps as an act of policy. This interval was not of long duration, and under the Qajar dynasty, which governed Iran from 1794 to 1925, the position of Jews deteriorated sharply. European travelers agree in describing the fear and degradation in which the Jews of Iran still lived.

In Iran as in Morocco, Jews found some compensation for outer misery through an inward spiritual life of their own. In both countries there was a significant literary output, in North Africa in Judaeo-Arabic, in Iran in Judaeo-Persian. The latter indeed forms one of the more original and interesting aspects of Jewish literary creativity during these centuries. Of particular interest are the rhymed narratives in Persian heroic style of Biblical and, sometimes, of current events.[61]

The position of Jews in Central Asia was in general rather better than in Iran, and in the 1840s, when the Jews of Meshed were subjected to forced conversion, some of them found refuge in the cities of Marv and Shahrisabz. The Bukharan Jews were, however, not exempt from such problems. In the mid-eighteenth century the rulers of Bukhara made the first of several attempts to Islamize them by force. As elsewhere, this and subsequent forced conversions produced groups of Marranos, who were rescued from this predicament only by the Russian conquest.[62]

As has been noted, by this time, some of our major sources of information are European travelers, visitors, and even residents—missionaries, merchants, tourists, and, increasingly, the resident communities of traders, bankers, entrepreneurs, and others. This is part of the general growth of European interest and activity, which soon inaugurated a new era in the history of the Middle East, and therefore of all the communities that lived in it.

FOUR

The End of the Tradition

IN NOVEMBER 1806 James Green, Esq., His Britannic Majesty's consul general "in all the dominions of the Emperor of Morocco," undertook an unusual demarche. At the request of a number of Jews in Gibraltar, subjects of His Britannic Majesty, he had asked the sultan "to annul certain order, said to be by his Imperial Majesty made, prohibiting all persons professing the Hebrew religion in general from appearing in any of his dominions wearing the European dress." Mr. Green reported that he had obtained an audience from the sultan, who "was pleased to declare that he annulled that order." The Gibraltarian Jews, anxious for a Moroccan as well as a British record of this annulment, sought an assurance from Mr. Green "to state whether such declaration of His Imperial Majesty is already published in his dominions, and whether we are now permitted to appear there with our usual dress, it being of much importance to us, who find ourselves occasionally under the necessity of going there on matters of Trade."[1]

The episode is significant in a number of respects. The Rock of Gibraltar had been in British possession since 1704, and despite a treaty commitment demanded of Britain by Spain not to permit "Jews or Moors" to establish themselves on the rock, the British authorities had winked at the establishment and development of a sizable Jewish community. Indeed, by the end of the eighteenth century Jews formed a major if not preponderant element of the civil population.[2] The great majority of these Jews had come from the neighboring kingdom of Morocco, where most of them still had family and business connections on which they depended for their livelihood. British Jews did not achieve full civil emancipation until the nineteenth century, but already in the eighteenth century Jews who were natural-born British subjects enjoyed substantial civil and human rights, among them the protection of His Majesty's representatives when traveling abroad.

The Moroccan authorities took a somewhat different view. In accordance with a practice followed by some Muslim states, they regarded treaties with Christian governments as applying only to the Christian subjects of those governments. Jews, irrespective of their political allegiance, were just Jews, and when Jews from foreign lands entered the Muslim domains they were regarded not as *musta'min*, enjoying the privileges attached to that status, but as *dhimmīs*, subject to the restrictions that term conveyed. In their own eyes and in those of the British authorities, the Jews of Gibraltar were British subjects, and it was normal for them to wear the same clothes as the rest of their compatriots. In the eyes of the sultan and his officers, they were Jews, and it was improper for them to wear anything but the distinguishing garb assigned to that status. At some point, presumably because of the intrusion of foreign Jews wearing European clothes to save themselves from the vexations to which they would otherwise have been exposed, the sultan apparently found it necessary to promulgate specific rules to this effect.

The Jews of Gibraltar were the first example in modern times of a Jewish community originating in a Muslim country and living under a European government of the Age of the Enlightenment—and this, moreover, at a distance of only a few miles from their country of origin. The resulting contrasts could not fail to have an unsettling effect.

The case is interesting in another respect. It is, it would seem, the first in which Jewish citizens of a European state call upon the representatives of their sovereign to intervene on their behalf with a Muslim power. In this, as in so much else, there was a reversal of roles since the days when an Ottoman sultan had written to the pope in Rome, the doge of Venice, and the king of France to protect the interests of his Jewish subjects.

In the course of the nineteenth century, with the emancipation of the Jews in all the civilized countries of Europe, and the acceptance of Jews as citizens with most of the rights of citizenship, such action by European governments on behalf of their own Jewish subjects became normal. A new situation arose when Jews in these Western countries, increasingly aware of the distressed condition of their coreligionists in the Middle East and North Africa, began to intercede and intervene on their behalf, using Jewish and where possible also political and diplomatic channels.

The involvement of the Western powers in the affairs of the Jews of the Islamic lands was by no means always to their advantage; sometimes, indeed, the reverse was true. While Jewish pressures and liberal principles sometimes combined to produce government action in favor of the Jews, there were other forces, hostile to both Jewish emancipation and nineteenth-century enlightenment, which worked in the opposite direction. These forces could also rely on a powerful combination of ancient prejudice and modern interest.

The new tripartite relationship of the West, Islam, and the Jews found its first dramatic expression in the famous Damascus affair of 1840. On February 5 of that year Father Tomaso, a Capuchin monk of Sardinian nationality, suddenly disappeared together with his servant. A Jewish barber was accused of murdering them and, after torture, declared himself ready to confess. The Father's fellow monks, instigated and encouraged by the French consul Ratti-Menton, proclaimed that he had been killed by the Jews for ritual purposes. On the urging of the consul, the governor Sharif Pasha arrested large numbers of notables and other Jews, many of whom were tortured. One communal leader, Joseph Laniado, died under questioning; another, Moses Abulafia, saved himself by embracing Islam. He and several others were induced by torture to confess whatever their accusers desired. The French consul, to justify and further his actions in Damascus, supported it with an active press campaign in France directed against the Jews in Damascus and Jews in general. Damascus was at that time under the rule of Muḥammad ʿAlī Pasha, the Ottoman governor of Egypt, who had succeeded in turning that country, with the addition of Syria, into a semi-inde-

pendent principality under purely nominal Ottoman suzerainty. In this policy he was supported by France and opposed
by Britain and other European powers.

These considerations of power politics may help to explain
why, while the representations of French Jewish leaders to the
government of France elicited unsatisfactory replies, similar
appeals in Britain produced a very different response. On June
22 Lord Palmerston, the British foreign secretary, informed
Parliament that he had warned Muḥammad ʿAlī Pasha of the
effect his "barbaric treatment" of the Jews of Damascus was
likely to have in Europe. On July 3 a mass meeting was held
at the Mansion House, the official residence of the lord mayor
of London, at which members of Parliament and dignitaries
of the church denounced the revival of this medieval libel and
the torture and murder of the innocent in its name. Other
Western governments, including that of the United States,
spoke and acted in support of the British position. A meeting
of prominent Jews in London, attended by the French Jewish
statesman Adolphe Crémieux, decided to send a delegation
to the Middle East, consisting of Crémieux himself, his com-
patriot, the orientalist Salomon Munk, and the Anglo-Jewish
knight, Sir Moses Montefiore.

Despite all the obstacles put in their way by the French
representatives in Cairo and Damascus, the delegation, with
considerable diplomatic support, achieved its purpose. On
September 6, in response to a joint note from nine European
consuls, Muḥammad ʿAlī Pasha sent orders to Damascus for
the release of the surviving Jewish prisoners. Shortly afterward
Muḥammad ʿAlī was forced to relinquish Damasacus and the
rest of Syria-Palestine, which were restored to full Ottoman
sovereignty. On their way home, the members of the Jewish
delegation were received by the Ottoman sultan who, at their
request, issued a *fermān* denouncing the accusation of ritual
murder as a baseless libel, and reaffirming the intention of the
Ottoman authorities to give full protection to Jewish life and
property.[3]

Several aspects of this affair call for comment. One of them
is the blood libel itself. The charge of using human blood for

ritual purposes first appears to have been leveled by pagans against the early Christians. It was then used by the Christians themselves against the Jews, and has been a familiar theme of Christian anti-Semitism from the earliest times to the present day. In classical Islamic times, this particular form of anti-Jewish calumny would seem to have been unknown. Its first appearance, under Islamic auspices, was during the reign of the Ottoman sultan Mehmed the Conqueror, and it almost certainly originated among the large Greek-Christian population under Ottoman rule. Such accusations had been common in the Byzantine Empire. They occurred at infrequent intervals under the Ottomans, and were usually condemned by the Ottoman authorities.[4]

The blood libel recurs in epidemic proportions in the nineteenth century, when such accusations, sometimes followed by outbreaks of violence, appear all over the empire. The Damascus affair of 1840 may have been the first. It was very far from being the last. For the rest of the nineteenth century and well into the twentieth, the blood libel becomes almost commonplace in the Ottoman lands, as for example in Aleppo (1810, 1850, 1875), Antioch (1826), Damascus (1840, 1848, 1890), Tripoli (1834), Beirut (1862, 1874), Dayr al-Qamar (1847), Jerusalem (1847), Cairo (1844, 1890, 1901-1902), Mansura (1877), Alexandria (1870, 1882, 1901-1902), Port Said (1903, 1908), Damanhur (1871, 1873, 1877, 1892), Istanbul (1870, 1874), Büyükdere (1864), Kuzguncuk (1866), Eyub (1868), Edirne (1872), Izmir (1872, 1874), and more frequently in the Greek and Balkan provinces.[5] In Iran and Morocco, in contrast, despite the general hostility toward Jews, this particular accusation for long remained virtually unknown, presumably because the Christian presence was smaller and the European influence later.[6]

Four features are worth noting. First, the libel almost invariably originated among the Christian population and was often promoted by the Christian, especially the Greek press; second, these accusations were sometimes supported and occasionally even instigated by foreign diplomatic representatives, especially Greek and French; third, Jews were usually able to count on the goodwill of the Ottoman authorities and on their help, where they were capable of providing it. Finally, and to an increasing extent, Jewish communities endangered by such accusations could often call on the sympathy and even the active support of the British representatives, and sometimes also of the Prussian and Austrian representatives.[7]

Although these accusations seem to have started in the Christian communities, they did not remain confined to them. By the early twentieth century they figured as part of an anti-Jewish campaign in some Egyptian Muslim newspapers, and have since then become a common theme in Muslim anti-Jewish literature, in the Middle East and elsewhere. The reports of the British representatives in Egypt, both before and after the occupation, express occasional concern at the dangerous consequences of such calumnies. They also express anger at the unhelpful and sometimes positively hostile attitude of the representatives of some other European powers.

British concern for the Jews of the Middle East and North Africa was not prompted solely by liberal and humanitarian principles, though the importance of these, in Victorian England, should not be cynically underrated. There were in addition, however, some further considerations. France and Russia, Britain's two main imperial rivals, had established virtual protectorates, the one over the Roman Catholics, the other the Orthodox Christians of the Ottoman Empire. Though the Orthodox were far more numerous, the Catholics were not negligible, and in Syria and Egypt in particular, Arabic-speaking Catholics and Uniates played an important cultural as well as commercial role. The special relationship established by the two powers with their coreligionists gave them—by abusive extension of treaty privileges—a virtual right of intervention with the Ottoman authorities whenever they so chose. It also gave them extremely useful points of contact and support in an important, active, and influential element of the Ottoman population.

Britain and later also Prussia-Germany were, in contrast, at a disadvantage. The Protestant subjects of the empire were few and insignificant and their protection was neither required

160 ▪ CHAPTER 4

by the protégé nor useful to the protector. At one point the British government seems to have flirted with the idea of extending its protection to the Druze, but nothing much came of this. In 1840, in response to an appeal from the Judaeophile Lord Shaftesbury, Palmerston listened with interest to Shaftesbury's ideas on a repatriation of the Jews to establish a national home in Palestine, and even lent a hand in that direction. Palmerston then proposed that, through the British vice consulate established in Jerusalem in 1838, Britain should become the protectress of Jewish interests, at least in Palestine. In curious anticipation of events in the following century, Palmerston linked the idea of Jewish repatriation with British protection. The Jews of Palestine, he suggested, should

> be allowed to transmit to the Porte, through British authorities, any complaints which they might have to prefer against the Turkish authorities. . . . It would be highly advantageous to the Sultan that the Jews who are scattered through other countries in Europe and Africa, should be induced to go and settle in Palestine; because the wealth and habits of order and industry which they would bring with them, would tend greatly to increase the resources of the Turkish Empire, and to promote the progress of civilization therein.

The function of British protection would be to avert

> the violence, injustice, and oppression to which the Jews have hitherto been exposed . . . and especially in Syria; . . . unless the Sultan would give the Jews some real and tangible security, he cannot expect the benefit which their immigration into Palestine would afford him.

These ideas were approved by the British government and by Queen Victoria, but foundered on the implacable resistance of the Turkish government, which—not surprisingly—saw no good reason to accept yet another foreign protector of yet another group of its own subjects. The British interest in the Ottoman Jews continued, however. The vice consulate in Jerusalem concerned itself very extensively with Jewish affairs, and the British government looked with favor on the activities of Sir Moses Montefiore. In 1843, for example, Colonel Hugh Henry Rose, the British consul general in Syria, reporting on Montefiore's visit to Palestine, noted that "they consider him as a sort of prince. This fact alone gives to Great Britain influence also with the Jews, not a circumstance to be lost sight of."[8] It is surely significant that when Montefiore was elevated from a knighthood to a baronetcy, the prime minister's letter spoke of the desire to aid his "truly benevolent efforts to improve the social condition of Jews in other countries"[9] as one of the reasons for this honor. The Jews in Palestine were apparently of sufficient importance for even the Russian government to offer them a protection it did not give to its Jewish subjects at home.

By the mid-century, Jews in Western Europe felt sufficiently secure in their own countries to be able to intervene more actively on behalf of their oppressed brethren, of whose predicament, thanks to modern communications and the growth of the newspaper press, they were becoming increasingly aware. A new phase began in 1860 with the establishment in Paris of the *Alliance Israélite Universelle*. Its founders were a group of French Jews, liberal in both religion and politics, who believed that, having gained a large measure of civic and to some extent even political equality with Christians in France, it was their duty to help their less fortunate coreligionists elsewhere. The aims of the society are stated in the first article of its statutes:

1. To work everywhere for the emancipation and the moral progress of the Jews.
2. To provide effective aid for those who suffer because of being Jews.
3. To encourage the publication of works contributing to these ends.[10]

The *Alliance*, as its name indicates, was intended to be an international Jewish organization. In fact, it rapidly became a specifically French organization, enjoying the benevolent attention of the French government, and itself sometimes acting in support of French interests. Shortly after its foundation, a proposal from the *Alliance* to the French government for the extension of French official protection to all Jews in Muslim countries, and especially in North Africa, was not accepted. Unlike Lord Palmerston in England, French statesmen were already adequately provided with protégés and had no need to seek further expansion in this field. But the activities of the *Alliance* in the Middle East and North Africa in creating primary and vocational schools for the Jewish communities, in which the language of instruction was French, were quickly recognized in official circles as an important extension of what they saw as the cultural mission of France. The competing cultural and material interests of other powers may have contributed to the formation of similar organizations elsewhere— the Anglo-Jewish Association in Britain in 1871, the *Israeli-tische Allianz* in Vienna in 1873, the *Hilfsverein der Deutschen Juden* in Berlin in 1901, and the American Jewish Committee in 1906. While these organizations usually cooperated fairly harmoniously in matters of purely Jewish interest, they were also acutely conscious of the conflicting interests of the countries of which they were citizens.

In retrospect, the activities of these organizations on behalf of their downtrodden brethren may seem a little quixotic. In the twentieth century, the once proud communities of Germany and Austria found themselves in far direr need than any of those whom they tried to help. Some of them sought and found refuge in Turkey. Even in France, the position of Jews, whether in public opinion or in official policy, was never very secure. In Damascus in 1840, one of the worst outbreaks of anti-Jewish hostility in the nineteenth century was instigated by the French consul, who enjoyed the full support of his government. Half a century later, amid the passion and polemics of the Dreyfus affair, the Jews of France achieved a momentary insight into the dangers that threatened them. Half a century after that the Vichy government made the threat a reality when it denied them even the second-class citizenship of the *dhimmī*, and, in another historic reversal, the sultan of Morocco protected his Jewish subjects against the malevolence of the Vichy authorities and their Nazi masters and mentors.[11] Only in Britain and, increasingly, in the United States did major Jewish communities survive which were able to maintain their own status and to intervene, directly and through the governments of their countries, on behalf of their brethren elsewhere.

Despite the vicissitudes of French Jewry and the somewhat equivocal attitudes of French governments, by far the most important effort in Muslim lands was made by the *Alliance*. There were more than sixty *Alliance* schools in the Ottoman Middle East, as well as others in Iran and in North Africa, in which poor Jewish children were provided with formal elementary education and vocational training. The *Alliance* representatives did not confine themselves to the purely educational function. They were also more generally concerned with the well-being of the communities among which they worked. Many of the teachers were natives of these regions, who were educated at the *Alliance* teachers training schools in Turkey and at the *Alliance* seminary in France and then sent back to teach, usually in some country other than their own. The network of *Alliance* teachers, inspectors, and advisers reported extensively on the condition of Jews in these countries and their relations with their neighbors and with the authorities.

These records, certainly the best and fullest source materials on the history of Ottoman, Iranian, and North African Jews in the late nineteenth and early twentieth centuries, present a depressing picture. Some correction to this picture must be made because of the nature of the documentation. This was a Jewish organization, concerned only with Jews. When its representatives report a persecution or ill treatment of Jews, as they do very frequently, it is not always clear whether this was indeed a persecution of Jews as such. Often it is a general outbreak against non-Muslims, directed at Christians as well as, or perhaps more than, Jews. Often it is no more than an expression of what had become the chronic disorder and chaos in many of these countries in which all—Muslim, Christian, and Jew alike—suffered. But even allowing for all these, and for the natural bias of a philanthropic institution looking for beneficiaries, what emerges is an unmistakable picture of grinding poverty, ignorance, and insecurity.

Western travelers, almost unanimously, confirm the impression that the period from the end of the eighteenth into the second half of the nineteenth century was the lowest point in the existence of the Jews in the Muslim lands. At first most of these travelers were Christians, since few European Jews were willing or able to undertake journeys in Muslim countries. In time, however, a few daring spirits ventured into these lands and added their testimony to that of their Christian predecessors.

At a time when Jews in Western Europe were beginning to enjoy the fruits of emancipation, several of the Christian travelers marked the contrast between the Jews they met in Muslim lands and those whom they knew at home. Thus Charles MacFarlane, who spent some time in Istanbul in 1828, notes that the Jews are "the last and most degraded of the Turkish Rayahs . . . loaded with the concurrent and utter contempt of Frank, Turk, and Armenian." Like many Western travelers, he reports the current stereotype of the eastern Jew as dirty and cowardly, and goes on to say:

> Throughout the Ottoman dominions, their pusillanimity is so excessive, that they will flee before the uplifted hand of a child. Yet in England the Jews become bold and expert pugilists, and are as ready to resent an insult as any other of His Majesty's liege subjects. A striking proof of the effects of oppression in one country, and of liberty, and of the protection of equal laws, in the other.[12]

The "uplifted hand of a child" could represent a mortal threat, as was noted in the same year by another English traveler, this time in Morocco, who, attributing a mean and degraded quality to the Moroccan Jews, ascribes it to

> the debasement to which they are subject even from the children of a true believer. I have seen a little fellow of six years old, with a troop of fat toddlings of only three and

four, teaching their young ideas [sic] to throw stones at a Jew, and one little urchin would, with the greatest coolness, waddle up to the man and literally spit upon his "Jewish gabardine." To all this the Jew is obliged to submit; it would be more than his life was worth to offer to strike a Mahomedan.[13]

Even in Istanbul the situation was hardly better. Julia Pardoe, in a description of "the city of the Sultan" in 1836, makes the point very vividly:

I never saw the curse denounced against the children of Israel more fully brought to bear than in the East; where it may be truly said that "their hand is against every man, and every man's hand against them."—Where they are considered rather as a link between animals and human beings, than as men possessed of the same attributes, warmed by the same sun, chilled by the same breeze, subject to the same feelings, and impulses, and joys, and sorrows, as their fellow-mortals.

There is a subdued and spiritless expression about the Eastern Jew, of which the comparatively tolerant European can picture to himself no possible idea until he has looked upon it. . . . It is impossible to express the contemptuous hatred in which the Osmanlis hold the Jewish people; and the veriest Turkish urchin who may encounter one of the fallen nation on his path, has his meed of insult to add to the degradation of the outcast and wandering race of Israel. Nor dare the oppressed party revenge himself even upon this puny enemy, whom his very name suffices to raise up against him.

I remember, on the occasion of the great festival at Kahaitchana (Kâthane), seeing a Turkish boy of perhaps ten years of age, approach a group of Jewesses, and deliberately fixing upon one whose delicate state of health should have been her protection from insult, gave her so violent a blow as to deprive her of consciousness, and level her to the earth. As I sprang forward to the assistance of this unfortunate, I was held back by a Turk of my acquaintance, a man of rank, and I had hitherto believed, divested of such painful prejudices; who bade me not agitate, or trouble myself on the occasion, as the woman was *only a Jewess!* And of the numbers of Turkish females who stood looking on, not one raised a hand to assist the wretched victim of gratuitous barbarity.[14]

Such practices survived into modern times, as may be gathered from a report written by the British vice consul in Mosul in January 1909, that is, after the Young Turk Revolution of 1908:

> The attitude of the Moslems towards the Christians and Jews, to whom as stated above, they are in a majority of ten to one, is that of a master towards slaves whom he treats with a certain lordly tolerance so long as they keep their place. Any sign of pretension to equality is promptly repressed. It is often noticed in the street that almost any Christian submissively makes way even for a Moslem child. Only a few days ago the writer saw two respectable-looking, middle-aged Jews walking in a garden. A small Moslem boy, who could not have been more than eight years old, passed by and, as he did so, picked up a large stone and threw it at them—and then another—with the utmost nonchalance, just as a small boy elsewhere might aim at a dog or bird. The Jews stopped and avoided the aim, which was a good one, but made no further protest.[15]

COMPARED to the Jews of Iran, the Jews of the Ottoman Empire were living in paradise. The verdict of the travelers is summed up by the Hungarian Jewish orientalist Arminius Vambery, who traveled extensively in Iran and Central Asia: "I do not know any more miserable, helpless, and pitiful individual on God's earth than the *Jahudi* in those countries. . . . The poor Jew is despised, belaboured and tortured alike by Muslim, Christian and Brahmin, he is the poorest of the poor, and is stripped by Armenians, Greeks and Brahmins."[16]

Perhaps the most informative of Western writers on nineteenth-century Iran was George, later Lord Curzon, whose great work *Persia and the Persian Question* appeared in 1892. Among numerous references to the Jews in that country, he has this to say on their situation in general:

> Throughout the Mussulman countries of the East these unhappy people have been subjected to the persecution which custom has taught themselves, as well as the world, to regard as their normal lot. Usually compelled to live apart in a Ghetto, or separate quarter of the towns, they have from time immemorial suffered from disabilities of occupation, dress, and habits, which have marked them out as social pariahs from their fellow creatures. The majority of Jews in Persia are engaged in trade, in jewellery, in wine and opium manufacture, as musicians, dancers, scavengers, pedlars, and in other professions to which is attached no great respect. They rarely attain to a leading mercantile position. In Isfahan, where there are said to be 3,700, and where they occupy a relatively better status than elsewhere in Persia, they are not permitted to wear the *kolah* or Persian head-dress, to have shops in the bazaar, to build the walls of their houses as high as a Moslem neighbour's, or to ride in the streets. In Teheran and Kashan they are also to be found in large numbers and enjoying a fair position. In Shiraz they are very badly off. At Bushire they are prosperous and free from persecution. As soon, however, as any outburst of bigotry takes place in Persia or elsewhere, the Jews are apt to be the first victims. Every man's hand is then against them; and woe betide the luckless Hebrew who is the first to encounter a Persian street mob. . . . During the absence of the Shah in Europe in 1889, a fanatical disturbance took place in Shiraz and Isfahan, largely instigated by the clerical firebrand, Sheikh Agha Nejefi, whom I have mentioned, in the course of which a Jew was killed in the streets, and his murderer was at first suffered to go scot-free, and finally only sentenced to the bastinado. The Sheikh, by way of improving or embittering the situation, took upon himself to promulgate a series of archaic disabling laws against the Jews of Isfahan, in which odious

restrictions were imposed upon their food, dress, habits, life, fortune, inheritance, and trade. The Zil-es-Sultan was afraid to move for fear of endangering his position. It was largely in consequence of this outbreak that an influential deputation from the Anglo-Jewish Association waited upon the Shah while in London, and presented to him a memorial on the subject of their co-religionists in Persia. The Shah gave assurances of protection, which were much needed, and which, it is to be hoped, will be carried out.[17]

Such descriptions—and many others could be added to them—no doubt helped to arouse the concern of Western Jews for their Eastern brethren. Some of these authors indeed explicitly urged them to action. Thus John MacGregor, who toured Syria, Palestine, and Egypt in 1869, remarked: "Jews amongst us Gentiles in England have refinement, cleanliness, luxury and elegance—why don't they send to the rabbis of Galilee, at any rate, besoms and soap?"[18]

The troubles of the Jews in Islamic lands in this period were not limited to poverty and degradation. For the first time in centuries they found themselves exposed to active hostility, not only in Iran, where such things were not uncommon in earlier times, but also in the Ottoman lands and Morocco. From the late eighteenth century through the nineteenth century, expulsion, outbreaks of mob violence, and even massacres became increasingly frequent. Between 1770 and 1786 Jews were expelled from Jedda, most of them fleeing to the Yemen. In 1790 Jews were massacred in Tetuán, in Morocco; in 1828, in Baghdad. In 1834 a cycle of violence and pillage began in Safed. In 1839 a massacre of Jews took place in Meshed in Iran followed by the forced conversion of the survivors, and a massacre of Jews occurred in Barfurush in 1867.[19] In 1840 the Jews of Damascus were subject to the first of a long series of blood libels in many cities. Other outbreaks followed in Morocco, Algeria, Tunisia, Libya, and the Arab countries of the Middle East.

With the increasing centralization of government through the nineteenth-century reforms, Ottoman rule became in many ways more effective. There was, for example, a notable improvement in the condition of the Jews in Tripolitania and Cyrenaica (the two provinces that later became Libya) after 1835, when direct Ottoman administration replaced the previous autonomous local regimes.[20] From the reforms until the end of the empire, through various changes of political order, the Ottoman authorities in general did their best to protect their Jewish subjects from the hostility of local populations and of rival minorities. Where they failed—as they sometimes did—it was through weakness or indolence rather than through active ill will.

The reforms and accompanying changes brought some alleviation to the deteriorating Jewish condition in the Middle East, which had become very marked by the early nineteenth century.

This deterioration may be attributed to a number of causes. Some have already been noticed: the internal decline of the Jewish communities; the falling standard of education before the arrival of the *Alliance* and the resulting loss of useful and marketable skills; the ousting of Jews from their traditional vocations by better-equipped, better-educated, and above all better-protected Christian competitors. To these may be added the general decline in Islamic power, and its effect on Muslim attitudes to the subject communities. By the early nineteenth century, Muslims were becoming aware of the advance of Europe and their own relative weakness. The Russians had conquered and annexed the Muslim lands around the Black Sea and in Transcaucasia and before long were able to advance into the old Muslim cities of Central Asia. In 1798 the French conquered Egypt with ease and held it for over three years; they had left it because of British, not Muslim, power. In 1830 the French invaded Algeria; in 1839 the British took Aden. These were only the first steps in the establishment of a British, French, and Russian stranglehold on the heartlands of Islam.

Nor was that all. The Russians in Transcaucasia, the French in Egypt, found among the local Christians willing and helpful coadjutors in establishing control over Muslim populations. Muslim resentment at these changes, seen as a violation of the old established principles of the *dhimma*, is clearly expressed in the literature of the time.[21] That resentment increased with the advance of Russian, French, British, and later also German penetration in the Middle East and North Africa, and the growing numbers of former *dhimmīs* who in one capacity or another served the European great powers. Loss of power led to loss of confidence, and this in turn to a loss of tolerance. What remained of Muslim tolerance was subjected to severe strains as the *dhimmīs* tried to combine the totally incompatible objectives of equal citizenship, foreign protection, and national independence. Sufferance gave way to mistrust, and the easy contempt of early times was replaced by an often well founded fear, sometimes mixed with envy.

In all this the Jew was not, in Muslim eyes, the principal offender. It was rather the native Christian who was seen as aiding and abetting the enemies of Islam. But from the mid-century onward, the Jew also began to enjoy his secondhand share of the fruits of empire when, thanks to new educational opportunities, Jews as well as local Christians were able to offer their services, in various capacities, to foreign governments and businesses. But if the Jew was not the principal malefactor, he was certainly the easiest victim. The Christians were numerous and well protected; the Jews were few, and enjoyed at best a slender and intermittent protection from outside powers. At a time of general, often undirected fear and resentment, it was natural that hostility should turn against the Jewish as well as the Christian *dhimmīs*, and that attacks should be directed to that quarter where there was the least chance of either immediate defense or subsequent retribution.

To make matters worse, it was not only the Muslims who turned against the Jews; it was also—and indeed more particularly—their Christian *dhimmī* compatriots, who, glorying in their new power and the protection of their mighty patrons, turned against their hapless Jewish neighbors, their ancient bigotry reenforced by modern ideologies. From the 1860s onward there was an ominous growth of European-style anti-Semitism among the Christian communities of the empire. This was strongest among the Greeks, but also affected other

Christians, including the Arabic-speaking Christians of the Levant and Egypt. One reason for this was certainly their increased openness to influences from Europe, including the precept and practice of European anti-Semitism; another was the educational and economic revival that was beginning among Ottoman Jews in the second half of the nineteenth century, and which confronted Christian merchants, shopkeepers, and artisans with competition from a quarter they had been accustomed to discount. Significantly, the appearance of anti-Semitic slogans and accusations was almost always accompanied by attacks on Jewish shops and workshops and calls for boycotts. The Muslim populations were the last to be affected by these incitements, and the Ottoman authorities usually gave what protection they could to their Jewish subjects. Almost to the end of the empire, numbers of Jews suffering or fearing persecution fled from Russia, Rumania, and other Balkan countries and found refuge in the Ottoman lands.

In Istanbul and other Turkish cities, there seems to have been a realization among Muslims that in this period the Jews were not the enemies but the fellow victims of the Turks. Turkish public opinion was not in general anti-Jewish, and Turkish official action was sometimes taken to protect the Jews from their local persecutors. In the Arab provinces of the Ottoman Empire, among a politically less sophisticated population, anti-Jewish outbreaks became more frequent. In the North African countries, where there was no native Christian population, the Jews were more useful to the imperial powers, and consequently more hateful to their Muslim neighbors.

In confronting these dangers, the Jews suffered from two major weaknesses; their unprotected status, which made them easy victims, and their low level of education, which left them without useful skills and therefore despised by Muslim and Christian, Easterner and Westerner alike.

It was to these two problems that the *Alliance Israélite Universelle* and its sister organizations principally addressed themselves. In both respects they achieved considerable successes. Their major public effort was devoted to improving the legal status of the Jews in these countries by securing better laws and their more effective application, and they proceeded by intercession or even intervention.

One important method was by publicity. In earlier times even large-scale persecutions could pass virtually unnoticed. In the age of the telegraph and the newspaper press, with a network of *Alliance* and other representatives all over the Middle East and North Africa, cases of ill-treatment or persecution were immediately known and made public. Such reports could cause grave embarrassment to Muslim rulers, especially at a time when most of them were bankrupt and in urgent need to raise loans on the European money markets. This gave an added force to the intercessions and interventions by Jewish individuals or organizations or by European governments, which from 1840 onward became increasingly frequent.

The opening of resident embassies from Muslim countries in European capitals opened a new line of access. The visits of Middle Eastern monarchs offered another kind of opportunity, and Nāṣir al-Dīn, shāh of Iran, in particular, was the subject of a number of Jewish complaints and requests during his three visits to Europe.[22] There is no evidence, however, that these had much effect on the position of the Jews in Iran, which remained miserable until the end of the Qajar dynasty in 1925.

The most effective form of intervention was, of course, through the official channels of a European great power. With the establishment of direct European control—the French in North Africa, the British in southern and eastern Arabia and then in Egypt—the powers themselves became responsible for their Jewish as for their other new subjects. There can be no doubt that the Jews—like the Christians, though not as much— benefited greatly from this change. Even the oppressive and anti-Semitic policies of the czars in Russian-dominated Central Asia represented an improvement on the rule of the amirs that had preceded it. In British-ruled Aden, Egypt, and Iraq, in French-ruled Algeria, Tunisia, and Morocco, in Italian-ruled Libya, imperial rule ushered in a new era of Jewish educational progress and material prosperity.[23] It also ensured the ultimate doom of these communities.

In the heartlands of the Middle East, however, two Muslim states, Iran and the Ottoman Empire, remained independent. Though their independence was often threatened and to some extent undermined by the European imperial powers, it was never completely lost, and both countries survived well into the twentieth century as working polities. Both of them were the home of ancient and important Jewish communities.

Ottomans

Historians of nineteenth-century Ottoman Jewry have focused attention on a few major events, some of them turning points in the history of the empire as a whole, others of purely Jewish significance. The first of these was the destruction, in 1826, of the Corps of Janissaries, for centuries the main component of the Ottoman infantry, and the ultimate military source of political power. In destroying this ancient and privileged institution, the reforming Sultan Mahmud II (1808-1839) was seeking to remove the main prop of opposition to his modernizing and Westernizing reforms, and to clear the way for a new-style army, trained, organized, and equipped along European lines, and wholly devoted to the person of the sultan and to the enforcement of whatever policies he might choose to promulgate.

One might assume that the removal of a military corporation that was the mainstay of reactionary and religious opposition to modernization would be of benefit to the Jews, as potential beneficiaries of liberal change. In fact, the reverse was the case, at least in the short run. In the course of time certain wealthy and prominent Jews had established a very close relationship with the Corps of Janissaries, and while this relationship was sometimes interrupted by conflicts and even murders, it remained effective. The quartermasters, purveyers, and merchants of the janissaries had to a large extent been Jewish, and the destruction of the corps was a major blow to the Jewish interest in Istanbul and elsewhere in the empire.[24]

It was also an important step forward for the Armenians, who had recently acquired a new importance and were beginning to oust the Jews from those functions they still re-

tained in the service of the empire. The advance and enrich-
ment of Ottoman Christians in the seventeenth and eighteenth
centuries had been accomplished mainly by Greeks and by
Syrian Catholics. The Armenians did, however, make some
progress, and from the last years of the eighteenth century
onward Armenian merchants, shipowners, entrepreneurs, and
bankers assumed an increasingly important role in the Ottoman economic structure. In doing so, they inevitably en-
croached on the few remaining Jewish footholds in the Ottoman economy. The Corps of Janissaries, and the small, close-
knit group of Jewish merchant families associated with them,
were the last redoubt of Jewish economic power. The destruction of the janissaries was followed by the ruin of their Jewish
associates, leaving the way open for the ultimately pyrrhic
Armenian victory.

Sultan Mahmud II was greatly concerned to centralize, or-
ganize, and rationalize the government of his empire. These
purposes also involved some change in the structure of the
Jewish communities that were subject to him. The two major
Christian communities, the Greeks and the Armenians, were
each organized in a hierarchical ecclesiastical structure, headed
by a supreme chief who exercised authority over all his faithful
throughout the Ottoman lands, and at the same time was
recognized by and answerable to the sultan. In contrast, the
Jews had no such central organization. Each city—and in cities
of any size, each community—had its own rabbi and wardens.
For some seventy years after the Turkish conquest of Constantinople in 1453, the sultans had recognized a chief rabbi
of the capital, not of the empire; after 1526 event his office
ceased to exist.[25] For the rest of the sixteenth, seventeenth,
and eighteenth centuries, there was no one who could speak
for the Jews of the empire as a whole, except self-appointed
dignitaries and men of affairs. Such anarchy was not acceptable to the tidy-minded sultan, and also began to seem dangerous to a Jewish community that felt itself isolated, weakened, and endangered. An imperial *fermān* of 1835 therefore
created the office of *hahambashi*, chief rabbi of the empire.
According to the rules established, the chief rabbi was to be

chosen by the Jews themselves, and appointed and ratified by the sultan.[26]

This new office, and the institutions that administered it, became the focus of a conflict that was affecting the Jews of other communities in nineteenth-century Turkey—what in another context has been called "the quarrel of the ancients and the moderns." One of the major themes of nineteenth-century Turkey was the struggle between those who desired modernization, which at that time and in that place meant those who wanted to Westernize their way of life, and those who saw such change as a mortal threat to their religious and other values and fought desperately to preserve the old order. Attention has naturally concentrated on the struggle between reformers and conservatives among the Turkish and Muslim majority. But there were parallel struggles among the non-Muslim communities of the empire. In most of these conflicts the reformers were, for a while at least, successful. They accomplished major reforms among the Greeks, somewhat later among the Armenians, and finally also among the Christian Arabs.

Among the Jews they failed. European, Turkish, and even Jewish movements of ideas passed the Turkish Jews by. There were few if any among them who had received the kind of European education that Greeks, Armenians, and Arabs in increasing numbers had been getting in Christian schools. The ideas of the French Revolution, and the whole intellectual ferment that followed in the early decades of the nineteenth century and caused such a tremendous stir among the Greeks and Armenians, seem to have had no impact among the Ottoman Jews, who continued undisturbed in their old ways. Nor were they influenced by the stirring of new ideas among the Muslim Turks. Though presumably most of the Jews in Turkey could speak some Turkish, they did so in a manner and with an accent that made them a favorite butt of popular humor. Only a tiny minority could read and write Turkish; however, with the nineteenth-century reforms, these became more numerous, and some found employment in government service, mostly as interpreters. They played no role in Turkish intellectual life, and were hardly touched by the movements and arguments that were agitating the Turks.

They were equally impervious to the movements that were transforming the outlook of European Jews—hasidism, the enlightenment, the Hebrew revival, religious reform, Zionism. All these, so important to the history of the Jews in Europe, for long left the Jews of the Ottoman Empire unaffected, even unaware.

Where there were some minimal signs of change, they were due mainly to external pressures or interventions. There were some Italian Jews who moved during the eighteenth and still more during the nineteenth centuries from various cities in Italy, especially Livorno, and settled in the Levant and North Africa. These Livornesi, or, as they were called in Hebrew, Gornim, became an important element in Jewish communal life in a number of cities, notably in Tunis.[27] They retained some contact with their countries of origin and helped to initiate the resumption of relations between the Jews of the Ottoman Empire and those of Europe. A role of some importance was played by a small community of Sephardic Jews from Turkey who, for commercial reasons, had settled in Vienna in the eighteenth century. These had retained their Ottoman nationality, which incidentally gave them a somewhat better status than that of the native Austrian Jews, and had also preserved close links with Istanbul.[28]

It was a well-meaning attempt by an Ottoman Jewish philanthropist from Vienna to secure some reform in Jewish communal life that brought the inner tensions of the community to a crisis point. The quarrel came into the open in 1862, perhaps the only occasion in the nineteenth century when the internal affairs of the Jewish community received some attention—even then minimal—in Turkish newspapers and historiography.[29] The crisis began with an attempt at reform, bitterly resisted by the ultra-conservative rabbinate controlling the institutions established by Ottoman law. The Jews began to riot and fight among themselves, to the point when the Ottoman authorities felt bound to intervene. At first this intervention resulted in a victory for the old guard and the imprisonment of some of the reformers. The authorities, however, seemed to have reconsidered the matter, and in 1865 the Jewish community was provided with a new communal constitution. This was not devised or proposed by the Jews themselves, but given to them by the Ottoman government. It was based on the constitution that had been enacted some years earlier for the Armenian community and which had been hammered out by the Armenians themselves after long and bitter arguments.

This new constitution differed from earlier arrangements in that it provided for a role to be played in communal affairs by the laity. Under the terms of this dispensation, the domination of the rabbinate, hitherto total and unchallenged, was to be limited, and in certain specified circumstances the rabbinate was required to consult with a council of laymen.

Even though it was backed with the force of an Ottoman imperial decree, the new arrangement did not work well. The rabbis did not like it, the faithful supported them—and the Ottoman government had more pressing matters requiring its attention. Before long, the constitution became a dead letter, and while the community retained its autonomy, the rabbinate was again in full control. It was not until the last years of the nineteenth century, when the activities of the *Alliance Israélite Universelle* produced a rising generation of French-educated Turkish Jews, that a new spirit began to work among the communities of the empire, and the first windows to the West were opened.

This process was paralleled and encouraged by the development of a new attitude among many Turks and Arabs, especially the Westernized and semi-Westernized urban elements most influenced by liberal and patriotic ideas. Among many of these there was a genuine desire to accord a measure of equality to non-Muslim compatriots, and to draw them into a common political allegiance and a shared social and cultural life. Both in Turkish and in Arab cities there was a mood of liberalism and optimism, and a widespread belief that the different communities of the empire, under a new political dispensation, could live in harmony and work for a common cause.

By the early years of the twentieth century, individual Jews were even beginning to play a role in politics—a new and radical departure from past precedent, and a striking indication of the changes that were taking place in the political attitudes and perceptions of both the majority and the minorities in the empire. The Jewish political role was incomparably smaller than that of other minorities. What was remarkable was that they played any role at all.

Even this small role was considered too much by some observers, outside as well as inside the empire. Popular mythology assigns an important role to the Jews in the conspiratorial committees that, working in secret under Sultan Abdulhamid II, eventually produced the Young Turk revolution of 1908. The charge that this revolution was due to Jewish machinations appeared almost immediately. In the Arab provinces in particular, the overthrow of the sultan's Islamic order was received with horror and alarm, and in several cities there were violent outbreaks against what were seen as the godless usurpers of the sultan's power.[30] One of the charges brought against the Young Turks was that they were transferring power to non-Muslims and, worst of all, to Jews. Some European journalists and diplomats, notably the British ambassador Sir Gerard Lowther and his chief dragoman Gerald H. Fitzmaurice, both addicts of conspiracy theories, took up the theme, and stories of a familiar type about Jewish masonic schemes and designs began to circulate. They were found useful during the First World War, when Allied propaganda sought ways to discredit the Young Turk regime in the Arab and more generally in the Islamic world.[31]

In fact the Jewish role in the Young Turk movement was small before the revolution, and virtually nonexistent after it. The leaders of the Young Turk movement that achieved the revolution of 1908 were overwhelmingly Muslim, mostly Turkish and Balkan, some Arab. They included comparatively minor groups of non-Muslims—Greeks, Armenians, Jews, and Christian Arabs. A few features combined to give an exaggerated and distorted impression of the role of these minorities in the movement. One was that they were more articulate in Western languages and more visible abroad than their Muslim colleagues. Another was that many of them were citizens or protégés of foreign powers and that their houses were therefore immune from search by the Ottoman police. This made them convenient meeting places for the conspirators; it did not imply that the owners of these houses had any great influence. Much the same may be said of the masonic lodges, in which Jews played a certain role, and which provided a useful cover for the Young Turks. Finally, the fact that the main center of Young Turk activity outside the capital was in Salonika, a major Jewish center, gave the impression of a large Jewish role. This impression was strengthened by the activities of one or two marginal Jewish figures, notably a certain Albert Carasso (also Karasu), a Salonikan Jew who was prominent in Young Turk councils before and during the revolution. A much more important figure was the economist Javid Pasha, who took part in the 1908 revolution and served several times as finance minister in Young Turk governments. He was not a Jew but a *dönme*.

Carasso was the only Jew, and his career did not last long. In the first Ottoman parliament of 1908 elected after the revolution, the members included 147 Turks, 60 Arabs, 27 Albanians, 26 Greeks, 14 Armenians, 10 Slavs (including Bulgarians, Serbs, Macedonians, etc.), and 4 Jews. These proportions remained more or less the same throughout the remaining years of the empire.[32]

The economic situation of Ottoman Jews remained, in general, bad. The occupations most frequently listed in *Alliance* school records for the parents of children are hawkers, ragmen, tinkers, bootblacks, match vendors, and water carriers. These are not high-income professions. To take a single example: the Jewish community of Silivri, a small town not far from Istanbul, was tabulated in detail by the *Alliance* representatives in the year 1907. Of 400 Jewish families in Silivri, they recorded the professions of 282, as follows: 130 hawkers, 50 bootblacks, 40 water carriers, 20 grocers, 12 tinkers, 4 butchers, 3 goldsmiths, 2 cobblers, 2 money-changers, 1 leather seller, 1 glazier, 7 clothiers, 3 barbers, 3 tavern keepers, 2 government employees, 1 mason, 1 box-maker, and a very large number of people who are described as doing "what they can," presumably odd jobs and occasional work. In addition, most of the Jewish girls in Silivri worked at making lace for various entrepreneurs in Istanbul. Only 12 of the 400 families are described by the *Alliance* representative as "notables . . . veritablement à l'abri du besoin"—really safe from need. It is a picture that can be paralleled in many other communities.[33]

They *Alliance* schools were bringing important changes. The taught their pupils trades, and they taught them French. Both of these were of the greatest importance in initiating an upward movement among the Jews of the Ottoman Empire that continued into the twentieth century, more especially after the revolution of 1908. Their position, however, remained comparatively weak. In this as in other respects, they did not rise with the Christians, but rather fell with the Turks on whose power their fortunes ultimately depended.

The final phase in the decline of Ottoman Jewry began with the occupation of the city of Salonika by the Greek army at the end of 1912, as a result of the Balkan war. Salonika, often called by Jews "a city and a mother in Israel," had indeed been a major Jewish religious and cultural center and certainly the most advanced Jewish community in the Ottoman Empire, giving leadership to Sephardic communities everywhere else. This city now passed from Turkish to Greek rule. The Jews of Salonika, familiar with the long record of commercial rivalry and anti-Semitic agitation of their Greek neighbors, viewed this change with considerable misgiving. Their fears about their possible fate under a Greek government proved to be misplaced. They were nevertheless doomed in that they had lost their raison d'être. The Jews of Salonika had enjoyed a symbiosis with the Turks, such as they could never hope to have with the Greeks. As part of the Ottoman Empire, Salonika had a natural economic hinterland in the Ottoman Balkans, which it no longer possessed as a northeastern outpost of the Greek kingdom. In 1914 the Ottoman Empire blundered into the First World War, and its Jews, like all its other subjects, were involved in its final collapse. The decay of the Jewish community of Salonika, cut off both from its economic and its Jewish hinterland, continued without interruption until its extermination by the Nazis.

The Jews of Iran in the same period suffered the same disadvantages and more, and enjoyed none of the same advantages as their brethren in the Ottoman lands. Isolated among a hostile and fanatical population, rarely protected by the public authorities, they had the further disadvantage of living in a remote country where few visitors, Christian or Jewish, would observe and report on their plight.

IRAN

However, there were some, and their descriptions, which generally agree, are confirmed by the reports of the *Alliance* representatives when schools were established in Iran from 1865 onward. The Jewish traveler J. J. Benjamin, who traveled in Iran at mid-century, summarized the misfortunes of the Persian Jews under fifteen headings:

1. Throughout Persia the Jews are obliged to live in a part of the town separated from the other inhabitants; for they are considered as unclean creatures, who bring contamination with their intercourse and presence.

2. They have no right to carry on trade in stuff goods.

3. Even in the streets of their own quarter of the town they are not allowed to keep any open shop. They may only sell there spices and drugs, or carry on the trade of a jeweller, in which they have attained great perfection.

4. Under the pretext of their being unclean, they are treated with the greatest severity, and should they enter a street, inhabited by Mussulmans, they are pelted by the boys and mobs with stones and dirt.

5. For the same reason they are forbidden to go out when it rains; for it is said the rain would wash dirt off them, which would sully the feet of the Mussulmans.

6. If a Jew is recognised as such in the streets, he is subjected to the greatest insults. The passers-by spit in his

face, and sometimes beat him so unmercifully, that he falls to the ground, and is obliged to be carried home.

7. If a Persian kills a Jew, and the family of the deceased can bring forward two Mussulmans as witnesses to the fact, the murderer is punished by a fine of 12 tumauns (600 piastres); but if two such witnesses cannot be produced, the crime remains unpunished, even though it has been publicly committed, and is well known.

8. The flesh of the animals slaughtered according to Hebrew custom, but as Trefe declared, must not be sold to any Mussulmans. The slaughterers are compelled to bury the meat, for even the Christians do not venture to buy it, fearing the mockery and insult of the Persians.

9. If a Jew enters a shop to buy anything, he is forbidden to inspect the goods, but must stand at a respectful distance and ask the price. Should his hand incautiously touch the goods, he must take them at any price the seller chooses to ask for them.

10. Sometimes the Persians intrude into the dwellings of the Jews and take possession of whatever pleases them. Should the owner make the least opposition in defence of his property, he incurs the danger of atoning for it with his life.

11. Upon the least dispute between a Jew and a Persian, the former is immediately dragged before the Achund [religious authority], and, if the complainant can bring forward two witnesses, the Jew is condemned to pay a heavy fine. If he is too poor to pay this penalty in money, he must pay it in his person. He is stripped to the waist, bound to a stake, and receives forty blows with a stick. Should the sufferer utter the least cry of pain during this proceeding, the blows already given are not counted, and the punishment is begun afresh.

12. In the same manner the Jewish children, when they get into a quarrel with those of the Mussulmans, are immediately led before the Achund, and punished with blows.

13. A Jew who travels in Persia is taxed in every inn and every caravanserai he enters. If he hesitates to satisfy any

demands that may happen to be made on him, they fall
upon him, and maltreat him until he yields to their terms.

14. If, as already mentioned, a Jew shows himself in the
street during the three days of the Katel (feast of mourning
for the death of the Persian founder of the religion of Ali)
he is sure to be murdered.

15. Daily and hourly new suspicions are raised against
the Jews, in order to obtain excuses for fresh extortions;
the desire of gain is always the chief incitement to fanaticism.[34]

The *Alliance* reports contain a number of accounts of the
occupational distribution of Persian Jews. Thus a report of
Shiraz in 1903 lists some 5,000 Jews as follows: 400 peddlers,
200 masons, 102 goldsmiths, 90 merchants, 80 wine sellers,
60 musicians, 20 grocers, 15 butchers, 10 vintners, 10 money-
changers, 5 drygoods merchants, 5 jewellers, 5 physicians,
2 surgeons. Another for Kermanshah in the same year, lists
70 grocery peddlers, 55 merchants, 44 textile peddlers, 27
dyers, 23 goldsmiths, 22 grocers, 15 porters, 10 weavers, 5
brokers, 3 wine sellers, 3 barbers, 3 synagogue beadles, 3 well
diggers, 2 vintners, 2 Hebrew teachers.[35]

The *Alliance* records include numerous stories of ill-treatment, humiliation, and persecution. Toward the end of the
century the shāh sometimes intervened to protect his Jews
from mob violence or religious hostility, but this was rare and
usually not very effective. Even the accusation of ritual murder, not known in the past, reached Iran, and a particularly
bad case occurred in Shiraz in 1910.[36] Appeals to foreign
rulers, the queen (later king) of England, the president of
France, the sultan of Turkey, were also of limited help. There
was no real change until after the constitutional revolution of
1905, and no substantial improvement until after the fall of
the Qajar dynasty in 1925.

In the Arab lands of the Middle East and North Africa, the
position of the Jews was for a while very much better and
benefited greatly from the prevalence, at that time, of liberal
ideas and aspirations among the political class. One of them,

the Egyptian James (Yaʿqūb) Sanua, better known by his pen name Abū Naddara (1839-1912), even played a certain role as a patriotic journalist and as a playwright. In general, the participation of Jews in Arab intellectual and cultural life, though greater than among the Turks, was—with the exception of Iraq—limited. In other respects, however, their educational standards and therefore their economic opportunities improved, while the new systems of government that were being created gave them an unprecedented degree of civil and political security. However, these improvements were linked with the establishment of Western predominance, either directly through imperial rule or indirectly through political and cultural influence. This association was ultimately to prove fatal to these communities, when that predominance weakened and ended. The Jewish communities in various Arab countries often differed quite considerably in the paths that they followed. In Iraq the Jewish community, while preserving an ancient tradition of Hebrew religious learning, was thoroughly Arab in language and culture, and profoundly integrated into the society; some of its members played an important part in the literary, musical, and artistic revival. The Jews of Egypt were at the opposite extreme. While the lower classes remained Arabic-speaking and Egyptian in sentiment, in the middle and upper classes Jews—like many Christians and even some Muslims—were often alienated in both culture and nationality, for the most part using Italian and later French rather than Arabic, sending their children to foreign-language schools, and often obtaining the citizenship of a European country. In the end, both Iraqi and Egyptian Jews suffered the same fate.

Western influence prepared the downfall of the Islamic Jewries in more ways than one—not only by violating the *dhimma* and thus exposing them to the hostility of the Muslim majorities, but also by providing new theories and forms of expression for this hostility. From the late nineteenth century, as a direct result of European influence, movements appear among Muslims of which for the first time one can legitimately use the term anti-Semitic. Hostility to Jews had, of course, roots in the past, but in this era it assumed a new and radically different character. The starting point was the very strong feeling that the proper relationship between believer and unbeliever, between Muslim and *dhimmī*, had been subverted. This feeling was fueled by growing resentment at the favor shown by European powers to members of the non-Muslim minorities and at the consequent successes achieved by members of these minorities, who attained positions of power and wealth under foreign rule or influence they would never have been able to achieve in the old Muslim order. This resentment was directed at Christians as much as Jews—indeed, rather more so. But a specific campaign against Jews, expressed in the unmistakable language of European Christian anti-Semitism, first appeared among Christians in the nineteenth century, and developed among Christians and then Muslims in the twentieth. Mention has already been made of the role of European consuls and traders, working with local Christian minorities, in ousting Jews and securing their replacement by Middle Eastern Christians. They were also active in the spread of certain classical themes of European anti-Semitism—for example, in the introduction of the blood libel, and in conjuring up fantasies of Jewish plots to gain world domination.[37]

The first anti-Semitic tracts in Arabic appeared toward the end of the nineteenth century. They were translated from French originals—part of the literature of the Dreyfus controversy. Most of the translations were made by Arab Catholics, Maronites, or other Uniate Christians. The first Arabic translation of the most famous of all anti-Semitic forgeries, the so-called *Protocols of the Elders of Zion*, was published in Cairo in 1927. This was followed by many other translations—indeed, there are now more translations and editions of the *Protocols* in Arabic than in any other language, and the text is still required reading in departments of comparative religion in a number of Arab universities. There is now also available in Arabic a vast literature of anti-Semitic works, translated or adapted from European originals. These include the Nazi classics that form the basis of a large proportion of current Arab writings on Jews, Judaism, and Jewish history, as well as other writers as diverse as Henry Ford and Karl Marx. The latter's essay on the Jewish question is now enjoying a new popularity in Arabic translation.

The result of all this is that some of the nastiest inventions of European anti-Semitism have been endorsed in Arab countries at the highest political and academic levels. The late President Nāṣir, in an interview with an Indian journalist on September 28, 1958, cited and recommended the *Protocols of the Elders of Zion* as a guide to Jewish designs,[38] and in another interview of May 1, 1964, with a German neo-Nazi newspaper, dismissed the Holocaust as a myth and expressed his regret at the Nazi defeat.[39] Dr. Ḥasan Zāzā, Professor of Hebrew at ʿAyn Shams University in Cairo, reached the conclusion, apparently on the basis of the Damascus affair of 1840, that Jews—in defiance of what he admits to be their own laws—use gentile blood for ritual purposes, and many other Arab writers on Judaism agree.[40] This approach is found not only in overtly polemical writings, but also in what purports to be scholarly work, concerned not with Israel or Zionism but with Jewish history and religion. The proceedings of the fourth conference of Islamic research, held at Al-Azhar in Cairo in September 1968, are full of these and similar accusations, often expressed in violent terms.[41] Even school books are affected. A UNESCO commission of three experts, one of them a Turkish Muslim, prepared a report on textbooks used in schools in the UNRWA camps in Jordan, Lebanon, the West Bank, and the Gaza strip. Among the criteria that the commission set was that:

> All terms contemptuous of a community taken as a whole should also be prohibited since this, obviously intolerable in itself, can among other consequences lead to the violation of the most sacred rights of the individual. Hence, liar, cheat, usurer, idiot—terms applied to Jews in certain passages, and part of the deplorable language of international antisemitism—cannot be tolerated.

Of 127 textbooks examined, the commission recommended that 14 be withdrawn entirely, 65 be used only after modification, and 48 be retained as they were. Among other problems, the commission found that in textbooks on religion and history,

> an excessive importance is given to the problem of relations between the Prophet Mohammed and the Jews of Arabia, in terms tending to convince young people that the Jewish community as a whole has always been and will always be the irreconcilable enemy of the Muslim community.[42]

The report was presented to the eighty-second session of UNESCO in Paris on April 4, 1969. It was never published.

Lebanon and Jordan are not among the most extreme in these matters. Far less restrained anti-Jewish statements appeared in Egyptian books, schoolbooks, and media, before and also after the peace treaty with Israel, not to speak of other more radical and more traditional states, each group with its own distinctive perceptions of relations with the Jews. A characteristic expression of the late King Fayṣal's understanding of the Jewish role in history occurs in an interview accorded to a widely circulated Egyptian picture magazine and published on August 4, 1972:

> Israel has had malicious intentions since ancient times. Its objective is the destruction of all other religions. It is proven from history that they are the ones who ignited the Crusades at the time of Saladin the Ayyubid so that the war would lead to the weakening of both Muslims and Christians. They regard the other religions as lower than their own and other peoples as inferior to their level. And on the subject of vengeance—they have a certain day on which they mix the blood of non-Jews into their bread and eat it. It happened that two years ago, while I was in Paris on a visit, that the police discovered five murdered children. Their blood had been drained, and it turned out that some Jews had murdered them in order to take their blood and mix it with the bread that they eat on this day. This shows you what is the extent of their hatred and malice toward non-Jewish peoples.[43]

The Saudi monarch, who used to present copies of the *Protocols* and other anti-Semitic tracts to his visitors,[44] had clearly traveled all or most of the way from the traditional contempt for the Jew as upstart to the modernized, Westernized nightmare of the Jew as the embodiment of evil. He was not alone in this.

The present-day Arabic reader has at his disposal the whole gamut of anti-Semitic mythology. His perceptions have also been modified by the introduction of European anti-Semitic iconography. Anti-Jewish cartoons, for some time now very common in the Arabic press, draw their themes and stereotypes entirely from central and eastern Europe. This is true even of cartoons in fundamentalist Islamic publications. Since there was no native tradition of anti-Jewish caricature, it required some education before readers of Arabic newspapers could be expected to understand the symbols. It would seem that this task of education has now been completed.

The propagation of anti-Semitic themes and notions was not left to chance, nor was it entirely entrusted to Middle Eastern enterprise. Anti-Semitism has been energetically propagated by various European groups. The most important in this century were the Nazis, who from the early 1930s until the defeat of Germany in 1945 devoted great efforts to the spread of anti-Semitic doctrines among the Arabs. Since the fall of the Nazis, some Arab countries have themselves become the major source of anti-Semitic publications, which are distributed all over the world.

A Turkish book, probably translated or adapted from the French, entitled *The Dreyfus Affair and its Secret Causes*, was published in Istanbul in 1898. The earliest anti-Semitic writer in Turkey would appear to be a certain Ebüzziya Tevfik, a prominent journalist and litterateur of the Young Turk period, and the editor of a magazine. He showed some interest in Jewish matters from an early stage, and already in 1888 he published a not unsympathetic booklet on the "Israelite *millet*," covering both ancient and recent history. In about 1911 he took up anti-Semitism and began publishing anti-Semitic tracts and articles, the material for most of which seems to have reached him from central Europe. In the same period the Jews found a defender among the Young Turk writers in Celâl Nuri

Ileri, whose writings include several sympathetic discussions of Jewish matters and problems.[45] Anti-Semitic arguments were used both against the Young Turks and later against Kemal Atatürk by conservative opponents seeking to discredit them in this way. Anti-Semitic writing of the European type has continued as a minor theme in Turkish polemics to the present day, mostly confined to the extreme Right and the extreme Left, though this has begun to increase of late as a result of the impact on Turkish media, politics, and trade of Arab concerns and influences.[46]

Obviously, a major element in the rise of Arab anti-Semitism is the Palestine question, and the consequent embitterment of relations between Jews and Arabs everywhere. In its origin this is a political conflict—not a matter of prejudice or bias, or intercommunal or interethnic hostility, but a specific and material conflict between two groups of people both claiming the same place. However, since Zionism and later Israel both happen to be predominantly Jewish, and since there were conveniently accessible Jewish minorities in Arab countries, and since furthermore anti-Semitism provided a ready-made system of themes, images, and vocabulary for attacks on Jews, the temptation was obviously very strong to make use of them. And, of course, there were skilled and experienced tempters to push them.

Palestin. cause

Arab leaders have reacted in various ways. Some have eagerly embraced these allies; others have denounced them with indignation; some have done both at the same time. While recognizing the obvious effect of the Palestine question in the deterioration of Arab-Jewish relations and, therefore, in the position of Jews in the Muslim world generally, its importance should not be exaggerated, in particular not to the neglect or exclusion of other factors. This deterioration is part of a larger change, affecting the general situation in the Muslim world and that of minorities within it. The general worsening of relations and loss of tolerance harmed others besides Jews. But it was worse for Jews because of the Palestine question, and because they were more vulnerable. Jews in Arab countries had, for the most part, been either indifferent or hostile to Zionism, which was seen as a predominantly European movement. The conversion of the Arab Jews to Zionism was subsequent and was, as in some other places, a direct result of persecution.

The process of their conversion was hastened by violence. In the summer of 1940, and again in February 1941, the mufti of Jersualem, Ḥāj Amīn al-Ḥusaynī, acting, he said, on behalf of an inter-Arab committee of governmental and nongovernmental representatives, presented proposals to the government of Germany for German-Arab cooperation to achieve common ends. If the German government would issue a declaration, a draft of which he provided, endorsing the mufti's aims, he could promise them effective Arab support. The earlier draft of the proposed declaration contains this clause, repeated with minor changes in the second:

> Germany and Italy recognize the right of the Arab countries to solve the question of the Jewish elements which exist in Palestine and in the other Arab countries, as required by the national and ethnic (*völkisch*) interests of the Arabs, and as the Jewish question was solved in Germany and Italy.[47]

The Germans, for a variety of reasons, never gave a clear answer to the mufti's requests, but there can be no doubt about the extent of Nazi influence, as expressed in the mufti's draft proposal, in the Arab nationalist camp at that time. Between 1941 and 1948 there were numerous outbreaks of anti-Jewish violence in Iraq, Syria, Egypt, Southern Arabia, and North Africa, in which hundreds of Jews were killed or injured, while far greater numbers found their work places sacked and their houses destroyed, leaving them homeless and destitute. All these events predated the establishment of the state of Israel and no doubt contributed to some extent to its creation. That, in turn, further undermined the position of Jews in Arab countries, already weakened through their perceived association with the West, and exposed to a new militancy that leaves no place for those who deviate from the rule. The result was a massive emigration of Jews from these countries, mostly in the late forties and early fifties. Of 300,000 Jews in Morocco, some 18,000 remain. Of 55,000 Jews in the Yemen, less than a 1,000 remain. Of the three major communities of Algeria, Iraq, and Egypt, previously estimated at 135,000, 125,000, and 75,000, respectively, only a few hundred old people remain in each.[48] Even in Turkey, a Jewish community once reckoned at some 80,000 to 90,000 has been reduced by emigration to about 23,000, while in Iran a return to the *dhimma* seems to be the best for which the Jews of that country can hope. Increasing numbers have preferred emigration, either to Israel or to the countries of the West.

There have been many chapters in the long history of the Jewish people. Greek Alexandria was the home of Philo, Babylon of the Talmud, medieval Spain of a rich Hebrew literature; the Jews of Germany and Poland wrote major chapters in modern Jewish history. They have all gone, and only their monuments and their memory remain. The Judaeo-Islamic symbiosis was another great period of Jewish life and creativity, a long rich, and vital chapter in Jewish history. It has now come to an end.

Notes

THE FOLLOWING abbreviations have been used in the notes:

AIU   *Alliance Israélite Universelle*
BAIU   *Bulletin de l'Alliance Israélite Universelle*
EI¹, EI²   *Encyclopaedia of Islam*, first and second editions
JQR   *Jewish Quarterly Review*
JWH   *Journal of World History*
REJ   *Revue des Études Juives*

ONE. ISLAM AND OTHER RELIGIONS

1. The position of the non-Muslim subjects of the Muslim state has been studied by A. S. Tritton, *The Caliphs and their Non-Muslim Subjects: A Critical Study of the Covenant of 'Umar* (London, 1930; reprinted 1970), and by Antoine Fattal, *Le Statut legal des non-musulmans en pays d'Islam* (Beirut, 1958). The literature on the different non-Muslim communities is uneven. Scholarly work on the Christians tends to be concerned with the history of Christianity and of the churches rather than with the actual life of the Christian communities. There is a quite extensive literature in Arabic. General works in Western languages include A. S. Atiya, *A History of Eastern Christianity* (London, 1968), and B. Spuler, *Die Morgenländischen Kirchen*, in *Handbuch der Orientalistik* (Leiden, 1964). On the history and historiography of the Jews in Islamic lands, there are two excellent recent publications: Norman A. Stillman, *The Jews of Arab Lands: A History and Source Book* (Philadelphia, 1979), and Mark R. Cohen, "The Jews under Islam: from the Rise of Islam to Sabbatai Zevi," in *Bibliographical Essays in Medieval Jewish Studies* (New York, 1976), pp. 169-229, reprinted with a supplement as Princeton Near East Paper Number 32, Princeton, 1981. On the writings of S. D. Goitein, by far the most important body of scholarly work on Judaeo-Arab history, see chapter 2, note 1 below, and passim. The history of both Jews and Christians under Muslim rule is discussed in A. J. Arberry, ed., *Religion in the Middle East* (Cambridge, 1969), where bibliographies are also given. For a selection of documents in

translation, see B. Lewis, *Islam from the Prophet Muhammad to the Capture of Constantinople*, II (New York, 1974), pp. 217-235. On Islamic tolerance in general, see Rudi Paret, "Toleranz und Intoleranz im Islam," *Saeculum* 21 (1970): 344-365; Francesco Gabrieli, "La Tolleranza nell'Islam," *La Cultura* 10 (1972): 257-266, reprinted in idem, *Arabeschi e Studi Islamici* (Naples, 1973), pp. 25-36; Adel Khoury, *Toleranz im Islam* (Munich, 1980). Two other works, which emphasize the negative aspects of the Muslim record, are Bat Ye'or (pseudonym), *Le Dhimmi: Profil de l'opprimé en Orient et en Afrique du nord depuis la conquête arabe* (Paris, 1980), and Karl Binswanger, *Untersuchungen zum Status der Nichtmuslime im osmanischen Reich des 16. Jahrhundert, mit einer Neudefinition des Begriffes "Dhimma"*(Munich, 1977). The latter is very critical of what he calls the "dogmatic Islamophilia" of many orientalists.

2. Cf. E. Gibbon, *Decline and Fall of the Roman Empire*, vol. 5, ed. J. B. Bury (London, 1909-1914), p. 332.

3. See, for example, the Āyatollāh Khomeinī's references to the position of the non-Muslims in the Islamic state. In his programmatic book on Islamic government, he indicates unequivocally that they would be required to pay the poll tax, in return for which they would profit from the protection and services of the state; they would, however, be excluded from all participation in the political process. See his *Ḥukūma Islāmiyya*, n.p. (Beirut), n.d., pp. 30ff.; *Vilāyat-i Faqīh*, n.p., n.d., pp. 35ff.; English version (from the Arabic), *Islamic Government* (U.S. Joint Publications Research Service 72663, 1979), pp. 22ff.; French version (from the Persian), *Pour un gouvernement islamique* (Paris, 1979), pp. 31ff. Another version in Hamid Algar, *Islam and Revolution: Writings and Declarations of Imam Khomeini* (Berkeley, 1981), pp. 45ff. Indeed, one of the Āyatollāh's main grievances against the shāh was that his legislation allowed the theoretical possibility (never in fact realized before the fall of the monarchy) of non-Muslims exercising political or judicial authority over Muslims.

4. On these matters, see B. Lewis, *Race and Color in Islam* (New York, 1971); revised and expanded French version, *Race et couleur en pays d'Islam* (Paris, 1982).

5. Muḥammad's dealings with the Jews have formed the subject of a considerable scholarly literature and, more recently, also of an extensive popular and semipopular literature in Arabic and other Islamic languages. See Cohen, "The Jews," pp. 176-179, and Stillman, *The Jews of Arab Lands*, pp. 3-21, 113-151.

Rather less attention has been given to Muḥammad's relations with the Christians. On his dealings with the Christians of Najran, see Werner Schmucker, "Die Christliche Minderheit von Naǧrān und die Problematik ihrer Beziehungen zum frühen Islam," in Tilman Nagel, Gerd-R. Puin, Christa-U. Spuler, Werner Schumucker, and Albrecht Noth, *Studien zum Minderheitenproblem im Islam*, I (Bonn, 1973), pp. 183-281. For brief general surveys, see *EI*[1] articles "Nadjrān" (by A. Moberg) and "Naṣārā" (by A. S. Tritton).

6. See *EI*[2], s.v. "Khaybar" (by Adolf Grohmann). On the expulsion of non-Muslims from Arabia, see Khoury, *Toleranz*, pp. 87-88.

7. W. Cantwell Smith, *The Meaning and End of Religion* (New York, 1964), pp. 58ff., 75ff.

8. R. Paret, "Sure 2,256: *la ikrāha fi d-dīn*, Toleranz oder Resignation," *Der Islam* 49 (1969): 299-300.

9. In two modern translations of the Qur'ān, these words are rendered "jusqu'à ce qu'ils paient la *jizya*, directement(?) et alors qu'ils sont humiliés" (R. Blachère); "bis sie kleinlaut aus der Hand Tribut entrichten" (R. Paret). Other recent renderings are: "until they give compensation (tax) for support from solidarity (shown by us to them), while they are in a state of lowliness" (F. Rosenthal); "until they pay the *jizya* out of ability and sufficient means, they (nevertheless) being inferior" (M. J. Kister); "until they give the reward due for a benefaction (since their lives are spared), while they are ignominious (namely, for not having fought unto death)" (M. Bravmann). See Rosenthal in *The Joshua Starr Memorial Volume* (New York, 1953), pp. 68-72; Bravmann and Kister in *Arabica* 10 (1963): 94-95; 11 (1964): 272-278; 13 (1966): 307-314; 14 (1967): 90-91, 326-327; cf. M. M. Bravmann, *The Spiritual Background of Early Islam: Studies in Ancient Arab Concepts* (Leiden, 1972), pp. 199-212.

10. Zamakhsharī, *Al-Kashshāf*, II (Cairo, 1353/1954), p. 147 (Beirut, n.d.), pp. 262-264; cf. Al-Bayḍāwī, *Commentarius in Coranum*, I, ed. H. O. Fleischer (Leipzig, 1846), pp. 383-384. On the manner of paying the *jizya*, see Fattal, *Le Statut*, pp. 286-288.

11. Ibn al-Naqqāsh, in Belin, "Fetwa relatif à la condition des dhimmis et particulièrement des chrétiens en pays musulmans depuis l'établissement de l'Islam jusqu'au milieu du 8e siècle de l'hégire," *Journal Asiatique* 4th series, 19 (1852): 107-108.

12. Abū ʿUbayd, *Kitāb al-Amwāl* (Cairo, 1353/1954), pp. 18ff., 52ff.

13. Abū Yūsuf, *Kitāb al-Kharāj* (Cairo, 1382/1962-1963), pp. 122-

125; English translation in Stillman, *The Jews of Arab Lands*, pp. 159-161.

14. See the important paper by G. E. von Grunebaum, "Eastern Jewry under Islam," in *Viator: Medieval and Renaissance Studies*, II (Berkeley-Los Angeles, 1971), pp. 365-372; in general, Salo W. Baron, *A Social and Religious History of the Jews*, III (New York, 1957), passim, especially pp. 120ff.

15. Some problems of Islamization have been examined in two recent volumes: a monograph by R. W. Bulliet, *Conversion to Islam in the Medieval Period* (Cambridge, Mass., 1979), and a symposium edited by Nehemia Levtzion, *Conversion to Islam* (New York and London, 1979), where further bibliography is given.

16. On the Sabians, and the various interpretations of this term, see *EI¹*, s.v. "al-Ṣābi'a" (by B. Carra de Vaux).

17. See *EI²*, article "Dhimma" (by Claude Cahen), where further bibliography is given.

18. For examples of the texts in which these restrictions are set forth see Lewis, *Islam*, II, pp. 217ff.

19. For a brief summary of Muslim law and doctrine on the holy war, see *EI²*, s.v. "Djihād" (by E. Tyan), where further bibliography is given. For examples of old and new legal texts, see Rudolph Peters, *Jihad in Mediaeval and Modern Islam* (Leiden, 1977); idem, *Islam and Colonialism: The Doctrine of Jihad in Modern History* (The Hague, 1979).

20. See *EI²*, s.v. "Amān" (by J. Schacht). On the disputes between foreign and Ottoman Jews about tax exemptions, as reflected in the Rabbinic responsa, see Eliezer Bashan's study in *East and Maghreb: A Volume of Researches*, ed. H. Z. (J. W.) Hirschberg (Ramat-Gan, 1974), pp. 105-166. On Russian Muslim subjects in Iran, see Marvin L. Entner, *Russo-Persian Commercial Relations, 1825-1914* (Gainesville, Florida, 1965), p. 14.

21. See D. Santillana, *Instituzioni di Diritto Musulmano*, 1 (Rome, 1926), pp. 69-71; L. P. Harvey, "Crypto-Islam in Sixteenth Century Spain," in *Actas del Primer Congreso de Estudios Arabes e Islámicos* (Madrid, 1964), pp. 163-178; al-Wansharīsī, *Asnā al-matājir fī bayān aḥkām man ghalaba ʿala waṭanihi al-naṣārā wa-lam yuhājir*, ed. Ḥusayn Muʾnis, in *Revista del Instituto Egipcio de Estudios Islámicos en Madrid* 5 (1957): 129-191. Cf. Bernard Lewis, *The Muslim Discovery of Europe* (New York, 1982), pp. 66ff., and Khoury, *Toleranz*, pp. 130ff.

22. Tritton, *The Caliphs*, and Fattal, *Le Statut*, passim, especially pp. 97ff.

23. On this badge, see *EI²*, article "Ghiyār" (by M. Perlmann); Tritton, *The Caliphs*, pp. 115ff.; Fattal, *Le Statut*, pp. 96-110.

24. S. D. Goitein, *A Mediterranean Society: The Jewish Communities of the Arab World as Portrayed in the Documents of the Cairo Geniza*, I (Berkeley and Los Angeles, 1967), p. 97; II (1971), pp. 380-394; idem, "Evidence on the Muslim Poll Tax from Non-Muslim Sources," *Journal of the Economic and Social History of the Orient* 6 (1963): 278-295.

25. Fattal, *Le Statut*, pp. 137ff.; Khoury, *Toleranz*, pp. 157ff.

26. Fattal, *Le Statut*, pp. 113ff., 344ff.; Khoury, *Toleranz*, pp. 162ff.

27. Tritton, *The Caliphs*, pp. 175ff.; Khoury, *Toleranz*, pp. 87ff.

28. Al-Qalqashandī, *Ṣubḥ al-Aʿshā*, XIII (Cairo, 1337/1918), p. 386; Fattal, *Le Statut*, p. 242; Khoury, *Toleranz*, p. 91.

29. Al-Nawawī, *Al-Manthūrāt*, ed. I. Goldziher, *REJ* 28 (1894): 94; English translation in Lewis, *Islam*, II, pp. 228-229.

30. Ibn Qutayba, *ʿUyūn al-Akhbār*, I (Cairo, 1962), p. 43; cited in part by A. L. Udovitch, "The Jews and Islam in the High Middle Ages: A Case of the Muslim View of Differences," in *Settimane di Studio del Centro italiano di studi sull'alto medioevo* (Spoleto, 1980), pp. 665-666. On the legal question of the employment of *dhimmīs* in government, see Khoury, *Toleranz*, pp. 91-92, 166ff.

31. Abū Yūsuf, *Kitāb al-Kharāj*, 3d ed. (Cairo, 1382/1962-1963), pp. 140-141; English translation in Lewis, *Islam*, II, pp. 223-224.

32. E. Ashtor, "The Social Isolation of the *ahl adh-dhimma*," in *Pal Hirschler Memorial Book* (Budapest, 1949), pp. 73-94; reprinted in idem, *The Medieval Near East: Social and Economic History* (London, 1978).

33. Cf. Qur'ān, II,61 and III,108. For a brief discussion, see M. Perlmann, "Eleventh-Century Andalusian Authors on the Jews of Granada," *Proceedings of the American Academy for Jewish Research*, 18 (1949): 289-290.

34. On anti-*dhimmī* propaganda, see M. Steinschneider, *Polemische und apologetische Literatur in arabischer Sprache* (Leipzig, 1877); R. Gottheil, "An Answer to the Dhimmis," *Journal of the American Oriental Society* 41 (1921): 383-457; M. Perlmann, "Notes on Anti-Christian Propaganda in the Mamluk Empire," *Bulletin of the School of Oriental and African Studies* 10 (1942): 843-861; Perlmann, "Eleventh-Century Andalusian Authors"; S. W. Baron, *A*

Social and Religious History of the Jews, V, pp. 95ff. Ibn Ḥazm's tract against Ibn Nagrella, cited by Perlmann, has been published; *Al-Radd ʿalā Ibn al-Naghrīla al-Yahūdī wa-rasā'il ukhrā*, ed. Iḥsān ʿAbbās (Cairo, 1380/1960). For other anti-Jewish poems, see W. J. Fischel, *Jews in the Economic and Political Life of Medieval Islam* (including some other contemporary attacks on Ibn Nagrella).

35. Sometimes the term "pig" is applied to both. The reference to apes may derive from the Qur'ān (II,61; V,65; VII,166). See Henri Pérès, *La Poésie andalouse en arabe classique au XIe siècle* (Paris, 1953), pp. 240-241; Perlmann, "Eleventh-Century Andalusian Authors," pp. 287-288.

36. In Ottoman usage the name Joseph was spelled *Yūsuf* for Muslims, *Yūsūf* for Christians, and *Yāsif* (or *Yāsef*) for Jews. David, Jacob, Abraham, and other Biblical names were similarly differentiated.

37. See Ignaz Goldziher, *Introduction to Islamic Theology and Law* (Princeton, N.J., 1981), pp. 213-216; idem, *The Zahiris, Their Doctrine and Their History* (Leiden, 1971), p. 58; Amedée Querry, *Droit musulman: Recueil de lois concernant les musulmans schyites*, I (Paris, 1871-1872), p. 44 (a translation of the *Kitāb Sharā'iʿ al-Islām*, by the Shiʿite jurist Najm al-Dīn Jaʿfar al-Ḥillī). On ritual purity, see *EI¹*, article "Ṭahāra" (by A. S. Tritton), and the sections on *Ṭahāra* (purity) and *Najāsa* (impurity) in the standard works on Islamic law and ritual.

38. Letter from Hamadān, dated 27 October 1892, in *AIU* archives, the text was published in Narcisse Leven, *Alliance Israélite Universelle, cinquante ans d'histoire*, I (Paris, 1911), pp. 376-377, and again by David Littman, "Jews under Muslim Rule: The Case of Persia," *Wiener Library Bulletin*, n.s. 32 (1979): 7-8; for an earlier version of the same rule, see J. J. Benjamin II, *Eight Years in Asia and Africa from 1846 to 1855* (Hanover, 1859), p. 212. As late as May 1907, one Sheikh Muḥammad Mahdī, leader of the religious party in Kermānshāh, with the support of the merchants and the artisans, issued sets of rules for both the Muslims and the Jews. The latter were required not to go out when it rained, always to wear the Jewish badge, not to build houses higher than those of the Muslims, not to cut their side whiskers, and not to ride horses (Report by Sagues, *AIU* archives, Iran II.C.4-8, Kermānshāh, Sagues, 1906-1907).

39. Rūḥullāh al-Mūsawī al-Khomaynī, *Risāla-i Tawżīh al-Masā'il* (Tehran, n.d. [1979?]), pp. 15, 18.

40. Cf. the observations of S. D. Goitein, *Interfaith Relations in Medieval Islam* (New York, 1973), pp. 28-29.

41. Cf. I. Goldziher, "Usages juifs d'après la littérature religieuse des musulmans," *REJ* 28 (1894): 324.

42. Text in Paul Horster, *Zur Anwendung des islamischen Rechts im 16. Jahrhundert* (Stuttgart, 1935), p. 37 (translation p. 76); also in M. Ertugrul Düzdag, *Şeyhülislâm Ebussuûd Efendi Fetvalari işiginda 16 asır Türk hayatı* (Istanbul, 1972), p. 94.

43. Fattal, *Le Statut*, pp. 232ff.; Khoury, *Toleranz*, pp. 90-91, 165ff. Some jurists permit the use of non-Muslim auxiliaries in warfare. "One may use them," says al-Sarakhsī, "as one would use a dog." The jurists agree, however, that *dhimmī* soldiers do not share the booty, but receive a stipend fixed by the Muslim authorities.

44. See, for example, Hanina Mizrahi, *Toldot Yehudê Paras* (Jerusalem, 1966), p. 36, and the document cited in note 38 above.

45. The use of the term "residing" (*sakin*) is significant. Muslim inhabitants of, say, Damascus or Jerusalem are simply called Damascenes or Jerusalemites. Muslims who have come from elsewhere, and all non-Muslims no matter how long they and their forebears have lived in the city, are denied the simple attributive ending (Turkish -*li*, Arabic -*ī*) and are designated as "residing in" the city in question. On a similar distinction in ancient Alexandria, see Pierre Vidal-Naquet, "Du bon usage de la trahison," introduction to Flavius Josèphe, *La Guerre des Juifs* (Paris, 1977), pp. 59-60.

46. Ahmed Refik, *Onuncu asr-i hicride Istanbul hayatı* (Istanbul, 1333), pp. 68-69; a French version in Abraham Galante, *Documents officiels turcs concernant les juifs de Turquie* (Istanbul, 1931), p. 114. See further, Binswanger, *Untersuchungen*, pp. 170ff.; idem, "Ökonomische Aspekte der Kleiderordnung im osmanischen Reich des 16. Jahrhunderts," *Prilozi za Orijentalnu Filologiju* 30 (1980): 51-65.

47. Ibn ʿAbdūn, *Risāla fiʾl-qaḍāʾ waʾl-ḥisba*, ed. E. Levi-Provençal (Cairo, 1955), pp. 43ff.; English translation in Lewis, *Islam*, II, pp. 162-163.

48. Littman, "Jews . . . Persia," p. 7.

49. Abdelmagid Turki, "Situation du 'tributaire' qui insulte l'Islam, au regard de la doctrine et de la jurisprudence musulmanes," *Studia Islamica* 30 (1979): 39-72; Khoury, *Toleranz*, pp. 164ff.

50. Horster, *Zur Anwendung*, text, pp. 32-33, German translation, pp. 74-75; Düzdag, *Şeyhülislâm Ebussuûd*, p. 102.

51. Edward William Lane, *An Account of the Manners and Customs of the Modern Egyptians*, 5th ed., II (London, 1871), p. 305.

52. Robert Brunschvig, "Justice religieuse et justice laïque dans la Tunisie des Deys et des Beys jusqu'au milieu du XIXe siècle," *Studia Islamica* 23 (1965): 68; reprinted in idem, *Etudes d'Islamologie*, II (Paris, 1976), p. 267. Accusations of this offense, often followed by arrest, imprisonment, and beating, continued through the nineteenth and into the twentieth centuries.

53. Cited in G. Levi Della Vida, "Un'Antica opera sconosciuta di Controversia Ši'ita," *Annali dell'Istituto Universitario Orientale di Napoli*, n.s. 14 (1964): 236.

54. Ibn al-Qalānisī, *Dhayl Ta'rīkh Dimashq*, ed. H. F. Amedroz (Beirut, 1908), p. 46.

55. Shaykh Aḥmad al-Budayrī al-Ḥallāq, *Ḥawādith Dimashq al-Yawmiyya*, ed. Aḥmad 'Izzat 'Abd al-Karīm (Damascus, 1959), p. 112 (cit. Sh. Shamir, "Muslim-Arab Attitudes towards Jews: The Ottoman and Modern Periods," in *Violence and Defense in the Jewish Experience*, ed. S. W. Baron and G. S. Wise [Philadelphia, 1977], p. 194).

56. Al-Balādhurī, *Futūḥ al-Buldān*, ed. M. J. de Goeje (Leiden, 1866), p. 162. For a somewhat different translation of the text, see P. K. Hitti, *The Origins of the Islamic State* (New York, 1916), p. 251. Cf. Goldziher, "Usages," p. 323.

57. Yaḥyā al-Antākī, *Annales*, ed. L. Cheikho, B. Carra de Vaux, and H. Zayyāt, in *Corpus Scriptorum Christianorum Orientalium, Scriptores Arabici*, 3d ser., VII (Paris, 1909), pp. 235-236; English translation in Lewis, *Islam*, II, pp. 227-228.

58. Al-Ḥasan ibn Manṣūr Qāḍīkhān, *Fatāwī*, III (Cairo, 1865), p. 616; English translation in Lewis, *Islam*, II, p. 228.

59. Cf. Uriel Heyd, "'Alilot dam be-Turkiya ba-me'ot ha-15 ve ha-16," *Sefunot* 5 (1961): 140ff.

60. The text of the poem is available in various versions and editions. See B. Lewis, "An Anti-Jewish Ode," in *Salo Wittmayer Baron Jubilee Volume* (Jerusalem, 1975), reprinted in B. Lewis, *Islam in History: Ideas, Men and Events in the Middle East* (London, 1973), pp. 158-165.

61. Al-Qalqashandī, *Ṣubḥ*, XIII, p. 368; English translation in Lewis, *Islam*, II, pp. 225-226.

62. Al-Ṭabarī, *Ta'rīkh al-Rusul wa'l Mulūk*, III, ed. M. J. de Goeje et al. (Leiden, 1879-1901), pp. 1389-1390.

63. See F. Babinger, *Mehmed the Conqueror and His Time*, tr. R. Mannheim (Princeton, 1978), pp. 494ff.

64. On this sultan, see *EI²*, s.v. "Bāyazīd II" (by V. J. Parry), where further literature is cited.

65. The source for this story is a passing reference in a report written by the Venetian Matteo Venier, archbishop of Corfu, 1586, and entitled *Relazione dello stato presente del Turco*. It was published by E. Alberi in *Le Relazioni degli ambasciatori veneti durante il secolo decimosesto*, series III, *Relazioni degli stati Ottomani*, II (Florence, 1844), p. 299, and cited in two standard works of nineteenth-century historiography, one on Turkey, the other on the Jews: J. W. Zinkeisen, *Geschichte des osmanischen Reiches in Europa*, III (Gotha, 1855), p. 372, and H. Graetz, *Geschichte der Juden*, IX (Leipzig, 1877), p. 439. Venier was a visiting priest, and his reports are not of the same quality as those of the Venetian ambassadors and consuls. This story, despite its inherent improbability, was repeated by several later historians, but with no additional evidence.

66. For discussions of the Almohad persecutions in the context of North African and of Jewish history, see H. Z. (J. W.) Hirschberg, *A History of the Jews in North Africa*, I (Leiden, 1974), pp. 123-139; J.F.P. Hopkins, *Medieval Muslim Government in Barbary* (London, 1958), pp. 59-70; Roger le Tourneau, *The Almohad Movement in North Africa in the Twelfth and Thirteenth Centuries* (Princeton, 1969), pp. 57ff., 77, etc.

67. See Roger Savory, *Iran under the Safavids* (Cambridge, Eng., 1980).

68. Cf. B. Lewis, "Some Observations on the Significance of Heresy in Islam," *Studia Islamica* I (1953): 43-63; revised version in idem, *Islam in History*, pp. 217-236.

69. On this episode, see Stillman, *The Jews of Arab Lands*, pp. 57-59, 211-225.

70. On these works, and more generally on mutual cultural influences between Judaism and Islam, see Hava Lazarus-Yafeh, *Some Religious Aspects of Islam* (Leiden, 1981), pp. 72-89.

71. Al-Jāḥiẓ, *Fi'l-radd ʿala 'l-Naṣārā* in *Thalāth Rasā'il*, 2d ed., ed. J. Finkel (Cairo, 1382), pp. 13-14, 17-18; English translation in Stillman, *The Jews of Arab Lands*, pp. 169-170. See also J. Finkel in *Journal of the American Oriental Society* (1927).

72. Charles Issawi, *The Economic History of Turkey, 1800-1914* (Chicago, 1980), pp. 13-14.

73. ʿAbd al-Raḥmān ibn Ḥasan al Jabartī, *ʿAjā'ib al-āthār fi'l-*

tarājim wa'l-akhbār III (Bulaq, 1297 [=1879-80]), pp. 11ff., 28, 44ff., 78, 109, 113, 208, etc., cf. Harald Motzki, *Dimma und Égalité: Die nichtmuslimischen Minderheiten Ägyptens in der zweiten Hälfte des 18. Jahrhunderts und die Expedition Bonapartes (1798-1801)* (Bonn, 1979), pp. 263ff., 324ff.

74. See, for example, the remarks cited by Cevdet Paşa, *Tezakir*, III, ed. Cavid Baysun (Ankara, 1963), pp. 236-237; English translation in Stillman, *The Jews of Arab Lands*, p. 361.

TWO. THE JUDAEO-ISLAMIC TRADITION

1. The formation of the Judaeo-Islamic tradition and the history of the Jews in the medieval Muslim world have formed the subject of an extensive scholarly literature. A few longer recent works will be mentioned here; guidance to the rest may be found in Mark Cohen's bibliographical studies, cited in Chapter 1, note 1. The only comprehensive surveys of the subject are still those contained in the larger, general Jewish histories; the latest, and by far the best, is S. W. Baron's *Social and Religious History of the Jews* (New York, 1952), in which the Islamic lands are examined both at length and in depth. Various aspects of relations between Jews and Muslims and between Judaism and Islam are discussed in E.I.J. Rosenthal, *Judaism and Islam* (London, 1961); A. I. Katsh, *Judaism in Islam* (New York, 1962); and, especially, S. D. Goitein, *Jews and Arabs; Their Contacts through the Ages*, 3d rev. ed. (New York, 1974). Goitein's *A Mediterranean Society: The Jewish Communities of the Arab World as Portrayed in the Documents of the Cairo Geniza* (3 vols., 4th in press: Berkeley and Los Angeles, 1967-) is a major achievement of scholarship, which, through the light it sheds on Jewish life in the medieval Islamic world, has brought a new dimension to the study of Islamic history itself. Though more limited in scope and purpose, Mark R. Cohen's *Jewish Self-Government in Medieval Egypt: The Origins of the Office of Head of the Jews, ca. 1065-1126* (Princeton, 1980) contributes substantially to the understanding of Jewish communal organization in the Islamic Middle Ages. Among books on specific countries, mention may be made of the works of E. Ashtor (Strauss) on the history of the Jews in Mamluk Egypt and Syria (3 vols., in Hebrew, Jerusalem, 1944-1970), and in Muslim Spain (2 vols., in Hebrew, Jerusalem, 1960-1966; English translation, Philadelphia, 1973-1979); and of J. W. (H. Z.) Hirsch-

berg on the Jews of North Africa (2 vols., in Hebrew, Jerusalem, 1965; English translation, Leiden, 1974-1982).

2. S. D. Goitein, "Jewish Society and Institutions under Islam," *Journal of World History* 11 (1968): 173. See also E. Ashtor, "The Number of Jews in Mediaeval Egypt," *Journal of Jewish Studies* 18 (1967): 9-42; 19 (1968): 1-22; idem, "Prolegomena to the Mediaeval History of Oriental Jewry," *JQR* 50 (1959): 55-68, 147-166; N. Golb, "The Topography of the Jews of Medieval Egypt," *Journal of Near Eastern Studies* 24 (1965): 251-270.

3. Geiger, *Was hat Mohammad aus dem Judenthum aufgenommen?* (Bonn, 1833, rev. ed., Leipzig, 1902); English translation, *Judaism and Islam* (Madras, 1898).

4. Hanna Zakarias, *L'Islam, entreprise juive de Moïse à Mohammed* (Cahors, 1955); idem, *L'Islam et la critique historique, la fin du mythe musulman et accueil fait aux ouvrages de Hanna Zakarias* (Cahors, 1960). According to Maxime Rodinson ("A Critical Survey of Modern Studies on Muhammad," in *Studies on Islam*, tr. and ed. Merlin L. Swartz [New York and London, 1981], p. 79, note 166), the author was a well-known Dominican scholar called G. Thery, who used a pseudonym because he was refused an imprimatur by his order.

5. Patricia Crone and Michael Cook, *Hagarism: The Making of the Islamic World* (Cambridge, Eng., 1977).

6. See *EI*[2], s.v.v. "Isrā'īliyyāt" (by G. Vajda), and "Banū Isrā'īl" (by S. D. Goitein). Gordon D. Newby, "Tafsir Isra'iliyat: The Development of Qur'an-Commentary in Early Islam in its Relationships to Judaeo-Christian Traditions of Scriptural Commentaries," *Journal of the American Academy of Religion* 47 (1979): 685-697. For a discussion of the views of different Muslim authorities on the lawfulness or otherwise of accepting information from Jewish sources, see M. J. Kister, "Ḥaddithū ʿan Banī Isrāʾīla walā ḥaraja: A Study of an Early Tradition," *Israel Oriental Studies* 2 (1972): 215-239; reprinted in his *Studies in Jahiliyya and Early Islam* (London, 1980). The references to Jews and Judaism in *ḥadīth* were studied in detail by G. Vajda, "Juifs et Musulmans selon le Hadit," *Journal Asiatique* 229 (1937): 57-127. The earlier studies by I. Goldziher are still of great value.

7. There is an extensive literature on this question. For a general survey, see *EI*[2], s.v. "al-Ḳuds" (by S. D. Goitein), where earlier publications are listed. For a more recent study, see Hava Lazarus-Yafeh,

Some Religious Aspects of Islam (Leiden, 1981), chapter 5, "The Sanctity of Jerusalem in Islam," pp. 58-71.

8. Aelia, the Roman name for Jerusalem, was also used in the early period of Arab rule, until it was replaced by the later al-Quds.

9. Al-Ṭabarī, *Ta'rikh*, I, pp. 2408-2409; English translation in Lewis, *Islam*, II, p. 3.

10. See pp. 96-97.

11. S. D. Goitein, *Studies in Islamic History and Institutions* (Leiden, 1966), chap. 5, "The Origin and Nature of the Muslim Friday Worship," pp. 111-125 (previously published in French in *Annales ESC* 3 (1958): 488-500.

12. Geiger, *Judaism*, pp. 68-69, citing *Mishna Berachot*, I,2. Cf. *The Soncino Talmud, Berachot*, pp. 48-49.

13. See *EI²*, s.v.v. "Ḳārūn" (by D. B. Macdonald); "Hām" and "Ilyās" (by G. Vajda). On the Curse of Ham, see also Lewis, *Race et couleur*, pp. 67-68, 141ff.; Ephraim Isaac, "Genesis, Judaism and the 'Sons of Ham,' " in *Slavery and Abolition* 1 (1980): 3-17; idem, "Concept biblique et rabbinique de la malédiction de Noé," *Service International de documentation judéo-chrétienne* 11 (1978): 16-35.

14. The evidence was very thoroughly examined by H. Z. (J. W.) Hirschberg, in his book *Israel be-Arav* (Tel-Aviv, 1946).

15. On the general background, see Sidney Smith, "Events in Arabia in the 6th century A.D.," *Bulletin of the School of Oriental and African Studies* 16 (1954): 425-468; and Janos Harmatta, "The Struggle for the Possession of Southern Arabia between Aksum and the Sasanians," in *IV Congresso Internazionale di Studi Etiopici*, I (Rome, 1974), pp. 95-106, especially pp. 103ff., on the role of the Yemenite Jewish king Dhū Nuwās, now much better known, thanks to the discovery and decipherment of two important Himyaritic inscriptions of A.D. 518-519.

16. On Judaeo-Arabic, see Joshua Blau, *Dikduk ha-ʿAravit ha-Yehudit shel yeme ha-benayyim* (Jerusalem, 1961); idem, *Judaeo-Arabic Literature: Selected Texts* (Jerusalem, 1980); idem, *The Emergence and Linguistic Background of Judaeo-Arabic* (Jerusalem, 1981).

17. On possible connections between Rabbinic and Islamic law, see Goitein, *Studies*, chap. 6, "The Birth-Hour of Muslim Law," pp. 126-134; idem, "The Interplay of Jewish and Islamic Laws," *Jewish Law in Legal History and the Modern World*, ed. Bernard S. Jackson (Leiden, 1980), pp. 61-77; Hava Lazarus-Yafeh, "Bayn halakha ba-yahudut le-halakha ba-Islam: ʿal kama hevdelim ʿiqariyim u-mishniyim," in *Tarbiz* 51 (1982): 207-225; Robert Brunschvig, "Her-

meneutique normative dans le Judaïsme et dans l'Islam," in *Atti della Accademia Nazionale dei Lincei*, series 8, *Rendiconti, class. Sci mor. stor. fil* 30 (1975) (Rome, 1976): 1-20; idem, "Voeu ou serment: Droit comparé du Judaïsme et de l'Islam," in *Hommage à Georges Vajda* (Louvain, 1980), pp. 125-134.

18. For a brief interpretative essay, see G. Vajda, "Le 'Kalām' dans la penseé religieuse juive du Moyen Age," *Revue de l'Histoire des Religions* (1973), pp. 143-160.

19. N. Wieder, "Hashpaʿot Islamiyot ʿal ha-pulhan ha-Yehudi," *Melila* 2 (1946): 37-120.

20. See L. A. Mayer, *L'Art Juif en terre d'Islam* (Geneva, 1959).

21. See Mordechai A. Friedman, "Polygyny in Jewish Tradition and Practice: New Sources from the Cairo Geniza," *Proceedings of the American Academy for Jewish Research* 49 (1982): 33-68.

22. See, for example, Ibn Isḥāq, *Sīrat Raṣul Allāh*, ed. F. Wüstenfeld (Göttingen, 1858-1860), pp. 684ff.; Engish translation by A. Guillaume, *The Life of Muhammad* (London, 1955), pp. 461ff. The treatment of the fate of the Banū Qurayẓa by modern scholars, both Muslim and Western, may serve as a touchstone of attitudes and preferences. An interesting point was made by Professor Rudi Paret, in his *Mohammed und der Koran* (Stuttgart, 1957), p. 112: "As regards the massacre of the Banū Qurayẓa, it must be borne in mind that the usages of warfare at that time were in many respects more brutal than those to which we are accustomed in the age of the Geneva convention. But Muhammad must be measured by the standards of his own time."

23. See *EI*¹, s.v. "Takīya" (by R. Strothmann).

24. Qur'ān, V,7: "The food of those who were given the Book is lawful for you." In practice this was usually restricted to Jews. For an Ottoman ruling, see Düzdag, *Seyhülislâm Ebussuûd*, p. 91. The Ottoman qāḍī's registers show that it was commonplace for Muslims to buy meat from Jewish butchers (see Amnon Cohen, *Jewish Life under Islam: Jerusalem in the 16th Century*, in press).

25. On the recent attempts to assign a new and larger significance to the Prophet's struggles with the Jews, see p. 187.

26. Moshe Perlmann, "The Medieval Polemics between Islam and Judaism," in *Religion in a Religious Age*, ed. S. D. Goitein (Cambridge, Mass., 1974), p. 106. On polemics in general, see M. Steinschneider, *Polemische und apologetische Literatur in arabischer Sprache zwischen Muslimen, Christen und Juden* (Leipzig, 1877); I. Goldziher, "Ueber Muhammedanische Polemik gegen Ahl al-Kitab," *Zeit-*

schrift der Deutschen Morgenländischen Gesellschaft 32 (1878): 341-387.

27. Al-Bāqillānī, *Al-Tamhīd*, ed. al-Khudayrī and Abū Riḍā (Cairo, 1366/1947), pp. 131-148; ed. R. J. McCarthy (Beirut, 1957), pp. 160-190; discussed by Robert Brunschvig, "L'Argumentation d'un théologien musulman du Xe siècle contre le Judaïisme," in *Homenaje a Millas-Vallicrosa*, I (Barcelona, 1954), pp. 225-241.

28. Ibn Ḥazm, *Al-Radd ʿala ibn al-Naghrīla al-Yahūdī wa-rasāʾil ukhrā*, ed. Ihṣān ʿAbbās (Cairo, 1380/1960); discussed in M. Perlmann, "Eleventh-Century Andalusian Authors on the Jews of Granada," *Proceedings of the American Academy for Jewish Research* 18 (1949): 271-284; and E. García Gomez, "Polémica religiosa entre Ibn Hazm y Ibn al-Nagrila," *al-Andalus* 4 (1936): 1-28. According to a story told by Yāqūt (*Irshād al-Arīb*, V, ed. D. S. Margoliouth, [London, 1911], p. 114), the Damascene historian Ibn ʿAsākir interrupted a series of discourses he was giving on the history of the early caliphate to dictate a discourse "in condemnation of the Jews and on their being doomed to eternal hellfire." No copy appears to have survived.

29. The view that all religions are equally false appears, as one would expect, not as an opinion that a writer puts forward as his own, but as an abominable error that he ascribes to an adversary. The best-known example occurs in a letter allegedly written by a tenth-century Ismaʿili leader, and cited by Sunni authors as an example of Ismaʿili sedition. See ʿAbd al-Qāhir al-Baghdādī, *Kitāb al-Farq bayn al-Firaq* (Cairo, n.d.), p. 281; English translation in A. S. Halkin, *Moslem Schisms and Sects* (Tel-Aviv, 1935), pp. 136-137. For a more epigrammatic version, which later also circulated in Europe, see Niẓām al-Mulk, *Siyāsat-nāme*, ed. Schefer (Paris, 1891), chap. 47, p. 197; French translation (Paris, 1893), p. 288; English translation by Hubert Darke, *The Book of Government* (London, 1960), p. 236. Similar sentiments are suggested in some of the quatrains of ʿUmar Khayyām. The more positive view, that all religions are true, appears in Sufi writings. For some examples, see Goldziher, *Introduction*, pp. 151-152. On some aspects of Muslim humanism, see also S. D. Goitein, "The Concept of Mankind in Islam," in *History and the Idea of Mankind*, ed. W. Wager (New Mexico, 1971), pp. 72-91.

30. Ibn Ṣāʿid al-Andalusī, *Kitāb Ṭabaqāt al-Umam* (Cairo, n.d.), pp. 131-136; another edition by Cheikho in *Machriq* (Beirut, 1912);

French translation by Régis Blachère, *Livre des Catégories des Nations* (Paris, 1935), pp. 155-161.

31. See Franz Rosenthal, "The Influences of the Biblical Tradition on Muslim Historiography," in *Historians of the Middle East*, ed. Bernard Lewis and P. M. Holt (London, 1962), pp. 35-45.

32. Karl Jahn, *Die Geschichte der Kinder Israels des Rašīd ad-Dīn* (Vienna, 1973) (introduction, text, translation, and commentary); cf. idem, "Die 'Geschichte der Kinder Israels' in der islamischen Historiographie," *Anzeiger der phil. hist. Klasse der Österreichischer Akademie der Wissenschaften* 109 (1972): 67-76.

33. W. F. Fischel, "Ibn Khaldūn: On the Bible, Judaism and the Jews," in *Ignace Goldziher Memorial Volume*, II (Jerusalem, 1956), pp. 147-171; idem, "Ibn Khaldun and Josippon," in *Homenaje a Millas-Vallicrosa*, I (Barcelona, 1954), pp. 587-589.

34. Goitein, *Mediterranean Society*, I, p. 211; idem, "Jewish society," *JWH*, pp. 175ff.

35. Text published by L. Ginzberg, *Genizah Studies in Memory of D. Solomon Schechter* (New York, 1928), pp. 310-312; discussed by B. Lewis. "On That Day: A Jewish Apocalyptic Poem on the Arab Conquests," in *Mélanges d'Islamologie: Volume dédié à la mémoire de Armand Abel* (Leiden, 1974), pp. 197-200; cf. idem, "An Apocalyptic Vision of Islamic History," *Bulletin of the School of Oriental and African Studies* 13 (1950): 308-338.

36. See *EI²*, s.v. "Abū 'Īsā" (by S. M. Stern); *Encyclopaedia Judaica*, s.v. (by Zvi Avneri).

37. Cited in S. W. Baron, *A Social and Religious History of the Jews*, VIII, p. 342, n. 91. Cf. *Judah Hallevi's Kitab al Khazari*, 2d ed., tr. Hartwig Hirschfeld (London, 1931), p. 69.

38. Moshe Perlmann, ed., *Saʿd b. Manṣur Ibn Kammūna's Examination of the Inquiries into the Three Faiths* (Berkeley and Los Angeles, 1967), p. 102.

39. See *EI²*, s.v. "Kaʿb al-Aḥbār" (by M. Schmitz).

40. See *EI²*, s.v.v. "Abū ʿUbayda" (by H.A.R. Gibb), and "Abū Ḥanīfa al-Nuʿmān" (by J. Schacht).

41. See *EI²*, s.v. "Ibn Killis" (by M. Canard).

42. Ibn Abī ʿUṣaybiʿa, *Kitāb ʿUyūn al-Anbāʾ fī Ṭabaqāt al-Aṭibbāʾ*, I (Cairo, 1299/1883), p. 260, in the biography of Ibn al-Tilmīdh; for the same author's biography of Abu'l-Barakāt, see pp. 278-280. See further *EI²*, s.v. "Abu'l-Barakāt" (by S. Pines).

43. See Goitein, *Mediterranean Society*, II, pp. 302ff.

44. Samaw'al al-Maghribī, *Ifḥām al-Yahūd*, ed. and tr. Moshe Perlmann (New York, 1964).

45. Ibn al-Qiftī, *Ta'rīkh al-Ḥukamā'*, ed. J. Lippert (Leipzig, 1903), pp. 317-319.

46. Ibn Ḥajar, *Al-Durar al-Kāmina*, III (Hyderabad, 1349), pp. 232-233; al-Maqrīzī, *Kitāb al-Sulūk*, II/3, ed. Muṣṭafā Ziāda (Cairo, 1958), pp. 189-190; al-Nuwayrī, *Nihāyat al-arab*, XXX, pp. 122-123; Dawlatshah, *The Tadhkirat ash-Shu'arā'*, ed. E. G. Browne (London, 1901), p. 330; Walter J. Fischel, "Azarbaijan in Jewish History," *Proceedings of the American Academy for Jewish Research* 32 (1953): 18-19.

47. See, for example, the ban imposed by the merchants' guild of Fez on Muslim craftsmen and merchants descended from Islamized Jews; details in *Enquête sur les corporations musulmanes d'artisans et de commerçants au Maroc* by Louis Massignon, reprinted from *Revue du Monde Musulman* (1925), pp. 221-224. Some of the Almohad rulers even subjected converted Jews and their descendants to certain restrictions on dress and on intermarriage with old Muslim families. See Hirschberg, *A History of the Jews in North Africa*, I, pp. 201ff.

48. From Maimonides' Epistle to the Jews of Yemen, written in 1172. English translation in Stillman, *The Jews of Arab Lands*, p. 241; text in *Iggeret Teman*, ed. A. Halkin (New York, 1952), p. 94; cf. S. D. Goitein, *Interfaith Relations in Medieval Islam* (New York, 1973), p. 27.

49. On "charges" of Jewish ancestry, see I. Goldziher, *Muhammedanische Studien*, I (Halle, 1889), pp. 203-205; English translation, *Muslim Studies*, I (London, 1967), pp. 186-188.

50. See *EI²*, s.v. "'Abdallāh b. Sabā" (by M.G.S. Hodgson). For earlier discussions, see I. Friedlander, "'Abd Allāh ibn Sabā'," in *Zeitschrift für Assyriologie* (1909), pp. 296-327; (1910), pp. 1-47; G. Levi Della Vida, "Il Califfato di Ali secondo il *Kitāb Ansāb al-Aśrāf* di al-Balādurī," in *Rivista degli Studi Orientali* (1912), p. 495, note 2.

51. See *EI²*, s.v. "Ibn al-Rāwandī" (by P. Kraus [G. Vajda]).

52. See *EI²*, s.v. "Abd Allāh b. Maymūn" (by S. M. Stern). On his alleged Jewish origins, see B. Lewis, *The Origins of Ismailism* (Cambridge, Eng., 1940; reprinted New York, 1975), pp. 67-69.

53. *Torlak* means an unbroken colt and hence, figuratively, a wild youth. Some early sources speak of "a *torlak* called Hu Kemal." On this rebellion, see F. Babinger, "Schejch Bedr ed-Din," *Der Islam* 2

(1921): 1-106; Abdülbaki Gölpinarlı, *Simavna Kadısı oğlu Şeyh Bedreddin* (Istanbul, 1966); J. Hammer, *Histoire de l'Empire Ottoman,* II (Paris, 1835), pp. 182-186; Ismail Hakkı Uzunçarşılı, *Osmanlı Tarihi,* I (Ankara, 1961), pp. 363-364, 531-532, 565.

54. Goitein, *Jews and Arabs,* p. 73.

55. Amnon Cohen, *Jewish Life.*

THREE. LATE MEDIEVAL AND EARLY MODERN PERIODS

1. For a discussion of the effects of the coming of the steppe peoples on the Muslim polity, see Lewis, *Islam in History,* pp. 179-198.

2. A critical bibliographical survey of scholarly publications on the history of all these communities, down to ca. 1670, will be found in the article by Mark R. Cohen, "The Jews under Islam," cited in chap. 1, note 1. For a comprehensive, classified bibliography on North Africa, see Robert Attal, *Les Juifs d'Afrique du Nord: Bibliographie* (Jerusalem, 1973). Bibliographical and documentary material will also be found in two Israeli periodicals devoted to the history and culture of Jews in the Islamic lands: *Sefunot* (1956-) and *Pe'amim* (1979-), both published by the Ben-Zvi Institute in Jerusalem. The University of Haifa has also published the first of what is announced as a series of collections of studies devoted to "research and monographs on the subject of Sephardic Jewry and Jews from Islamic countries" (*Mikkedem Umiyyam,* I [Haifa, 1981]). For a general survey, with documentary and bibliographical appendices, of the history of the Jews in Islamic lands from the end of the Middle Ages to the mid-nineteenth century, see Yosef Tobi, Jacob Barnai, and Shalom Bar-Asher, *Toldot ha-Yehudim be-artzot ha-Islam,* ed. Shmuel Ettinger (Jerusalem, 1981). Graetz's account of the Ottoman Jews, though based exclusively on Jewish and European sources, is still of value. Baron's history has already covered the Islamic lands in the later Middle Ages; volume 18, dealing with the Ottomans, appeared when this book was already in proof.

3. These responsa were extensively used by some earlier scholars, notably Joseph Nehama, *Histoire des Israelites de Salonique,* 5 vols. (Salonika and Paris, 1935-1959); I. S. Emmanuel, *Histoire des Israélites de Salonique,* I (Paris, 1936); S. Rozanes, *Divrê Yemê Yisrael be-Togarma* (= *Korot ha-Yehudim be-Turkiya ve-artzot ha-Qedem*), vol. I² (Tel-Aviv, 1930); vols. 2-5 (Sofia, 1934-1938); vol. 6 (Jerusalem, 1945); and more recently in a series of articles by J. Hacker. For a bibliography of responsa collections, see Boaz Cohen, *Kuntres*

ha-Teshuvot (Budapest, 1930; reprinted Westmead, 1970). In general, see Jacob M. Landau, "Hebrew Sources for the Socio-Economic History of the Ottoman Empire," *Der Islam* 54 (1977): 205-212, where further bibliography is given.

4. A curious exception is a manuscript of an early Turkish anonymous chronicle, transcribed in Hebrew letters; Ugo Marazzi, *Tevarih-i Al-i Osman: Cronaca anonima ottomana in trascrizione ebraica* (Naples, 1980).

5. The two works are (1) Eliyahu Kapsali, *Seder Eliyahu Zuta*, 2 vols., ed. Aryeh Shmuelevitz et al. (Jerusalem, 1975-1977); some excerpts were published at a much earlier date by M. Lattes, *De Vita et scriptis Eliae Kapsalii* (Padua, 1869); (2) Joseph ha-Cohen, *Sefer Divrê ha-Yamim le-malkhê Tsarefat u-malkhê bêt Ottoman ha-Toger*, printed in Sabbionetta in 1554 and reprinted in Amsterdam in 1733 and in Lemberg in 1859. An English translation by C.H.F. Bialloblotsky (*The Chronicles of Rabbi Joseph ben Joshua ben Meir the Sephardi*, 2 vols. [London, 1836]) is hopelessly inaccurate. For discussions of these (and other) Jewish historiographical works, see Moritz Steinschneider, *Die Geschichtsliteratur der Juden* (Frankfurt, 1905), pp. 93-94, 102.

6. R. D. Barnett, "The Correspondence of the Mahamad of the Spanish and Portuguese Congregation of London during the Seventeenth and Eighteenth Centuries," in *Translations of the Jewish Historical Society of England* 20 (1964): 1-50, especially pp. 23ff.

7. For examples of studies based wholly or in part on these archives, see A. C. Wood, *A History of the Levant Company* (London, 1935; reprinted 1964); Paolo Preto, *Venezia e i Turchi* (Florence, 1975); Erik Årub, *Studier i Engelsk og Tysk Handelshistorie* (Copenhagen, 1907); André Raymond, *Artisans et commerçants au Caire au XVIIIᵉ siècle*, 2 vols. (Damascus, 1973-1974); Robert Mantran, *Istanbul dans la seconde moitié du XVIIᵉ siècle* (Paris, 1962); A. H. de Groot, *The Ottoman Empire and the Dutch Republic: A History of the Earliest Diplomatic Relations, 1610-1630* (Leiden-Istanbul, 1978). These and other similar works throw some light on the frequent commercial and occasional diplomatic role of Jews in Ottoman-European relations.

8. An excellent guide to the travel literature may be found in Shirley Howard Weber, *Voyages and Travels in Greece, the Near East and Adjacent Regions, Made Previous to the Year 1801* (Princeton, 1953); idem, *Voyages and Travels in the Near East Made During the XIX Century* (Princeton, 1952). For Jewish travelers, Abraham Ya'ari's

bibliographies and collections have to a large extent superseded the earlier works of J. Eisenstein and others.

9. See, for example, the chronicles of Rashid, anno 1077 (1666-1667), on the execution of a Jew and a Turkish woman for fornication; 1128 (1716), on the execution of three Jews for beating a Turkish boy; Çelebizade, 1139 (1726-1727), on the removal of Jewish dwellings to make room for the Yeni Jami mosque; 1159 (1746), on the execution of several Jews for assaulting a Turk.

10. For general accounts of the archives, see *EI²*, "Başvekâlet arşivi" (by B. Lewis); Paul Dumont, "Les Archives ottomanes de Turquie," in *Les Arabes par leurs archives (XVIᵉ-XXᵉ siècles)*, ed. Jacques Berque and Dominique Chevallier (Paris, 1976), pp. 229-243; S. J. Shaw, "Archival Sources for Ottoman History: The Archives of Turkey," *Journal of the American Oriental Society* 80 (1960): 1-12; Midhat Sertoglu, *Muhteva bakımından Başvekâlet Arşivi* (Ankara, 1955); Atillâ Çetin, *Başbakanlîk Arşivi Kılavuzu* (Istanbul, 1979); J. Reychman and A. Zajaczkowski, *Handbook of Ottoman Turkish Diplomatics* (Hague-Paris, 1968). On the Tapu series, see Ö. L. Barkan, "Les grands recensements de la population et du territoire de l'Empire ottoman," *Revue de la faculté des sciences économiques de l'Université d'Istanbul* 2 (1940): 21-34, 168-179; idem, "Essai sur les donnés statistiques des registres de recensement dans l'Empire ottoman au XVIème et XVIIème siècles," *Journals of the Economic and Social History of the Orient* (1957), pp. 36-39; idem, "Daftar-i Khākānī," in *EI²*.

11. Ömer Lûtfi Barkan, "Quelques observations sur l'organisation économique et sociale des villes ottomanes des XVIᵉ et XVIIᵉ siècles," in *Recueils Société Jean Bodin, La Ville*, II (Brussels, 1955), p. 295.

12. Mark Alan Epstein, *The Ottoman Jewish Communities and Their Role in the Fifteenth and Sixteenth Centuries* (Freiburg, 1980).

13. B. Lewis, "Judaeo-Osmanica," in *Thought and Action: Essays in Memory of Simon Rawidowicz on the 25th Anniversary of his Death*, ed. A. A. Greenbaum and Alfred L. Ivry (1983), pp. I-VIII.

14. Amnon Cohen, *Yehudê Yerushalayim ba-mea ha-shesh'esreh lefi te'udot Turkiyot shel bet ha-din ha-Shar'i* (Jerusalem, 1976). For an example of this type of documentation, from the registers of Bursa, see Halil Inalcik, "Osmanlı Idare, Sosyal ve Ekonomik Tarihiyle ilgili Belgeler," *Belgeler: Türk Tarih Belgeleri Dergisi* 10 (1980): 1-91, especially documents 2, 9, 24, 46, 75, 89, 107, 115, 118, 134, 151, 156. The 190 documents published in this study were all written between February 1484 and January 1486. For regesta, without texts,

from the registers of Ankara, from March 1583 to February 1584, see Halit Ongan, *Ankara'nın I Numaralı Şer'iye Sicili* (Ankara, 1958), especially numbers 107, 654, 997, 1112, 1114. Examples from Sofia in Galab D. Galabov, *Die Protokollbücher des Kadiamtes Sofia*, ed. H. W. Duda (Munich, 1960); index, s.v. "Jude."

15. A number of articles dealing with various aspects of Ottoman Jewish history will be found in *Christians and Jews in the Ottoman Empire*, 2 vols; ed. Benjamin Braude and Bernard Lewis (New York, 1982). A short classified bibliography is appended. This, and the relevant sections of Mark Cohen's articles, include the writings of early modern chroniclers such as Franco, Rozanes, and Galante; the second generation studies in Rabbinic responsa (e.g., Goodblatt, Emmanuel, and Zimmels); and more recent scholarly monographs based on Turkish archives (Heyd, Ankori, Amnon Cohen, Epstein, etc.). To these should be added a number of articles by Haim Gerber, dealing with the economic life of Ottoman Jewry, especially in Bursa, and based on both Turkish and Rabbinic sources. See especially *Sefunot* m.s. 1 (1980); *Zion* 14 (1980); *Michael* 7 (1982), and, in English, *JQR* 71 (1981).

16. Braude and Lewis, *Christians and Jews*, I, pp. 11-12, 117ff. (by J. R. Hacker); Barkan, "Osmanlı Imparatorluğunda bir iskân ve Kolonizyon Metodu olarak sürgünler," *Istanbul Üniversitesi Iktisat Fakültesi Mecmuası*, 11 (1949-1950): 524-561; 13 (1951-1952): 56-78; 15 (1953-1954): 209-236; idem, "Les déportations dans l'Empire ottoman," *Revue de la faculté des sciences économiques de l'Université d'Istanbul* 2 (1949-1950): 67-131; Halil Inalcik, "Ottoman Methods of Conquest," *Studia Islamica* 2 (1954), especially pp. 122ff.; idem, *EI²*, s.v. "Istanbul," Epstein, index. For a study, with documents, of deportations to and from Manisa, in Anatolia, see M. Çagatay Uluçay, "Sürgünler," *Belleten* 15 (1951): 507-592. Several of Uluçay's documents refer to the deportation or pardoning of Jewish malefactors (e.g., pp. 519, 532, 543, 554, 587, 591).

17. Jewish evidence in Kapsali, *Seder Eliyahu Zuta*, I, pp. 81ff.; cf. Rozanes, *Divrê Yemê*, I, pp. 21-22, and Galante, *Histoire des Juifs d'Istanbul*, I (Istanbul, 1941), pp. 3-5.

18. Topkapı Palace Archives D9524. This document was apparently first published, in excerpts, in the Turkish newspaper *Vatan*, of July 26, 1948. It was analyzed from there by Alfons Maria Schneider, "Die Bevölkerung Konstantinopels im XV. Jahrhundert," *Nachrichten der Akademie des Wissenschaften in Göttingen: Phil. Hist. Klasse* 9 (1949): 240ff.; and again, from the original and at

greater length, by Ekrem Hakkı Ayverdi, *Fatih devri sonlarında Istanbul mahalleleri, şehrin iskânı ve nüfusu* (Ankara, 1958), pp. 80-81. See further, Halil Inalcik, *EI²*, s.v. "Istanbul," pp. 238-239; and Robert Mantran, "Règlements fiscaux ottomans: La police des marchés de Stamboul au début du XVIᵉ siècle," *Cahiers de Tunisie* 14 (1956): 238, note 68.

19. Arnold von Harff, *Die Pilgerfahrt des Ritters A.v.H. . . . in den Jahren 1496 bis 1499 vollendet,* ed. E. von Groote (Cologne, 1860); English translation by Malcolm Letts (London, 1946), p. 244; Cristóbal de Villalon (attrib.), *Viaje de Turquia* (Madrid, 1905), p. 146 (the author of this work was in fact not Villalon but Andrés Laguna; see Marcel Bataillon, *Le Docteur Laguna: Autour du Voyage en Turquie* [Paris, 1958], pp. 712-735); *The Travels of John Sanderson in the Levant, 1584-1602,* ed. Sir William Foster (London, 1931), pp. 82-83; Uriel Heyd, "The Jewish Communities of Istanbul in the Seventeenth Century," *Oriens* 6 (1953): 299-314; Epstein, *Ottoman Jewish Communities,* pp. 178-188.

20. See, for example, S. D. Goitein, " 'Eduyot qedumot min ha-Geniza 'al qehillat Saloniki," *Sefunot* 2 (1971-1978): 11-33.

21. Lewis, "Judaeo-Osmanica," pp. V-VI; idem, *Notes and Documents from the Turkish Archives* (Jerusalem, 1952), pp. 25-28; Epstein, *Ottoman Jewish Communities,* passim. See further, Heath W. Lowry, "Portrait of a City: The Population and Topography of Ottoman Selânik (Thessaloniki) in the year 1478," *Diptykha* (Athens) 2 (1980-1981): 254-292.

22. Documents from the *Muhimme* registers, edited and translated in Lewis, *Notes and Documents,* pp. 28-34. In an important article, Uriel Heyd ("Teʿudot Turkiyyot ʿal Yehudê Tsefat ba-meʾa ha-16," *Yerushalayim* 2/5 [1955]: 128-135) published the texts of five further documents from the *Muhimme* registers, as follows: (1) 981/1573, penal deportation to Cyprus; (2) 986/1579, deportation dropped; (3) 986/1578, confirms; (4) 987/1579 (order to Cyprus), authorizing the settlement there of Jews intercepted on their way from Salonika to Safed; (5) 992/1584 (order to Damascus), calls for an investigation of the synagogue in Safed. (Some translated in Heyd, *Ottoman Documents on Palestine 1552-1615* [Oxford, 1960], pp. 167-169.)

23. *Tarih-i Peçevi,* I (Istanbul, 1280/1863-1864), p. 99.

24. Joseph ha-Kohen (1496-1575), *Divrê ha-Yamim le-Malkhê Tsarefat u-vêt Ottoman he-Toger,* II (Amsterdam, 1733), p. 76; Bialloblotsky, *Chronicles,* II (London, 1835-1836), p. 58. Cf. A. Galante,

Turcs et Juifs (Istanbul, 1932), pp. 28-29; idem, *Türkler ve Yahudiler* (Istanbul, 1947), p. 17.

25. Demetrius Cantemir, *A History of the Growth and Decay of the Ottoman Empire (1300-1683)*, from Latin into English by N. Tindal (London, 1734), p. 281, note 10; Galante, *Türkler*, p. 18.

26. Braude and Lewis, *Christians and Jews*, pp. 24ff.; see also the contributions by Benjamin Braude and Mark A. Epstein in this volume. On the structure of the rabbinate in the Ottoman Empire, see the study by Leah Bornstein, based on rabbinical sources, in Hirschberg, *East and Maghreb*, pp. 223-258.

27. B. Lewis, "The Privilege Granted by Mehmed II to His Physician," *Bulletin of the School of Oriental and African Studies* 14 (1952): 554. For a critical and annotated edition of the Hebrew text of this responsum, see *Melila* (Manchester) 5 (1955): 169-176.

28. Lewis, "The Privilege," passim.

29. Izzet [Kumbaracızade], *Hekim-Başı odası, ilk eczane, Baş-Lala kulesi* (Istanbul, 1933); Uriel Heyd, "Moses Hamon, Chief Jewish Physician to Sultan Süleyman the Magnificent," *Oriens* 16 (1963): 156-157; Eleazar Birnbaum, "Hekim Yâqub, Physician to Sultan Mehemmed the Conqueror," *Harofe Haivri: The Hebrew Medical Journal* 1 (1961): 222-250. According to an Ottoman document written ca. 1607-1608, the palace medical staff consisted of forty-one Jewish and twenty-one Muslim physicians. By the mid-seventeenth century the numbers and proportions had shrunk to four Jews and fourteen Muslims.

30. Heyd, "Moses Hamon," pp. 168-169.

31. Metin And, *A History of Theatre and Popular Entertainment in Turkey* (Ankara, 1963-1964).

32. See B. Lewis, *The Emergence of Modern Turkey*, 2d ed. (London, 1968), pp. 41-42, 46-47, 50-52, where further sources are cited.

33. The relationship between the Jews and the janissaries has been discussed by both early and recent historians. See, for example, Franco, *Essai*, pp. 130, 133-134, 139; S. A. Rozanes, *Korot ha-Yehudim be-Turkiya uve-artzot ha-Qedem* (Jerusalem, 1945), pp. 13ff.; A. Galante, *Histoire des juifs d'Istanbul*, II (Istanbul, 1942), pp. 55ff.; Lûtfi, *Tarih-i Lûtfi*, I (Istanbul, 1290-1328), pp. 245-246; II, pp. 203-204; Ismail Hakkı Uzunçarşılı, *Osmanlı Devleti Teşkilâtından Kapıkulu Ocakları*, I, *Acemi Ocağı ve Yeniçeri Ocağı* (Ankara, 1943), pp. 406-410, 495; Robert W. Olson, "Jews in the Ottoman Empire and Their Role in Light [sic] of New Documents," *Tarih Enstitüsü Dergisi* (Istanbul) 7-8 (1976-1977): 119-144; cf. idem in *Jewish*

Social Studies 42 (1979): 75-88. On the supply of cloth to the janissaries, see Halil Sahillioğlu, "Yeniçeri çuhası ve II Bayezid'in son yıllarında yeniçeri Çuha Muhasebesi," *Güney-Doğu Avrupa Araştırmaları Dergisi* 2-3 (1973-1974): 415-467.

34. *Navigations* (Antwerp, 1576), p. 246.

35. Vicente Roca, *Historia en la qual se trata de la origen y guerras que han tenido los Turcos* . . . (Valencia, 1556), fol. li verso; cited in *The Turks in MDXXXIII: a series of drawings made in that year at Constantinople by Peter Coeck of Aelst . . . reproduced . . . in facsimile with an introduction by Sir William Stirling Bart* (London and Edinburgh, 1873), p. 50.

36. Franz Kobler, ed., *Letters of Jews* . . . , I (London, 1953), pp. 283-285. Cf. H. Graetz, *Geschichte der Juden*, VIII (Leipzig, 1875), pp. 423-425. The Hebrew text was published by A. Jellinek (*Kuntres Gezerat 4856 [= 1095-96] . . . zur Geschichte der Kreuzzüge* [Leipzig, 1854], pp. 14ff.). Graetz dates the letter ca. 1454.

37. Samuel Usque, *A Consolaçam as Tribulacões de Israel*, III, ed. Mendes Remedio (Coimbra, 1906), liii; cf. English translation by Martin A. Cohen, *Consolation for the Tribulations of Israel* (Philadelphia, 1965), p. 231.

38. F. von Pastor, *The History of the Popes*, XIV (London, 1924), pp. 274ff.; Graetz, *Geschichte der Juden*, IX (Leipzig, 1877), pp. 42-43, 349ff. There is an extensive modern literature, most of it somewhat romanticized, on Gracia Mendes and Joseph Nasi. For some Turkish documents, see Saffet, "Yosef Nasi," in *Tarih-i Osmani Encümeni Mecmuasi*, 3d year (1328), pp. 982-993; idem, "Doña Gracia Mendes," ibid., pp. 1158-1160; A. Galante, *Don Joseph Nassi, duc de Naxos, d'après de nouveaux documents* (Istanbul, 1913).

39. Examples in Binswanger, *Untersuchungen*, pp. 160ff. and passim.

40. John Sanderson, *Travels*, p. 202; Joseph P. de Tournefort, *A Voyage into the Levant*, II (London, 1718), p. 74; French text in idem, *Voyage d'un botaniste*, II, ed. Stéphane Yerasimos (Paris, 1982), p. 92.

41. Michele Febure (attrib.), *Teatro della Turchia* (Venice, 1681), pp. 314-315; cf. Mantran, *Istanbul*, pp. 60-62. The author of this book was in fact a French Capuchin called Jean-Baptiste de Saint-Aignan (see Clemente da Terzorio, "Il vero autore del *Teatro della Turchia* e *Stato Presente della Turchia*," *Collectanea Franciscana* 3

(1933): 384-395; cf. Paolo Preto, *Venezia e i Turchi* (Florence, 1975), pp. 293-294.

42. A. Ubicini, *Lettres sur la Turquie*, II (Paris, 1854), pp. 377ff.

43. B. Lewis, "A Letter from Little Menahem," in *Studies in Judaism and Islam Presented to Shelomo Dov Goitein* (Jerusalem, 1981), pp. 181-184.

44. See J. H. Mordtmann, "Die jüdischen Kira im Serai der Sultane," *Mitteilungen des Seminars für orientalischen Sprachen zu Berlin* 32/II (1929): pp. 1-38; further details in Orhan Burian, *The Report of Lello: Third English Ambassador to the Sublime Porte* (Ankara, 1952), and Sanderson, *Travels*, pp. 85, 185, 188, 201-204.

45. See Attilio Milano, *Storia degli Ebrei Italiani nel Levante* (Florence, 1949).

46. Jabartī, ʿAjāʾib, I, pp. 21ff. Jabarti gives the text of a contemporary "poem," celebrating the downfall of the Jew.

47. Raymond, *Artisans et commerçants au Caire*, pp. 88, 452, 459-464, 487-488, 498-499, 625-626, 746-747.

48. A. C. Wood, *A History of the Levant Company* (London, 1964), pp. 155-156, 214-215.

49. The best treatment of his career, and of its significance in Jewish history, will be found in the great work of G. Scholem, *Sabbetai Ṣevi: The Mystical Messiah 1626-1676* (London, 1973; Hebrew original, Tel Aviv, 1957), Turkish sources are cited by Ibrahim Alâettin Gövsa, *Şabatay Sevi* (Istanbul, n.d.), especially pp. 46-52, and Abraham Galante, *Nouveaux Documents sur Sabbetai Sevi* (Istanbul, 1935). For a discussion, see Geoffrey L. Lewis and Cecil Roth, "New Light on the Apostasy of Sabbetai Zevi," *JQR* 52 (1963): 219-225.

50. For a brief account see *EI²*, s.v. "Dönme" (by M. Perlmann). For a Turkish view, see Selahattin Galip, *Belgelerle Türkiye'de Dönmeler ve Dönmelik* (Istanbul, 1977).

51. Texts edited by Heyd, "'Alilot," *Sefunot* 5 (1961): 137-149; cf. Yaakov Barna'i, "'Alilot dam ba-Imperiya ha-Ottomanit ba-me'ot ha-15-19," in *Sin'at Yisra'el le-doroteha* (Jerusalem, 1980), pp. 211-216.

52. Stillman, *The Jews of Arab Lands*, pp. 78-79.

53. Ibid., pp. 281-286.

54. This rule persisted until the French occupation. See Leven, *Alliance*, 1, pp. 348-372, and letters cited by David Littman in *Wiener Library Bulletin* 29, n.s. 37/38 (1976): 12ff.

55. Stillman, *The Jews of Arab Lands*, p. 84.

56. Details in W. J. Fischel, *Jews in the Economic and Political Life of Mediaeval Islam* (London, 1937), pp. 120ff.

57. On the Jews under Safavid rule, see W. J. Fischel, "Toldot yehudê Paras biyemê shoshelet ha-Safavidim," *Zion* 2 (1936-1937): 273-293; idem, "Ha-Yehudim be-Iran ba-meot ha-16-19," *Pe'amim* 6 (1980): 5-31; Amnon Netzer, "Redifot ushemadot be-toldot Ye-hudê Iran ba-mea ha-17," ibid., pp. 33-56. For a brief review of the literature of the history of the Jews in Iran and Central Asia, see Mark R. Cohen, "The Jews," p. 187 and bibliography.

58. W. Bacher, "Les Juifs de Perse au XVIIᵉ et au XVIIIᵉ siècle," *REJ* 103 (1906): 248. On these events, see further, Ezra Spicehandler, "The Persecution of the Jews of Isfahan under Shah 'Abbas II (1642-1666)," *Hebrew Union College Annual* 46 (1975): 331-356; Vera B. Moreen, "The Persecution of Iranian Jews during the Reign of Shah 'Abbas II (1642-1666)," ibid., 52 (1981): 275-309 (citing and examining a number of Jewish, Muslim, and Christian sources).

59. Jean de Thevenot, *Travels . . . into the Levant* (London, 1687), p. 110.

60. See I. Markon, "Otličitel'ni Znak dlya Evreev v Persii," *Zapiski Vostočnavo Otdelenya Imperatorskavo Russkavo Arkheologiskavo Obščestva* 23 (1915): 364-365. The wearing of a distinguishing patch is attested by both Western and Jewish travelers.

61. On Judaeo-Persian literature, see W. J. Fischel, "Israel in Iran," in *The Jews, their History, Culture, and Religion*, 3d ed., II, ed. L. Finkelstein (New York, 1960), pp. 1149-1190.

62. M. Zand, "Bukhara," in *Encyclopaedia Judaica Yearbook* (Jerusalem, 1976), pp. 183-192.

FOUR. END OF THE TRADITION

1. Stillman, *The Jews of Arab Lands*, p. 367, citing FO 174/10, in the Public Record Office.

2. See Sir Joshua Hassan, *The Treaty of Utrecht and the Jews of Gibraltar* (London, 1970); A.B.M. Serfaty, *The Jews of Gibraltar under British Rule* (Gibraltar, 1933).

3. On the Damascus affair, see Stillman, *The Jews of Arab Lands*, pp. 105-106, 393-402; and A. J. Brawer in *Encyclopaedia Judaica*, V, pp. 1249-1252, where a full bibliography is given. Scholarly stud-ies on the subject are based almost entirely on Jewish and Western documents. For a contemporary account by a Syrian Arab Christian,

see Mikhā'īl Mishāqa, *Al-Jawāb ʿala iqtirāḥ al-Aḥbāb*, ed. A. J. Rustum and Abū Shaqra (Beirut, 1955), pp. 132-136.

4. Heyd, "ʿAlilot," *Sefunot* 5 (1961): 137-149. For possible exceptions, see Galante, *Histoire des juifs d'Istanbul*, II, p. 125, citing *REJ* 17 (1888), on an alleged incident in San'a, Yemen, in 1633; idem, *Histoire des juifs d'Anatolie*, I (Istanbul, 1937), pp. 183, 185, on a minor incident in Izmir in 1774.

5. On blood libels, see J. Landau, *Jews in Nineteenth-Century Egypt* (New York, 1969), index; Franco, *Essai*, pp. 220-233; Leven, *Alliance*, I, pp. 387-392; A. Galante, *Histoire des Juifs d'Anatolie, les Juifs d'Izmir (Smyrne)* (Istanbul, 1937), pp. 183-199; idem, *Histoire des Juifs d'Istanbul*, II, pp. 125-136; idem, *Documents officiels turcs*, pp. 157-161, 214-240; idem, *Encore un nouveau recueil de documents concernant l'histoire des Juifs de Turquie: Etudes scientifiques* (Istanbul, 1953), pp. 43-45; Barna'i, "ʿAlilot dam." An anti-Jewish disturbance in Urmia, in Iran, was described by Charles Stuart, *Journal of a Residence in Northern Persia* (London, 1854), pp. 325-326: "Last month a Persian child was found dead in front of the house of a Jew at Ooroomiah. It had evidently died a natural death, but popular prejudice accused the Jew of murder, and the mob wished to massacre every member of that nation settled at Ooroomiah. The Ameer was applied to for permission to perpetrate this crime; he forbade the sanguinary bigots to touch a single Jew, but, impatient of delay, they had murdered, and afterwards burnt, the accused individual, before the return of the messenger. The remainder escaped death, but were forced to pay a considerable fine. I have not heard of any punishment being inflicted on the assassins." Such accusations and persecutions are not unusual, in both east and west. There is no indication, however, that the allegation of murder was given a ritual significance.

6. On a case in Shiraz, in 1910, see the reports of M. Nataf in *BAIU*, 3d series, 35 (1910): 179-191, cited in D. Littman, "Jews under Muslim Rule: The Case of Persia," *The Wiener Library Bulletin* 32 (1979), n.s. 49/50: 12-14. No cases appear in the standard works on North Africa. The reports in the *AIU* files on the blood libel in Damascus in 1890 are particularly full and instructive.

7. For examples, see Stillman, *The Jews of Arab Lands*, pp. 399-400, 403-405; and Landau, *Jews in . . . Egypt,* passim.

8. Harold Temperley, *England and the Near East: The Crimea* (London, 1936), pp. 443-444, citing FO/427, Palmerston to Ponsonby, no. 33 of 7 February 1841, and FO 78/535, report from Rose,

no. 28 of 29 March 1843. See further, F. S. Rodkey, "Lord Palmerston and the Regeneration of Turkey, 1830-1841," *Journal of Modern History* 2 (1930): 215-216.

9. Paul Goodman, *Moses Montefiore* (Philadelphia, 1925), p. 96, citing Louis Loewe, *Diaries of Sir Moses and Lady Montefiore* (London, 1890), p. 388.

10. Elie Kedourie, "The Alliance Israélite Universelle, 1860-1960," *Jewish Journal of Sociology* 9 (1967): 94. Two major histories of the *Alliance* were published on its fiftieth and hundredth anniversaries, by Narcisse Leven, *Alliance Israélite Universelle, cinquante ans d'histoire*, 2 vols. (Paris, 1911-1920), and by André Chouraqui, *Cent ans d'histoire: L'Alliance Israélite Universelle et la renaissance juive contemporaine (1860-1960)* (Paris, 1965). On the Islamic lands, see in particular Leven, 1, pp. 147-170, 340-396; 2, pp. 72-272; and Chouraqui, pp. 101-128. More recently, Paul Dumont has published a series of important articles on late Ottoman Jewish history, based in the main on the *Alliance* archives. See especially his "Jewish Communities in Turkey during the Last Decades of the Nineteenth Century in the Light of the Archives of the Alliance Israélite Universelle," in Braude and Lewis, *Christians and Jews*, I, pp. 209-242; "Une source pour l'étude des communautés juives de Turquie: Les archives de l'Alliance Israélite Universelle," *Journal Asiatique* 267 (1979): 101-135; "La structure sociale de la communauté juive de Salonique à la fin du dix-neuvième siècle," *Revue Historique* 263 (1980): 351-393. For material from the *Alliance* archives on North Africa and Iran see David Littman's articles in *The Wiener Library Bulletin* 27 (1975): 65-76; 29 (1976): 1-19; 32 (1979): 2-15; cf. idem, "Quelques aspects de la condition de dhimmi juifs d'Afrique du Nord avant la colonisation," *Yod: Revue des Études Hebraïques et juives modernes et contemporaines* 2 (1976): 1-32; idem, "Les Juifs en Perse avant les Pahlevi," *Les Temps Modernes* 34 (1979): 1910-1935. Much useful information will be found in the Bulletin of the *Alliance*, cited as *BAIU*.

11. Cf. the comments of Elie Kedourie, "The Alliance Israélite Universelle."

12. Charles MacFarlane, *Constantinople in 1828*, I (London, 1829), pp. 115-116.

13. G. Beauclerk, *Journey to Morocco* (London, 1828), p. 280.

14. Miss (Julia) Pardoe, *The City of the Sultan; and Domestic Manners of the Turks, in 1836*, II (London, 1837), pp. 361-363.

15. H. E. Wilkie Young, "Notes on the City of Mosul," enclosed

with dispatch no. 4, Mosul, January 28, 1909, in F. O. 195/2308; published in *Middle Eastern Studies* 7 (1971): 229-235 (cit. p. 232).

16. Arminius Vambery, *The Story of My Struggles* (London, n.d.), p. 395.

17. (Lord) George N. Curzon, *Persia and the Persian Question*, I (London, 1892), pp. 510-511; cf. I, pp. 165-166, 333, 380, 567; II, pp. 240, 244, 493. Among Jewish travelers the most informative by far is Jakob Eduard Polak, *Persien: Das Land und seine Bewohner*, 2 vols. (Leipzig, 1865). Polak, who spent some time in Iran as physician to the shāh and teacher at the medical school in Tehran, also wrote a separate article on the Jews. The history of the Jews in nineteenth-century Iran has been little studied, and before the coming of the *Alliance* representatives there are few documents. Such studies as exist rely mainly on Jewish and European travelers, supplemented by the local oral tradition. In addition to Littman's articles cited above, reference may be made to W. J. Fischel, "The Jews of Persia, 1795-1940," *Jewish Social Studies* 12 (1950): 119-160; Hanina Mizrahi, *Toldot Yehudê Paras u-meshorerêhem* (Jerusalem, 1966); Ḥabīb Levi, *Tārīkh-i Yahūd-i Irān*, III (Tehran, 1960). The *AIU* reports from Iran, where the school directors, for various reasons, became more involved in public affairs than their colleagues in the Ottoman Empire and North Africa, are particularly instructive.

18. John MacGregor, *The Rob Roy as the Jordan: A Canoe Cruise in Palestine, Egypt, and the Waters of Damascus* (London, 1869; 8th ed., 1904), p. 356.

19. On the expulsion from Jedda, see M. Abir, "Jewish Communities in the Arabian Peninsula between the End of the 18th and the Middle of the 19th Centuries," *Sefunot* 10 (1966): 635ff. (citing J. L. Burckhardt, *Travels in Arabia* [London, 1829], p. 15, and J. R. Wellsted, *Travels in Arabia* [London, 1838], p. 210). On Tetuan, see Stillman, *The Jews of Arab Lands*, p. 308, and idem, "Two Accounts of the Persecution of the Jews of Tetuan in 1790," *Michael: On the History of the Jews of the Diaspora* 5 (1978): 130-142 (citing Austrian and Arabic sources). On Baghdad, see Stillman, *The Jews of Arab Lands*, p. 347, and Abir, "Jewish Communities," p. 636. On Safed, see Stillman, *The Jews of Arab Lands*, pp. 340ff., and articles by M. Abir and I. Ben-Zvi in *Sefunot* 7 (1963). On Meshed, see Benjamin, *Eight Years in Asia and Africa*, pp. 195ff.; Curzon, *Persia and the Persian Question*, pp. 165-166; J. Wolff, *Narrative of a Mission to Bokhara in 1843-1845*, I (London, 1845), pp. 238-239; and II, pp. 172ff. On the outbreak, in Barfurush, see Curzon, I, p.

380, and A. H. Mounsey, *Journey through the Caucasus* (London, 1875), pp. 273-282. On this occasion, the *Alliance* made its first distribution of relief funds in Iran, through the good offices of the British minister.

20. Renzo De Felice, *Ebrei in un paese arabo: Gli ebrei nella Libia contemporanea tra colonialismo, nazionalismo arabo e Sionismo (1835-1970)* (Bologna, 1978), pp. 19ff.

21. Cf. above, pp. 64-65.

22. See, for example, the appeal submitted by the Jews of England to the shāh when he visited London in 1873; text in Littman, *Wiener Library Bulletin* (1979), pp. 5-7. The shāh received similar petitions in Paris, Berlin, Vienna, Amsterdam, Brussels, Rome, and Istanbul (*BAIU*, 1873[2], pp. 93-113).

23. There are few extensive modern studies on the history of the Jews in the Middle East and North Africa in the nineteenth and twentieth centuries. Egypt is the most comprehensively covered, by J. M. Landau, *Jews in Nineteenth-Century Egypt* (New York, 1969), and Gudrun Krämer, *Minderheit, Millet, Nation? Die Juden in Ägypten 1914-1952* (Wiesbaden, 1982). The Jews of Libya have been treated by a distinguished Italian historian, Renzo De Felice, *Ebrei in un Paese arabo*, cit. note 20 above. André N. Chouraqui, *Between East and West: A History of the Jews of North Africa* (Philadelphia, 1968), is mainly concerned with the modern period. The now extensive literature on North Africa is listed in Robert Attal, *Les Juifs d'Afrique du Nord: Bibliographie* (Jerusalem, 1973). For a general bibliography of the modern period, see *Asian and African Jews in the Middle East, 1860-1971*, ed. by H. J. Cohen and Zvi Yehuda (Jerusalem, 1976).

24. See Franco, *Essai*, pp. 130-135; Rozanes, *Ḳorot*, pp. 13ff.; Galante, *Histoire des Juifs d'Istanbul*, II, pp. 55-58; Ahmed Lûtfi, *Tarih-i Lûtfi*, I (Istanbul, 1290-1328/1873-1910), pp. 245-246; II, pp. 203-204.

25. See above, pp. 126-128.

26. Galante, *Documents officiels turcs*, pp. 7-27; idem, *Histoire des Juifs d'Istanbul*, I, pp. 76ff.; Rozanes, *Ḳorot*, pp. 27ff.

27. Attilio Milano, *Storia degli Ebrei*, pp. 169ff.

28. See J. Fraenkel, ed., *The Jews in Austria* (London, 1967), pp. 327-346.

29. Şinasi, *Külliyat*, IV (Ankara, 1960), pp. 43-46 (first printed in the newspaper *Tasvir-i Efkâr*, no. 52 of 4 Rajab 1279/26 December

1862); cf. Franco, pp. 164-166 and 278; Rozanes, *Korot*, pp. 70ff.; Galante, *Histoire des Juifs d'Istanbul*, I, pp. 130-131.

30. Anti-Jewish incidents in Iraq and Syria are reported toward the end of 1908, both in the diplomatic reports and in the Arabic press (e.g., *al-Muqattam*, no. 5933 of 1 October 1908, and no. 5973 of 19 November 1908). Cf. Neville Mandel, "Turks, Arabs and Jewish Immigration into Palestine, 1882-1914," in *St. Antony's Papers—Number 17, Middle Eastern Affairs Number 4*, ed. Albert Hourani (Oxford, 1965), pp. 94-95; idem, *The Arabs and Zionism before World War I* (Berkeley and Los Angeles, 1976), pp. 66ff.

31. Elie Kedourie, "Young Turks, Freemasons and Jews," *Middle Eastern Studies* 7 (1971): 89-104, reprinted in idem, *Arab Political Memoirs and Other Studies* (London, 1974), pp. 243-262. Lewis, *Emergence*, pp. 211-212; E. E. Ramsaur, *The Young Turks: Prelude to the Revolution of 1908* (Princeton, N.J., 1957), pp. 103-109. On the Young Turks and the Jews, see further Kandemir in *Yakın Tarihimiz*, II, pp. 243-244; and Feroz Ahmad, "Unionist Relations with the Greek, Armenian and Jewish Communities of the Ottoman Empire 1908-1914," in Braude and Lewis, *Christians and Jews*, I, pp. 425-428.

32. Feroz Ahmed, *The Young Turks: The Committee of Union and Progress in Turkish Politics, 1908-1914* (Oxford, 1969), pp. 28, 155.

33. Dumont, *Journal Asiatique* (1979), p. 112. The report cited by Dumont is one of a large number of similar type sent in from various centers, and prepared in response to a questionnaire sent out from *Alliance* headquarters in Paris.

34. Benjamin, *Eight Years in Asia and Africa*, pp. 211-213. Similar descriptions of the conditions of the Jews in Iran are given by other Jewish travelers, e.g., Ephraim Neimark, *Masaʿ be-eretz ha-Kedem*, ed. A. Yaʿari (Jerusalem, 1946), pp. 72-97; David d'Beth Hillel, *Travels from Jerusalem . . . to Madras* (Madras, 1832); J. E. Polak, *Persien, das Land und seine Bewohner* (Leipzig, 1865).

35. *BAIU*, no. 28, 2d series (1903), pp. 115-128, especially p. 123. For a report on the occupational distribution of the Jews in Kashan in 1907, see *BAIU*, no. 32, 3d series (1907): 68-81.

36. See p. 218, note 6.

37. The most detailed examination of Arabic anti-Semitic literature is contained in Y. Harkabi, *Arab Attitudes to Israel* (Jerusalem, 1971; original Hebrew edition, Tel Aviv, 1968). See also Sylvia G. Haim, "Arabic Anti-Semitic Literature," *Jewish Social Studies*, vol. 17, no.

4 (1955): 307-312; Dafna Alon, *Arab Racialism* (Jerusalem, 1969); Yehoshua Ben-Hananya, "Sifrut ʿAravit anti-tsiyonit," *Hashiloah*, 43 (1935): 272-279; Yehoshaphat Harkabi, "La'anti-shemiyat ha-ʿaravit me-hadash," in *Sin'at Yisrael le-Doroteha*, pp. 247-259; Norman A. Stillman, "New Attitudes toward the Jew in the Arab World," *Jewish Social Studies* 37 (1975): 197-204; Shimon Shamir, "Muslim-Arab Attitudes toward Jews in the Ottoman and Modern Periods," in Salo W. Baron and George S. Wise, eds., *Violence and Defense in the Jewish Experience* (Philadelphia, 1977), pp. 191-203; Moshe Ma'oz, "The Image of the Jew in Official Arab Literature and Communication Media," in *World Jewry and the State of Israel*, edited by Moshe Davis (New York, 1977), pp. 33-51. A good specimen of this literature is ʿAbdallah al-Tell's 400-page book, *The Menace of World Jewry to Islam and Christendom*, published in Cairo in 1964. A very laudatory review, by Muḥammad ʿAbdallāh al-Sammān, appeared in the distinguished Egyptian literary magazine, *Al-Risāla*, 7 January 1965, pp. 54-56. Such publications are not limited to the Arab countries, but may also be found in other Islamic lands. See, for example, a Pakistani publication in English, *Jewish Conspiracy and the Muslim World*, ed. Misbahul Islam Faruqi (Karachi, February 1967). The subject is treated from time to time in *Patterns of Prejudice* and in *The Wiener Library Bulletin*, both published in London.

38. Interview with R. K. Karanjia on September 28, 1958, reported in *Al-Ahrām*, September 29, 1958; English translation in *President Gamal Abdel Nasser's Speeches and Press-Interviews, 1958* (Cairo, 1959), p. 402.

39. *Deutsche National-Zeitung und Soldaten-Zeitung* (Munich), 1 May 1964.

40. Interview in *Ākhir Sāʿa*, 14 November 1973. Cf. his book *Al-Fikr al-Dīnī al-Isrāʾīlī: Aṭwāruhu wa-madhāhibuhu* (Cairo, 1971), pp. 222-227. For other examples, see Stillman, "New Attitudes toward the Jews," pp. 202-203.

41. Al-Azhar Academy of Islamic Research, *The Fourth Conference of the Academy of Islamic Research Rajab 1388/September 1968* (Cairo, 1970); Arabic original, *Kitāb al-Muʾtamar al-Rābiʿ li-majmaʿ al-Buḥūth al-Islāmiyya*, 3 vols. (Cairo, 1388/1968). Selection from the official English translation in D. F. Green, *Arab Theologians on Jews and Israel* (Geneva, 1976).

42. UNESCO Document 82 EX/8, annex II, p. 9, section III, par-

agraph 6, and annex I, p. 3, section III, paragraph (4) [sic]. Cited in Stillman, "New Attitudes toward the Jews," pp. 203-204.

43. *Al-Muṣawwar*, 4 August 1972, translation by Stillman in "New Attitudes toward the Jews," p. 197.

44. *Le Monde*, 29 January 1974.

45. Ali Reşat-Ismail Hakkı, *Dreyfus meselesi ve esbab-i hafiyesi* (Istanbul 1315/1898-1899) (not seen); Ebüzziya, *Kütübhane-i Ebüzziya*, no. 66 (Istanbul, 1305/1888); "*Millet-i Israiliye.*" It includes a rather striking passage in which Ebüzziya describes how he discovered, to his astonishment, that a French Jew considered himself a Frenchman. At the time of the French defeat in the Franco-Prussian War, he says, he called on a French Jewish bookseller in Istanbul, and found him overcome with grief. "The following conversation took place between us: 'I: What is the matter with you. Is something afflicting you? The bookseller: Don't you know of the misfortune which my country has suffered? Can there be any greater affliction? I (smiling): But you are not a Frenchman. What is it to you? The bookseller: How? If I am not a Frenchman, then what am I? I: But aren't you Jewish? The bookseller: Excuse me sir! In France everything is French.' " Ebüzziya goes on to describe his embarrassment and his shame at having, through ignorance, insulted a genuine patriot (pp. 57-59). See further the later issues of the Ebüzziya collection and, for an opposing viewpoint, Celâl Nuri, *Tarih-i Istikbal*, III (Istanbul, 1332/1913), pp. 99-108. For studies of Turkish attitudes toward Zionism in the late nineteenth and early twentieth centuries, see (Mim) Kemal Öke, *II Abdülhamid, Siyonist'ler ve Filistin Meselesi* (Istanbul, 1981); idem, *Siyonism ve Filistin Sorunu (1880-1914)* (Istanbul, 1982); idem, "The Ottoman Empire, Zionism, and the Question of Palestine," *International Journal of Middle East Studies* 14 (1982): 329-341.

46. See, for example, Hikmet Tanyu, *Tarih Boyunca Yahudiler ve Türkler*, 2 vols. (Istanbul, 1976), and the numerous writings of Cevat Rıfat Atılhan, listed, along with other productions of the same kind, by Öke. Professor Tanyu was the dean of the Faculty of Divinity in the University of Ankara. In most of these writings the blood libel, the *Protocols of the Elders of Zion*, and the rest of the apparatus of European anti-Semitism are taken for granted and serve as the main basis of exposition.

47. Translated from the German documents in Fritz Grobba, *Männer und Mächte im Orient* (Göttingen, 1967). English translation in *Documents on German Foreign Policy*, series D, vol. X (London and

Washington, 1950-1964), no. 403, pp. 559-560, and vol. XI, no. 680, pp. 1151-1155. Cf. Lukasz Hirszowicz, *The Third Reich and the Arab East* (London, 1966), [Polish original (Warsaw, 1963)], pp. 82-84, 109-110. Cf. Bernd Philipp Schröder, *Deutschland und der Mittlere Osten im Zweiten Weltkrieg* (Frankfurt, 1975), pp. 44-48, 53, 65-66, where, however, the references to "solving the Jewish problem" are not mentioned.

48. After the establishment of Israel in 1948, even Jewish visitors from elsewhere were unwelcome. Virtually all the independent Arab states included a question about religion on their visa application forms, and routinely refused visas to all who declared their religion as Jewish. Some even demanded proof from West European and American applicants that they were not Jewish, and thus presented the strange paradox of strongly Islamic governments demanding baptism certificates from would-be travelers. In recent years some Arab states have dropped this policy of exclusion. Some have begun to apply it more selectively. Some still maintain it with full rigor.

Index

Cohen, Boaz, *Kuntres*, 209-10 n. 3
Cohen, H. J., *Asian and African Jews*, 221 n. 23
Cohen, M. R., 212 n. 15, *Jewish Self-Government*, 202 n. 1, "The Jews," 193 n. 1, 194 n. 5, 202 n. 1, 209 n. 2, 216 n. 57
Cohen, Martin A., 215 n. 37
Commander of the Faithful, 47-48
comprador, 63
concubinage, 82
Constantine, 5
Constantinople, 47, 109, 120, 122-23, 126-27, 135, 174, 212 n. 18, 215 n. 35, 219 n. 12. *See also* Istanbul
conversion, converts, 9-10, 12, 16, 26, 34, 40, 47, 52, 61, 71-72, 78, 83, 87, 89, 92-101, 130, 135, 146-47, 151, 153, 156, 196 n. 15, 208 n. 47
Cook, Michael, *Hagarism*, 203 n. 5
Copts, 64-65
Cordova, 100
Corfu, 126, 201 n. 65
Crémieux, Adolphe, 157
Crete, 114
Crimea, 111, 218 n. 8
Crone, Patricia, *Hagarism*, 203 n. 5
Crusaders, Crusades, 23-24, 32, 43, 51, 54, 58, 61, 71, 102, 187, 215 n. 36
Ctesiphon, 75
Curzon, Lord (George), *Persia and the Persian Question*, 166-67, 220 nn. 17, 19
Cyprus, 123-24, 213 n. 22
Cyrenaica, 169
Czar, 22, 172

Daftar-i Khākānī, 211 n. 10
Damanhur, 158
Damascene, Damascus, 41, 96, 117, 129, 134, 156-58, 162,

168, 199 n. 45, 200 nn. 54, 55, 206 n. 28, 213 n. 22, 218 n. 6, 220 n. 18
Damascus Affair, 156, 158, 186, 217 n. 3
Dār al-Ḥarb, 21
Dār al-Islām, 21, 23
Darke, H., 206 n. 29
Davis, M., *World Jewry*, 223 n. 37
Dawlatshah, *Tadhkirat*, 208 n. 46
Dayr al-Qamar, 158
De Felice, Renzo, *Ebrei*, 221 nn. 20, 23
de Goeje, M. J., 200 nn. 56, 62
de Groot, A. H., *The Ottoman Empire and the Dutch Republic*, 210 n. 7
Defter-i Hakani, 117
Dervish Revolt, 104
Deutsche National-Zeitung und Soldaten-Zeitung, 223 n. 39
dhilla, dhull, 14, 32
dhimma, 21-22, 24, 30, 38, 40-44, 57, 64-66, 106, 150-51, 170, 184, 191, 194 n. 1, 196 n. 17. *See also Ahl al-Dhimma, dhimmī*
dhimmī, 14-16, 21-22, 24-29, 32, 35-48, 50-52, 58, 61, 63, 85, 90, 98-99, 102, 106, 116-17, 137-38, 147, 155, 162, 170, 185, 197 nn. 30, 34, 199 n. 43, 219 n. 10
Dhū Nuwās, 204 n. 15
dīn, 12-13, 195 n. 8
doge, 155
dönme, 147, 179, 216 n. 50
dragoman, 130-31, 146, 178
Dreyfus Affair, 162, 185, 188, 224 n. 45
Druze, 160
Duda, H. W., 212 n. 14
Dumont, P., "Jewish Communities," 219 n. 10, "La Structure sociale," 219 n. 10, "Les Archives . . . Turquie," 211 n. 10,

Lûtfi, A., *Tarih-i Lûtfi*, 214 n. 33,
221 n. 24

MacDonald, D. B., "Kārūn," 204
n. 13
MacFarlane, Charles, 164, *Con-*
stantinople, 219 n. 12
MacGregor, John, 168, *The Rob*
Roy, 220 n. 18
Machriq, 206 n. 30
Madras, 222 n. 34
Maghrib, 126, 196 n. 20. *See also*
North Africa
mahalle, 126
Mahdī, 51
Mahmud II, 173-74
Maibaum, Ignaz, 78-79
Maimonides, 76, 84, 100, 102,
106, 208 n. 48, *Iggeret*, 208 n.
48
Majar, 126
Mālikī, 23, 39-40, 151
Mandel, N., *Arabs and Zionism*,
222 n. 30, *Jewish Immigration*,
222 n. 30
Manisa, 212 n. 16
Mannheim, R., 201 n. 63
Mansura, 158
Mantran, R., *Istanbul . . . du XVII*ᵉ
siècle, 210 n. 7, 215 n. 41, "Rè-
glements," 213 n. 18
Ma'oz, M., "The Image of the
Jew," 223 n. 37
al-Maqrizi, *Kitāb al-Sulūk*, 208 n.
46
Maranids, 149
Marazzi, Ugo, *Tevarih-i Ali-i Os-*
man, 210 n. 4
Margoliouth, D. S., 206 n. 28
Markon, I., "Otlicitel'ni," 217 n.
60
Maronites, 185
Marranism, Marranos, 84, 94, 100,
134, 137, 153

martyros, 83
martyrdom, 5, 8, 40, 82-83, 146
Marv, 153
Marx, Karl, 186
masonic lodge(s), 179, 222 n. 31
Masoretes, 81
Massignon, L., *Enquête*, 208 n. 47
Mayer, L. A., *L'Art Juif*, 205 n. 20
McCarthy, R. J., 206 n. 27
Mecca, 70-71
medicine, 56, 60, 90-91, 98-102,
129-31, 135, 139, 144, 183, 214
nn. 27, 29, 220 n. 17
Medina, 10-11, 59, 70, 83, 96
de Medina, Samuel, 128
megorashim, 127
Mehmed II ("the Conqueror"), 49,
126-27, 130, 139, 147, 158, 214
nn. 27, 29
Mehmed III, 43
Melila, 214 n. 27
Mendes, Doña Gracia, 136, 215 n.
38
mellaḥ, 149-50
Meshed, 152-53, 168, 220 n. 19
messianism: Islamic, 51-52; Jewish,
93-94, 146-47, 216 n. 49
Michael, 212 n. 15, 220 n. 19
Mikkedem Umiyyam, 209 n. 2
Milano, A., *Storia*, 216 n. 45, 221
n. 26
Millas-Vallinciosa, *Homenaje*, 206
n. 27, 207 n. 33
millet, 125-26, 221 n. 23, 224 n.
45
minhag, 120
Miques, João. *See* Joseph Nasi
Mīrānshāh, 101
Mishāqa, M., *al-Jawāh*, 218 n. 3
Mishna, 73, 204 n. 12. *See also*
Gemara, Talmud
Mizrahi, Eliyahu, 128
Mizrahi, H., *Toldot*, 199 n. 44,
220 n. 17

Library of Congress Cataloging in Publication Data

Lewis, Bernard.
The Jews of Islam.

Includes index.
1. Judaism—Relations—Islam. 2. Islam—Relations—Judaism. 3. Jews—
Islamic countries. 4. Islamic countries—Ethnic relations. I. Title.

BP173.J8L48 1984   297′.1972   84-42575
ISBN 0-691-05419-3